RECLAIMING
the NATIVE
HOME
of
HOPE

RECLAIMING *the* NATIVE HOME *of* HOPE

COMMUNITY, ECOLOGY AND THE AMERICAN WEST

Edited by ROBERT B. KEITER

Foreword by PAGE STEGNER

THE UNIVERSITY OF UTAH PRESS

SALT LAKE CITY

Reclaiming the native home of hope : community, ecology, and the
    American West / edited by Robert B. Keiter ; foreword by Page Stegner.
            p.   cm.
        "The outgrowth of two symposiums sponsored by the University of
Utah College of Law's Wallace Stegner Center for Land, Resources and
the Environment"—Ack.
        Includes bibliographical references.
        ISBN 0-87480-558-9 (alk. paper)
        1. West (U.S.)–Environmental conditions. 2. Environmental
management—West (U.S.)   I. Keiter, Robert B., 1946–   .
II. University of Utah.   Wallace Stegner Center for Land, Resources, and
the Environment.
GE155.W47R43   1998
333.7'15'0978—dc21   97-49564

For Murray, Barbara, Yancey, and Cindy

CONTENTS

FOREWORD
Page Stegner

If one were looking for a unifying identifier to apply to the Intermountain West, one might settle on Boom and Bust country, and quote Ed Marston's recurrent lament in the *High Country News* that "so many communities in the Rockies are tied to extractive industries, and that those industries lead nowhere but to booms and busts." Or one might settle on the Raided Region and invoke Wallace Stegner's observation that "the whole history of the West is a series of consecutive raids"—raids that began with the beaver and moved on through gold, grass, timber, and uranium to today's ongoing assault on coal, oil, and gas deposits.

However one thinks about the territory that lies between the front range of the Rockies and the Sierra Nevada and Cascade Ranges, there is a remarkable longevity to the problems that plague it and to the issues that divide its citizenry into fundamentally two ideological camps—the antifederalists, with their state's rights, sagebrush rebellion variations on a theme, and the environmentalists, with their variations on wilderness preservation and federal control. The former tend to be rural, conservative, and development (or at least job) oriented; the latter tend to be urban and liberal, and to support public land preservation efforts.

Regardless of one's preference or outright affiliation, the attempt to transfer the public domain from federal to state management, and thence into private or corporate hands is certainly the most dominant western theme of this century, and there is no indication that it is soon going to stop. In fact, the rhetoric coming from Congress over the past four years strikes one as déjà vu all over again . . . all over again . . . all over again. The "take back" federal lands proposals, like the 1995 legislation, H.R. 2032, to transfer 270 million acres of our lands to the western states, sounds like Nevada representative Santini's 1979 bill, H.R. 7837, to transfer all BLM lands to the states containing them, and like the subsequent bill introduced a few days later by Utah senator Orrin Hatch to return to the states not only all BLM lands but national forestlands as well.

Recent arguments for closing or privatizing national parks, and for opening the Arctic Wildlife Refuge to oil drilling sound like James Watt. In his first four months as secretary of the Interior, Watt suggested we had too many parks and diverted Land and Water Conservation funds to maintenance instead of the acquisitions they were intended for; tried to turn management of the parks over to the concessioners; and tried to open for lease sale at least four offshore basins along the Pacific Coast that had been closed to drilling.

The recent declaration by Nye County, Nevada, that it owns all the federal lands within its borders (apparently it couldn't wait for legislation from its antigovernment friends in Congress) sounds like the law passed by the Nevada legislature in June of 1979—an equally empty assertion—that declared "subject to existing rights, all public lands in Nevada and all minerals not previously appropriated are the property of the State of Nevada and subject to its jurisdiction and control."

And the recently withdrawn Utah Wilderness Bill, H.R. 1745, sponsored by the Utah delegation to designate a measly 1.8 million of the 5.7 million eligible acres as wilderness, thereby opening up the rest to development, sounds like all the other variations on antifederalist, antiprotectionist themes. While it died in a filibuster, one can feel confident that it will be reintroduced . . . all over again . . . as soon as the political climate in Washington seems right.

If the present debate over land and resource management is a repeat of past debates, which are themselves reissues of still more distant debates, is there any reason to hope for anything but more of the same in the century that is nearly upon us? Perhaps there is, because there is definitely something new in the mix, something that has been attracting increasing attention (particularly during the symposiums from which this volume emerges), something that in the long run may have a profound effect on the traditional confrontations and conflicts throughout the Intermountain West, and may tip the scales in favor of environmental quality rather than economic development.

That something is a profound change in demographics. The Grand Canyon Trust recently published a book called *Charting the Colorado Plateau*, which looks at economic and social changes over the past twenty-five years, and points out that national park visitation alone jumped 95 percent over the past twelve or so years. But more important, the resident population doubled between 1960 and 1990, and grew another 13 percent between 1990 and 1994. What has occurred between 1994 and 1997 is a real estate agent's dream.

This demographic shift is an in-migration of major proportion. I don't refer here to the industrial strength tourism that makes so many of the natives restless (legitimately so), but rather to a massive influx of people fleeing the urban/ suburban rat race, looking for what they allude to as a better "quality of life" —by which they mean clean air, clean water, clean living, photo-op scenery, out-the-door recreational opportunities, peace and quiet. They come from different economic and social circumstances than the historical residents, very often with considerable educational advantages, and as anybody who lives in the Inter-mountain West knows, they continue to come in droves.

The thing about urban transplants is that although they change their habitat, they seldom change their habits, and they bring with them cultural attitudes that are often distinctly different from those held by the locals. Not only do they want NPR and decaf lattes, they want that "high-quality life"—which generally doesn't include a lot of pipelines, transmission towers, dams, roads, and strip mines in the backyard. And increasingly, since many of these resident in-migrants become involved in small-business operations that depend on tourism, there is going to evolve an understanding (if it hasn't already evolved) that the greatest economic resource available to much of the West is the quality of its environment.

I think there is no question that the political climate is slowly changing in many western communities, and will change in others. Ten years ago you would not have found Bill Hedden as one of the Grand County commissioners. Maybe ten years hence you will find entirely different western congressional delegations. As one who camps with the environmental crowd, I am possessed of a cautious optimism when something like the Grand Canyon Protection Act is passed and H.R. 1745 is defeated. And I can be guardedly optimistic about the myriad, smaller cooperative efforts that western communities and citizens are engaging in with the goal of promoting a more environmentally sensitive and economically sustainable future . . . even as I reflect gloomily on the history of western resource management and remember that the region under discussion has been greatly reduced and diminished.

I am hopeful, too, that the kind of thoughtful deliberation and discourse provided by those who participated in the inaugural symposiums at the Wallace Stegner Center for Land, Resources and the Environment, and whose work is presented in the pages that follow, will enable all of us to find a way to live respectfully with the land, subordinate our presence wherever and whenever possible, and convey to our descendants the gift of such wilderness as remains without having disfigured and consumed it.

ACKNOWLEDGMENTS

Robert B. Keiter

This book—the outgrowth of two symposiums sponsored by the University of Utah College of Law's Wallace Stegner Center for Land, Resources and the Environment—would not have been possible without the assistance of numerous organizations and individuals. This acknowledgment, attached to the first book produced from Stegner Center programs, seems an appropriate place to recognize and thank those who have helped bring the center into existence as well as the many others who were vital to the symposiums and the book itself.

The Stegner family made the center possible by enthusiastically endorsing the idea of an interdisciplinary center in Wallace Stegner's memory at the College of Law, even though Wally was not a lawyer. But as Page Stegner so eloquently put it at the center's dedication, what other American writer has a law school center named after him, and what could be more appropriate given the law's dedication to principle.

Longtime Stegner family friend, the late Lowell Durham, who also directed the Tanner Humanities Center at the University of Utah, was unfailingly supportive of the law school's early efforts to establish the center in Wally's memory and of the initial symposium programs. Bonnie Mitchell deserves credit for encouraging us to see Wallace Stegner's legacy as linked to the College of Law's natural resource and environmental law program.

The R. Harold Burton Foundation has provided critical financial assistance that has allowed the center to plan and coordinate major symposium programs. With the Burton Foundation's assistance, the center was able to bring important literary, governmental, scientific, legal, and other figures to Salt Lake to participate in these events. In addition, the S. J. and Jessie E. Quinney Foundation has provided the center with vital endowment funds to support its various programs.

At the College of Law, numerous individuals have given unsparingly of their time and energy to the Stegner Center's inaugural activities. Dean Lee Teitelbaum has placed the law school administration squarely behind the center's programs, providing full encouragement at every step along the way. My faculty colleagues—Bob Adler, Susan Poulter, Bill Lockhart, Ileana Porras, and Tony Anghie—have spent many hours initially conceiving the center and then bringing it to fruition through programs like the annual symposium. The college's administrative staff, namely Kathleen Morgan, Karen McLeese, Margaret Billings, Lisa Stewart, Pamela Starley, Natalie Nell, and Joro Walker, has filled roles too numerous to list and are responsible for seeing that the symposiums from which this volume grew were well organized and enjoyed by all who attended.

The authors whose work is represented in these pages not only met the schedule for bringing this edited volume to print but did so generously and with a commitment to the project that greatly facilitated my job as editor. My secretary, Elizabeth Kirschen, endured endless manuscript revisions and still kept the volume together while maintaining an enthusiasm for the project to the end. University of Utah Press acquisitions editor Dawn Marano has been a true pleasure to work with; the manuscript has benefited enormously from her suggestions and thoughtful review.

My wife, Linda, has both supported and indulged this project, as she has so many others over the years, for which I am abidingly grateful.

INTRODUCTION

Robert B. Keiter

Wallace Stegner wrote: "All of us have the obligation somehow to have some kind of concern for the species, for the culture, for the larger thing outside of ourselves." In that spirit, the Wallace Stegner Center for Land, Resources and the Environment, located at the University of Utah College of Law, was conceived as an interdisciplinary forum for exploring anew Stegner's beloved and self-contradictory West. Through regular symposiums and related activities, the Stegner Center is engaged in bringing diverse and thoughtful perspectives to bear on the contemporary western landscape, its institutions, and its populace. This volume represents an edited compilation of symposium presentations, and reflects the Stegner Center's commitment to promoting better understanding and dialogue among those concerned about the West's future.

Drawing upon Wallace Stegner's writings for inspiration and insight, the essays that follow explore critical issues that confront westerners today. Stegner's timeless observations on community, place, geography, and wildness provide the unifying themes, which are examined from a contemporary perspective. While the West is clearly experiencing significant change, Stegner's work affords a firm basis for comprehending the past and anticipating the future. Indeed, his insights are of such enduring quality and clarity that they are still remarkably reliable guides in our efforts to understand the West as it edges ever closer to the 21st century.

Wallace Stegner himself wore many labels: teacher, historian, biographer, novelist, essayist, mentor, and environmental advocate. His breadth of knowledge, vision, and concern is reflected in his many published works, which span the better part of the 20th century and a similar range of topics. He wrote novels about the settlement and development of the American West, biographies of John Wesley Powell and Bernard DeVoto, histories of the Mormon migration and settlement of Utah, and essays about his personal experiences growing up western. His extraordinary career and voluminous literary output have indelibly shaped our collective understanding of the West's unique environment and diverse citizenry. At the Department of the Interior, two presiding secretaries have cited Stegner as a singular influence in expanding their own views, and unabashedly called upon him for inspiration and expertise.

In his incisive biography of John Wesley Powell, Wallace Stegner pens a powerful description of Powell's impact:

Order is the dream of man. It was a dream of John Wesley Powell more than of most, and he never questioned that an order could be discovered or perhaps to some degree created, by the human mind and the scientific method. The larger syntheses that he attempted in several areas . . . turned out always to be working syntheses only, sure to be periodically discarded and replaced.

Arthur Schelsinger, Jr., pays Stegner a similar compliment: "His ambition was . . . to delineate the historic continuities between past and present and thereby to help transform natural chaos into human order." In the best tradition of Powell and Stegner and the others who came before, these essays too seek to illuminate "historic continuities" and to identify "larger syntheses" emerging today in the fields of natural resources and environmental thought and policy.

The themes addressed in this volume reflect Stegner's personal concern for the West, the place that he regarded as home and understood perhaps better than anyone else. The papers honor Stegner by continuing his exploration of the West, its character and its peculiar geography. Representing such diverse disciplines as literature, history, science, economics, law, and policy, the authors bring their talent and personal experience to bear on today's West. Through this interdisciplinary exploration, the volume presents thought-provoking ideas on how to surmount the West's persistent conflicts to achieve the unitary society that Stegner envisioned—one that matches its scenery. The hope is that the collective ideas will serve as a catalyst in stimulating public dialogue and understanding of the complex issues now confronting the West. The goal is for more informed, wise, and just decisions to resolve the region's pressing quandaries.

The book focuses on the West's continuing struggle over its public land and natural resource heritage. The opening essays explore the essential dimensions of a western ethic—those basic values and beliefs at the core of the West's experience. The next essays share personal experiences with newly evolving cooperative approaches to managing the West's lands and with the government's emerging commitment to ecosystem management. Further redefining the human relationship with the western landscape, the essays then identify and assess the important new concept of ecological restoration, suggesting that it may be the order of the 21st century. Then the essays examine how these concepts apply in specific locations that are confronting particularly fractious controversies, namely the debate over wilderness on Utah's Colorado Plateau, the conflict over wolves and grizzly bears in the northern Rockies, and the role of people, livestock, and nature in the Great Basin. The volume concludes with two personal essays, one exploring continuities with the past and the other describing one family's struggle to come to terms with the contemporary West of endangered species and urban growth. Whether read individually or as a whole, the essays provide a penetrating review of the ideas and forces that are shaping western public land and natural resource policy.

Although the collected essays confirm that major natural resource conflicts still simmer across the West, they also recast the region's dilemmas into a more focused and tractable frame of reference. Most important, they suggest that Wallace Stegner's characterization of the West as the "native home of hope" has not outlived its metaphoric usefulness. While multiple-use versus preservation arguments may still dominate the political discussion in southern Utah, the gradual transformation of the region's economy is inexorably changing the terms of that debate, just as new cooperative management efforts are confirming the region's essential unity. In the northern Rockies, the debate over endangered species preservation now focuses less on the value of grizzly bears and wolves and more on how the region's diverse interests might structure a workable recovery effort. Similarly the Great Basin's livestock interests have found it essential to adapt to the dry landscape's inherent limitations and thus acknowledge that ecological concerns will inevitably define their relationship to the land. In sum, these developments illustrate how deeply an ecological ethic has penetrated the West's collective conscience.

To be sure, impassioned debates still rage over how far ecological preservation and restoration efforts should go and what effect they will have on local communities. No one would assert confidently that southern Utah is on the verge of an ecologically sensitive wilderness compromise or that the reintroduced wolves are now entirely secure in the Yellowstone region, but the momentum is certainly moving in that direction. Proof can be found in the collaborative efforts of a diverse group of citizens to achieve sustainability on the Tipton ranch in central Nevada; further proof is suggested by the adoption of a desert tortoise habitat conservation plan for one of Utah's fastest-growing communities. Moreover, the fact that the 104th Congress was unable to pass a minimal-acreage Utah wilderness bill, or to dismantle the Endangered Species Act, or to relinquish federal ownership of the public lands is further evidence of this shift. In the larger sense, these developments suggest that wilderness, its wild inhabitants, and their ecological needs are becoming an accepted and ever more important part of the West's sense of place.

Because the West's public lands still furnish a setting where ecological and economic sustainability are within reach, the immediate challenge is to design institutional arrangements capable of achieving these important objectives. With the West's open spaces shrinking and its citizens fighting over ever smaller pieces of the public domain, westerners are finally learning that they will have to live with one another and jointly map out the future of the surrounding landscape. If ecological and economic realities are to be given their due and if an ecologically functional landscape is to be realized, then new institutional arrangements that transcend traditional, geopolitical boundaries are required. While entrenched interests may be reluctant to release what leverage they currently enjoy, these new institutional arrangements must include everyone in a redefined relationship to the land and to each other. For the present, the move toward cooperative, citizen-based management arrangements offers a hopeful model for transcending traditional ideological positions and for addressing the needs of the land, its ecological systems, and its human inhabitants.

As this cooperative management effort unfolds, however, these new institutional arrangements must be ground-tested to ensure that they truly do incorporate new ecological concerns alongside traditional ones. If the Forest Service's ecosystem management program cannot accommodate meaningful wilderness in the Yaak Valley, then it cannot be squared with the new ecological imperative and should be restructured. If a citizen-based grizzly bear recovery effort in Idaho cannot guarantee the long-term survival of the bear, then it too violates basic ecological principles and must be reconfigured or jettisoned. And when a Utah wilderness proposal ignores the region's important ecological, remoteness, and spiritual values, then it deserves to be resisted. The basic commitment must be to fashion workable arrangements that accommodate the land's ecological and special values, as well as the equally important needs of its human residents. In this process, the goal must be to dignify all components of the landscape, including its natural as well as human communities.

The potential benefits are substantial. If the West's citizenry can design and implement such workable institutions, then the West will be on the verge of recapturing a measure of control over its own destiny. If the West can ensure both the welfare of its shared landscape and the vitality of its communities, then it can rightfully lay claim to important sovereign prerogatives. If the West is prepared to commit itself to an evolutionary perspective, then it will be well positioned to begin constructing a sustainable society. In short, the West will be on the way toward reclaiming the native home of hope.

PART I

The
NASCENT
WEST

TOWARD A WESTERN ETHIC

The quest for a western ethic—one that captures the essence and spirit of today's heated clashes over the use and preservation of the West's natural heritage—is the subject of these essays. Wallace Stegner wrote that "the West is still nascent," an eloquent way of acknowledging that the West has yet to define itself fully or to achieve its full innate potential. The three opening chapters take up that challenge and offer insightful observations into how the West might shape its own destiny. Former Missoula mayor Dan Kemmis, with a sweeping survey of western history as well as American political thought, posits that the West's simmering controversies can best be understood in geopolitical terms; he boldly calls upon westerners to break down conventional jurisdictional boundaries and to transcend historical ideological schisms in order to construct a new vision of regional self-determination and thus reclaim the West's sovereignty. Utah State University English professor Tom Lyon, drawing widely upon insights from psychology, religion, literature, and other fields, deftly employs emotional and rational argumentation to construct a western sense of place that rests upon the region's connectedness and the important role of wilderness in sustaining this wholeness. University of Utah law professor Bob Keiter, upon reviewing the evolution of American public land law, concludes that the human relationship to the landscape is undergoing a profound transformation, with an ecological ethic ascending to a dominant position on the management agenda and public involvement assuming a key role in defining natural resource priorities. Besides reconfirming the inherent connections between people and the surrounding landscape, the opening essays affirm that important, evolutionary changes are occurring, which will require the public to engage in the civic enterprise of redefining the West's basic governmental structure, the role of wilderness, and priorities on the public domain.

Chapter 1

A DEMOCRACY
TO MATCH ITS LANDSCAPE

Daniel Kemmis

OF WOLVES AND SOVEREIGNTY

Nothing in recent years has stirred western energies and emotions or nonwestern images and myths about the region like the reintroduction of wolf packs into various areas of the northern Rockies, including Yellowstone Park: The fierce opposition of ranchers and farmers to bringing back animals their grandparents had done everything they could to exterminate, and finally, with the assistance of federal bounties, had exterminated. The threats of violence and even death to the new federal agents who now proposed to bring back these same predators to take up exactly where they had left off with killing their precious sheep and cattle. The days of delay while the caged Canadian wolves were held on the ground at a Montana airport while a last-minute petition for an injunction against their release met its slow, deliberate demise in the federal courts. The electronic convergence at the release site, where every television network staked out a location for its remote van and crew, competing not only with one another but with the dozens of documentary crews all vying for the best angle to capture what they were guessing to be the wolves' own angle of escape into the surrounding forest. The wolves themselves electronically leashed to their own remote vans, the frequencies programmed into their radio collars carefully separated from those of the cellular phones attached to the modems in the laptop computers of the print journalists. All these legal, electronic, and biological crosscurrents left no doubt that the West the wolves were being introduced into was not the West their kin had been exterminated from.

Yet the way the wolves moved into and through all our minds as they learned their way into the awaiting landscape could only remind us that the newer things get, the older they have to be. Everyone who gave the wolves even a passing thought, from whatever pro, con, or merely curious angle they encountered them, must know that the moment the wolves darted from their cages, they began sniffing their way along ancient, well-marked pathways in our own minds. All the rekindled folklore of the Big Bad Wolf, of Little Red Riding Hood and poor, ingested Granny drew us back, and still farther back, through the story of Romulus and Remus, back into our own species' being and our own species' hard-earned inhabiting of ancient landscapes.

And as the howls, silenced for generations, began to echo again in the canyon of the Yellowstone, claiming the countryside in all the ways the mountains had taught thousands of generations of wolves to exercise the sovereignty to which they had evolved, the pathways of western minds began opening to new understandings of what sovereignty might mean for us in this dawning age of the reinhabitation of a sovereign landscape.

How strange that we should need wolves, bald eagles, king salmon, elk, and grizzlies to remind us of what human sovereignty might be all about. The word itself has become faint in our minds, carrying, when it comes up at all, mere fragments of itself, as tired and worn and battered as all the other good old words of a full-bodied democracy. But one deep-throated, sustained howl and answering howl across the canyon could stir in us a memory of what it means to stand with our feet firmly planted on home soil and to say to those others with whom we had established our range, "We are here, and here we intend to stay and to be about the business of making a life on this land."

Yet, by the time the wolves had left their cages, mankind had long since laid claim to the landscape it had spread into (that was, in other words, history). The rest was just the unfolding of the done deed across the continent until everything was in place, the survey pins all driven, the land platted and fenced and plowed, the wolves poisoned, the tribes penned on reservations, annoying the calm sense of order with an occasional claim of tribal sovereignty, all too often over a worn-out stretch of prairie or a tobacco shop or casino. Real sovereignty had been centralized in a ten-square-mile swamp at the tidal opening of the Potomac, and the rest of the Spirit of '76 was merely a memory or less, a nagging, painful reminder of what it might still mean to be a democratic people, a festering inversion now of democracy in which every exercise of sovereignty, whether by the tribes or the feds, only left more westerners more angry, as they showed themselves angry at the wolf reintroduction hearings.

But the wolves were out there now, howling, multiplying, eating deer and now and then killing a calf sure enough, being wolves in other words and therefore being sovereign because that is what wolves had been shaped to be. And as they went about laying their claim and declaring their sovereign presence, another word began to emerge. What made the wolves, like the grizzlies, so politically difficult was the fact that if they were to exist at all, they would have to have access to a sufficient range to sustain them. That range had a name: it was called a region, and the recollection of what region meant gave deeper meaning to the sovereignty of all the wide-ranging, majestic "charismatic megafauna," from grizzly to eagle. Everything about the wolf was attuned to its region, from the incredible strength and endurance of its powerful hindquarters, evolved to carry it tirelessly across miles of mountainous landscape to where the howl it had just answered told of a kill that needed defending, to the throat itself, shaped by the mountains and their lakes to reach across them to secure its reign. It was that response of wolf to landscape that shaped the wolf slowly into the majestic form of a ruler over the region whose Roman name itself (*regere*, to rule) echoed of sovereignty.

SOVEREIGNTY AND THE WEST

But just as democratic human sovereignty had been atrophied by decades of bureaucracy, so too, had any connection of region to sovereignty been obliterated by what Bernard DeVoto called "the course of empire." As wolf and grizzly reintroduction, spotted owl, and endless other controversies deepened the West's restless discontent with the imperial writ, the issue of sovereignty began to emerge in every form but the one that was rooted deeply enough in the landscape to make a difference. Freemen and militiamen wove theories of democratic fundamentalism into what for most of us remained puzzling claims of their sovereign right not only to resist, but to indict, try, and convict those justices of the peace and other magistrates who attempted to hold them accountable to a set of laws whose legitimacy they stoutly denied. The counties movement added a kind of feudal twist by finding in counties (of all places) a residual sovereignty that no one had ever noticed before, but which they now claimed required federal officials to clear all their actions in advance with the local sheriff. Less bizarrely but still not quite to the point, a broad flanking movement of states' rights has churned it way out of the Rockies, ranging from a series of bills to "return" federal lands to the states to a flurry of resolutions in western state legislatures claiming a broad range of state powers under the Tenth Amendment and culminating in a movement led by Utah's governor Michael Leavitt to convene an "assembly of the states." Perhaps this is a call for a constitutional convention to address the festering issues of sovereignty underlying all these stirrings of western discontent.

Why exactly is it that these issues of sovereignty never quite get settled in the West? We move toward the answer by noticing that the turmoil and discontent seem always to center on questions of who has the say over land and land use. Much of this focus can and must be attributed to the remarkable amount of public land in the West. But what accounts for that phenomenon? What accounts for it is also, perhaps, the real source of the continual eruption of issues of sovereignty in the West. For the fact is that in the Rockies, more than anywhere else in the country, all politics are fundamentally geopolitics. Here the lay of the land determines as it always has determined everything else.

In his culminating trilogy on the West, Bernard DeVoto made the most commanding case yet for the doctrine of Manifest Destiny—the geopolitical logic that compelled the United States to expand from its early subcontinental nestling between the Appalachians and the Atlantic to occupy and assert sovereignty over a continental domain. In *The Year of Decision*, DeVoto describes the various westward vectors that converged in the 1846 decision to claim, in the face of Mexican, Russian, and British opposition, an American Pacific shoreline. In *Across the Wide Missouri*, the commercial torque of this imperial thrust is illustrated in the activities of the western fur trappers who built eastern fortunes while they traced out the skeleton of imperial expansion into the Rockies. Finally, working his way a step further back in history, DeVoto concentrates on the Lewis and Clark expedition in *The Course of Empire*. He elucidates clearly the geopolitical aim of the project in terms of the effort to secure for the United States the supposed "height of land," the short, easy portage from which the continental waters flowed west, east, and perhaps even south, the king-of-the-mountain possession that would ensure its possessor control of that Pacific fur trade, which was only the first of a long series of depleting extractions of vast wealth from the West. Empire, in other words.

So for two centuries, the continent-commanding geography of the Rockies has combined with the region's breathtaking richness to produce the defining politics of the West. Those politics have been and still are fundamentally imperial. To call them national is to ignore what DeVoto saw so clearly: that at the "height of land," nation could only become empire. To call the politics federal, or to name the imperial holdings federal lands is to forget that a federation is an association of sovereigns. The whole point of American nationhood has been to ensure that only the sovereignty exercised from the Potomac would amount to anything. Finally, to call the politics of the West democratic (as Frederick Jackson Turner did) is to see beneath the imperial grip a landscape that has told its best observers that it had something other than imperial domination in mind.

Which is to venture that the "course of empire" is not necessarily the last word on the topic of sovereignty in the West. How else do we account for the fact that DeVoto spent most of his last years resisting the efforts of western congressmen to return federal lands to state control, or that DeVoto's intellectual heirs are now once again engaged in exactly the same resistance? It might be worth asking what Thomas Jefferson would have had to say about these recurring patterns of western rebelliousness.

DeVoto gives Jefferson credit for being our foremost geopolitician and knowing exactly what he was doing in buying Louisiana and sending Lewis and Clark in search of the "height of land." But Jefferson was also our best democrat, and his democratic instincts would always trump any geopolitics; in the end he would favor no system that threatened self-determination. If he had seen a West continually challenging the empire, his democratic antennae would home in on that phenomenon, leading him to ask why this insistence on challenging the established order? If Jefferson the scientist had known the mountain-building theory of plate tectonics, he would have applied it geopolitically to the Rockies to reinforce his argument that political systems can only remain democratic if they keep moving. To DeVoto and the other celebrants of the imperial ordering of the West (sometimes even to Wallace Stegner) Jefferson would almost certainly have raised the question: Is this state of affairs really the angle of repose, or is there still more movement in these mountains?

Even without the clear-sightedness of a Jefferson, we know the end of this century to be a period of great nation-shattering turmoil, all of it in the name of self-determination. Not since the upheavals of the American and French Revolutions has the issue of sovereignty been so universally up for grabs; never has nationhood been so beset, both from above, in the undeniable emergence now of global economic and ecological imperatives, and in the accompanying, nation-eroding emergence of continental trading structures, but also in the hundred-and-one assertions of regional autonomy from Chechnya to Northern Italy, from Basque Spain to Palestine to Quebec. In the midst of all this movement, America stands aloof, either smugly or numbly unaware that when the plates shift anywhere, they shift everywhere.

Only in the Rocky Mountain West, where the issue of sovereignty refuses to die, does America still whisper to itself the Jeffersonian question of 1776: Does the structure we woke with in the morning still serve us at mid-afternoon? Only here, at the "height of land," where nationhood emerged most undeniably in its imperial form, has the presence of empire continued to chafe as it chafed Sam Adams and Patrick Henry. Here the remoteness, the harshness, the aridity of the place selected for independence, the imperative of self-determination, refuses to be legislated or regulated or scolded out of existence.

Yet no one is quite sure how seriously to take any of this, and above all, the question recurs of how serious any of these western challengers to established sovereignty really are. One way of putting that question would be to compare their resolve with that of a newly freed wolf in the Idaho wilderness. One look into the cold, determined eyes of one of these sovereigns will erase any doubt that might arise about the wolves' seriousness. They will do exactly what it takes to establish their manifest role across their region. By comparison, the activities of most of the western challengers of established sovereignty carry a flickering pulse of gaming self-indulgence, a suggestion that this may be a pursuit more of the pleasures of challenging sovereignty than of the hard work of actually claiming and exercising it as Thomas Jefferson and his compatriots claimed it with unmistakable seriousness.

The first step toward getting serious about something of this order of magnitude is to stare down all distracting forms of self-indulgence. And the one preeminent self-indulgence the West would have to overcome on the path to claiming its own territory is the indulgence of ideology. Conservatives can call to conservatives across the narrow chasms that might separate them; liberals can join in a chorus of commiseration with other liberals, but if the West is to get serious about its own destiny, we will have to learn to speak in one western voice, a voice clear and strong enough to carry up and down the spine of the continent.

Do western conservatives care enough about self-determination to admit that greed and unrestrained private property rights and a healthy dose of racism do not quite add up to a formula for the good life that a robust majority of westerners can finally subscribe to? Can western liberals acknowledge to themselves that there is something soothingly self-indulgent in their never-ending discovery of new classes of victims and villains, or that there is something self-contradictory in western Democrats' deeply antidemocratic refusal to trust themselves and their neighbors to govern the land they inhabit together? Above all, could left and right, setting aside their respective forms of self-indulgence, begin to look at the West in terms of possibilities that would necessarily transcend the comfortable half-truths of their worldviews?

ASSESSING THE STAKES

What none of us can see, yet, is what could be at stake, large enough and compelling enough to induce all westerners to speak and act in concert. What follows is merely a suggestion of what might in fact be at stake.

Global Positioning

That we inhabit a global economy has become commonplace. What is not so universally understood is that the organic integration of the global economy is drawing into play suborganisms that refuse to be ordered by anything other than their internal logic. The emergence of continental economies is one clear instance of this, and one indisputable mark of the declining importance of nation-states, whose boundaries these organic economies simply refuse to be bound by. That the emergence of natural, land-based economies should carry from the global to the continental level and then stop is counterintuitive, and it is clear that organic subcontinental economic regions are rapidly emerging. Slowly but steadily, for example, Seattle and Vancouver are organizing what some call Cascadia as a major global economic power, oblivious to the international border that cannot be allowed to interfere with this natural region's efforts to maximize its global competitive advantages. The city-states of northern Italy, recognizing that their region can only consolidate its natural competitive advantage on the continent by acting like a region, have organized a serious self-determination movement, which may well lead to the region's secession from Italy.

In this rapidly restructuring global and continental context, the Rocky Mountain West faces two stark choices: either it will be dragged into the new globalism as a vassal to more highly organized coastal regions, or it will look to its own regional advantages and prepare itself to play a more independent global role. But three forms of internal fracturing now prevent the West from playing the mature global role to which it is naturally suited.

The first is ideological. One ideology would make the West's natural resources readily available to any highest bidder in the global marketplace with the fewest possible restrictions on their extraction, while the other would either lock resources out of the market altogether or restrict their extraction through the remote, inefficient, and deeply resented mechanism of a federal command-and-control regulatory structure. The point here is not to determine which ideology is right, but rather to acknowledge the fact that the unrelenting, winner-take-all struggle between the two ideologies puts the West at a severe competitive disadvantage in the global marketplace. The inordinate uncertainty that such political struggles create is the bane of investment and entrepreneurship, which means that the only kind of economic activity a volatile place like the West can expect is not investment, or anything else that might contribute to sustainable prosperity, but raw, get-it-while-you-can-and-get-out exploitation.

This does not need to be the West's role in a maturing global economy. Its resources can be made to last, to provide a sustainable generation of wealth over many centuries. Its cities and their universities can produce the intellectual capital on which the economy runs. If it maintains the attractiveness of its landscape, and tends to the livability of its communities, the West can attract a steady stream of good businesses whose chief location consideration is a healthy, satisfying setting for their owners and employees. But none of these global advantages can be effectively seized by a region so blinded by its ideological divisions that it cannot think straight.

Rural West vs. Urban West

To organize its economy for a global role, the West must not only learn to think and act outside its ideological channels it must also overcome its deep-seated antagonism between city and countryside. Only through the economically focusing power of one or more major cities can any subcontinental region hope to secure its global niche. There is a growing body of research proving that those cities that learn to build prosperity with (rather than at the expense of) their surrounding small towns and rural areas are gaining a global competitive advantage over those that continue to ignore or abuse that relationship. The mythical but politically still potent independence of "the rural West"—from the Denvers, Salt Lake Cities, and Albuquerques, which the region has always treated as intruders on the landscape—has become an indulgence the West can no longer afford.

The Dysfunctional States

What is becoming increasingly clear is that none of these debilitating divisions can be addressed in the context of the existing jurisdictional framework. Nowhere is this clearer than in the region's state capitols. Anyone who goes into communities around the West will encounter one steady refrain: that of the maddening dysfunctionality of western legislatures. Here the warfare of pro-development vs. pro-environment forces and of urban vs. rural interests produces endless variations on the gridlock pattern, which steadily undermines westerners' belief that anyone is really minding the store.

What no one on either side of these battles recognizes is how severely the jurisdictional framework exacerbates the problem. The continental and subcontinental forms to which the global economy responds are without exception organic (that is, they reflect the realities of land forms), while states, especially in the West, where straight lines studiously ignore natural forms, are anything but organic. Within an arbitrary, abstract, right-angled jurisdiction like Colorado, Denver's relationship to its region can be twisted into the dysfunctional form of competing urban and rural interests. The jurisdiction that has a stake in developing Denver's natural, prosperity-enhancing relationship to its land-based, nonlinear region does not exist, which means that relationship is never constructively explored. Which means in turn that the West steadily squanders its natural global advantages, to the benefit of other regions that do not so self-injuriously set city against countryside.

Managing Growth

All this becomes a vicious circle. Not able to organize itself in ways that would build sustainable prosperity, the West bloodies itself in endless fights over whatever can momentarily pass as "economic development." In this way, the whole issue of growth has become both unintelligible and unmanageable. While some few sectors (most notably construction and real estate) profit in the short term from the fact that the Rockies have become the fastest-growing region in the country, there is ample reason to believe that unplanned, uncontrolled growth that blights the West's natural beauty will do far more long-term economic harm than good. Here again, the ideological fracturing of the region is most pronounced in state legislatures, where even modest efforts at growth management turn into battles over what constitutes the "taking" of private property. And again, the focusing of attention in the clumsy, largely irrelevant jurisdictions of the states guarantees that the continental and subcontinental nature of the growth issue is never recognized or addressed.

What the region is actually dealing with is nothing more or less than a migration from the coast into the mountains—a migration pushed more than marginally by the continental migration north across the Rio Grande. Trying to deal with a subcontinental phenomenon as if it had anything to do with states has exactly the same effect as trying to deal with the globalization of the economy in state capitols: It simply hardens the already dysfunctional ideological battle lines and heightens the frustration of a citizenry already weary with those hopelessly unproductive sparrings.

To play an effective global role economically or to deal with downstream regions on issues like migration, the West would have to be willing and able to constitute itself as a self-determining region—which is to say that it must be willing to confront some fundamental constitutional issues (especially around the imperial reach of the commerce clause.) That will return us to the issue of sovereignty by way of a uniquely western phenomenon: the never-ending debate over public lands.

The Imperial Presence of "Federal" Lands

It is the public lands more than anything else that makes the West so much more alert to sovereignty concerns than any other region. And it is this issue that is most likely to trigger a serious constitutional engagement that could then address growth management and sustainable economics. In a number of ways, the public lands reveal what can in other contexts be more successfully denied: the fact that the national government does not have the capacity to perform across the range for which it claims responsibility. Even in the heyday of federal expansiveness, it is doubtful whether Washington had the capacity to "manage" the millions of acres of federal domain in the West. With the steady, drastic downsizing of that government, the issue is no longer seriously in doubt. But this is not simply a matter of money or manpower. The inability of the Congress to pass comprehensive wilderness legislation for most western states revealed years ago to the West what the repeated shutdowns of the federal government have more recently disclosed to the rest of the country: This is a government of appallingly shaky legitimacy.

The national government operates in the same way on the wilderness issue that state governments do on issues not suited to their jurisdiction: It fractures into partisan posturing for the sole sake of gaining political advantage, and it therefore remains incapable of straightforwardly solving problems. The alternative to this dysfunctional pattern is one currently unthinkable in any quarter. It would involve westerners, left and right, finding a quiet spot where they could begin talking intelligently and honestly about what makes most sense for the region in the broad, global context and in the long, sustainable run. It may well involve the West making a deal with the national government, roughly of this nature: "Since we have finally surmounted our ideological divisions sufficiently to glimpse how we could do a better job of managing the public lands than you can (provided we are also given the capacity to control growth, to guide the economy, etc.), we propose that you turn over that control to a duly constituted regional body, subject to a public trust binding us to manage our lands in an environmentally sustainable and socially responsible manner."

RETRACING THE PATH TOWARD SELF-DETERMINATION

The preceding paragraphs have hinted at how, in a number of arenas like economics, rural-urban relations, growth management, and public lands, there are interlinking opportunities for the development of good public policy, which cannot even be imagined, let alone enacted, except by thinking and acting regionally. Once we begin to see these possibilities, we can see more clearly how poorly our current governmental structure serves us. It is perhaps time we devoted some attention to the West's inordinate power in the U.S. Senate, and to how the region might use that forum to bargain for a more appropriate alignment of sovereignty. To be able to think such unaccustomed thoughts, another round of historical triangulation may prove helpful. A dispassionate appraisal of the daily doings inside the Beltway would lead us to the conclusion that the deepest fears of both George Washington and Thomas Jefferson have braided themselves together into a structure that serves adequately neither the West nor any other region. Washington's fear was of the corrosive effect of partisanship. Watching now the minute partisan calculations of how every move on every issue can give one party some advantage over the other, noticing the lack of any ability to deal honestly and straightforwardly with the problems we encounter, we have to ask ourselves whether we have let our attachment to established forms blind us to how dysfunctional they have become.

And that was the Jeffersonian fear: that the Constitution would overshadow the democratic core of the Declaration of Independence. He foresaw that Americans would want to make a religion of the Constitution; that they would come to treat as sacrosanct what was all too obviously the work of human hands, thereby denying themselves the fundamental democratic ability to ask whether the forms they had inherited any longer served them.

Jefferson fully appreciated the complexity of that question. Seldom are things as simple as ideologues would have them be, and that is especially true of the ultimate democratic question. Since no constitution and no government are ever perfect, well-established forms must be cultivated and nudged toward greater responsiveness rather than simply abandoned every time they let us down. But that attitude, taken to an extreme, can mutate into the kind of subservience to existing forms that caused Jefferson so much anxiety.

Thomas Paine wrote more bluntly in "Common Sense" an appeal to the colonists to begin "laying aside all national pride and prejudice in favor of modes and forms," to commence "an inquiry into the constitutional errors in the English form of government, . . . for as we are never in a proper condition of doing justice to others, while we continue under the influence of some leading partiality, so neither are we capable of doing it to ourselves while we remain fettered by any obstinate prejudice."

What Jefferson and Paine identify as a "prejudice" in favor of established forms has clearly become a bar to our capacity to imagine what forms actually might enable us to bring our human resourcefulness to bear on the problems and opportunities we face. Above all, we have lost the ability to make the lay of the land our ally in the enterprise of democracy. We have done this most detrimentally by the forced abolition of regional self-determination from our catalogue of constitutional possibilities. On this score, it is perhaps time we had a word with Mr. Lincoln, the more so since, in terms of national sovereignty, the West begins exactly where the Civil War ends.

There is probably no one who ever understood better what Jefferson meant about the democratic imperative of constantly reinventing ourselves than Abraham Lincoln. The Gettysburg Address is now widely understood as a bold and brilliant rewriting of the Declaration of Independence. Its closing concern that democratic government "shall not perish from the earth" is a quintessentially Jeffersonian concern. That the way to keep the democratic spirit alive is periodically to give it a "new birth in freedom" is no less Jeffersonian. But to bring forth new vessels for democracy necessarily means changing or transcending those fashioned earlier. So Lincoln moved beyond Jefferson, in at least two crucial ways.

The one that has attracted the greatest attention was Lincoln's ability to accomplish what Jefferson could not: the abolition of slavery. But what that in turn required was what Lincoln was really after, and what would have given Jefferson the greatest pause: the decisive centralizing of sovereignty in the national government and the concomitant closing off of regional alternatives.

The point is not to argue whether that tectonic shift in sovereignty was well conceived. That it occurred, and having occurred, deepened, and having deepened, began to ossify—these are the facts—and the democratic question now is whether it is time for us to say, with Thomas Paine, "there was a time when it was proper, and there is a proper time for it to cease." If nationhood is steadily losing its ability to solve problems, and if there is reason to believe that in the new global and continental context, self-determining regions may have an unexpected ability to do what neither nations nor states can accomplish, then it is time to acknowledge that a new regional self-determination may be what is required to ensure that American democracy does not perish in a swamp of Potomac-bred cynicism.

In 1943, Bernard DeVoto finished and published his *Year of Decision*, a celebration of American nationhood, which, while it focused on the imperial triumphs of 1846, was clearly written for the America of a century later and written, Stegner implies in his biography of DeVoto, as that frustrated warrior's major contribution to the war effort. The nation then muscling its way across the Sahara and onto the beachheads of Guam and Corregidor had decisively confirmed its nationhood eighty years earlier at Gettysburg, but DeVoto was convinced that the only geopolitically acceptable answer to the question of national sovereignty had actually been established by 1846, when the American flag was firmly planted on Pacific sands.

Geography dictated that this would be a continental empire, DeVoto argued, and no amount of sectional rebelliousness could stand in the way of that imperative. Later, then, looking back to the Lewis and Clark expedition, DeVoto found in Thomas Jefferson's geopolitical acumen about seizing the "height of land" an even earlier foreclosing of any but the imperial solution. But to reach that conclusion and give it the appearance of angle-of-repose finality, DeVoto had to silence certain Jeffersonian doubts that Jefferson himself could not put down. Looking to what he knew as the West—the rapidly filling catchment of the Mississippi—and watching how insistently its stream of settlers kept recurring to thoughts and threats of their own independence if the East kept yanking at their bit, Jefferson wrote: "Whether we remain in one confederacy or form into Atlantic and Mississippi confederacies, I believe not very important to the happiness of either part . . . and did I now foresee a separation at some future day, yet I should feel the duty & the desire to promote the western interests as zealously as the eastern." DeVoto trumps this musing of Jefferson's with Lincoln's own geopolitics set forth in his first inaugural address where he maintained that "physically speaking we cannot separate. We cannot remove our respective sections from each other nor build an impassable wall between them. A husband and wife may be divorced and go out of the presence and beyond the reach of each other, but the different parts of our country cannot do this."

The land does not change, he was saying, and therefore we cannot argue with its imperatives. He declares that "as our case is new, so we must think anew and act anew," and with a touch on the lever, he sweeps all this (and vastly more) state sovereignty into Washington.

But if Lincoln balanced national sovereignty on the deep democratic principles of the Declaration and on the equally profound imperatives of the continental land form, he would also be the first to understand how nationhood could become more of a hindrance than an aid to democratic self-determination.

Jefferson and Paine had argued that the real test of a democratic people lies in its ability to recognize when the system it has inherited no longer serves the pursuit of human well-being. But the real question is: Do you have it in you to seize the situation and rehumanize it? Can you get beyond dreaming, beyond complaining, beyond taunting and scheming; can you assume that full-bodied responsibility for all your circumstances, which would enable you to say with the self-assured dignity of a sovereign that you "are, and of right ought to be" in full charge of your own homeland?

What it comes down to, finally, is how much westerners really care about the West. If what most of us care most about is gaining the upper hand for one or another ideology, then that game will continue to be played out to whatever its conclusion may be. But if we were to conclude that our current course leaves too much to chance, promotes too fierce a struggle, we might choose instead the path of self-determination.

But this is no path for the fainthearted. Self-determination carries deeply rooted imperatives, just as the topography of the West does, and only those willing to countenance all possible unfoldings should set foot on the path.

The West's best observers, from Jefferson to Frederick Jackson Turner, from John Wesley Powell to Wallace Stegner have always detected some emanation of democratic spirit from the western landscape. A key component of that culture is a bold open-mindedness, a refusal to be trapped in box canyons of any kind.

With the Civil War, America assumed that it had concluded something: that regional self-determination was no longer an option on this continent. But that conclusion is just the kind of box canyon or dam that a democratic people would never allow itself to be denied the opportunity to challenge. The plates move; the dam cracks; the "course of human events" moves forward, even as the wolves move with sovereign determination to claim their realm.

Chapter 2

AN ETHIC OF PLACE
Thomas J. Lyon

SENSE OF PLACE

The sense of place is a kind of enlightenment, a natural loosening of the boundary of self. It comes through the pores, as Wallace Stegner wrote in *Wolf Willow*; nothing intellectual about it. Nothing that you, as an ego, can will into existence. Place and inherent nature do the work, and the magic connection flows through the "soft animal of your body," in Mary Oliver's phrase. "You walk a stranger in a vegetating world," as Mary Austin described a stroll through piñon-juniper woodland, "and then with a click the shutter of some profounder awareness opens, admitting you to sentience of the mounting sap."[1] That awareness is mind-heart-body-nature awareness, the life and flow of the universe realized in human terms. In this state, the "landscape [is] beaming with consciousness like the face of a god," as John Muir once wrote. In this state of continuity, nature is not "natural resources."

ENLIGHTENMENT

The temptation is to see such experience—place enlightenment—as unusual. We have accepted self-hood and egoistic consciousness so completely that we have become professional fragments of intellect, standing apart from the stream of life. We have categories for everything: we list Mary Austin and John Muir under "landscape mysticism," and go about our business, untouched. We have accepted the paradigm of separate self-hood so completely that we tend to doubt the relevance of our own experience of place. That, if it should happen, we put in the category labeled "nostalgia." Sigmund Freud referred to it (at second hand) as the oceanic feeling, and said that it had never happened to him and was probably greatly overrated. A rational skeptic, he stood firmly with reason and analysis. He went so far as to say that in fact it is the human condition, the given, to feel and to be apart from nature. This Freud stated in 1930, in *Civilization and Its Discontents*,[2] just a year after Joseph Wood Krutch had asserted a similarly conclusive judgment on the heroically alienated state of humankind in *The Modern Temper*.[3]

This theory of alienation is still very much with us, and still in conflict with the sort of experience Mary Austin described. The polarity of ego consciousness and place- or nature-embeddedness gives rise to perhaps the most anciently perceived human contradiction. Herman Melville called it "head" and "heart" ("I stand for the heart. To the dogs with the head!" he wrote to his friend Nathaniel Hawthorne).[4] Many centuries before Melville, the Chinese philosophers of the Hwa Yen school of Buddhism stated that if one looks at the world in what they termed the Svabhava way, one will see independent objects, whereas if one looks in the Nihsvabhava way, one will see interdependent systems. The Svabhava way shows a static collection of things, or shows them knocking into each other in simple, linear cause and effect. The Nihsvabhava way shows a dynamic inter-impingement. This is where the sense of place lives. Two different ways of looking result in two different worlds. J. Krishnamurti's metaphor for the polarity of consciousness was simple: To see the world as separate objects (and oneself as the subject of that world) was, he said, thought. To experience the world as an inclusive totality was intelligence. In his 1946 study, *The Meeting of East and West*, F. C. S. Northrop identified the two aspects of consciousness as the "determinate theoretic component" and the "undifferentiated aesthetic component."[5] In 1972, in *The Psychology of Consciousness*, Dr. Robert Ornstein located the poles of consciousness in the left and right halves of the cortex, a formulation that subsequent research found applied mainly to right-handed adult males but one that has proven influential. Ornstein's left-right dualism is consonant with Krishnamurti's thought and intelligence, Northrop's two differing components, Hwa Yen Buddhism's Svabhava and Nihsvabhava, and Melville's head and heart. The point is not so much where the two main capabilities of human consciousness are located physiologically, but simply that they do exist.

It seems clear that Freud and Krutch were using the determinate theoretic component in making their analyses of the human condition. As they sat in their studies, their left brains were dominant. They were strangers in the world then, as Austin might have seen them, and their theories simply reflected the way their minds were working. Krutch later got out and did some walking in the desert, and changed his ideas about the human condition, but that is another story. What I would like to explore now is the differing ethical impetus implicit in the two sides of human consciousness.

THE OBJECTIVE WORLD

If I see the world as object, I see myself as subject. I possess the same sort of entity as anything I look at: lodgepole pine; Volvo station wagon. I am one of the objects of the objective world. I am special, though, because I possess this consciousness that I shine out upon objects. They do not have my consciousness, my peculiar, personal, sentient I-ness. In my thinking, thoughtful separateness, leaning toward the Svabhava side of consciousness, dwelling in thought, I experience the emotions of my state, the emotions of the self. Identified with the thought stream, I feel tragic separateness, heroic separateness; neediness; fear; righteousness. Lacking feel for the relational world, I am inherently self-referential and hierarchic. Perfectly inevitably, I join a world economy ignorant of the codependent, relational nature of nature. As a separate being, I experience nagging discomfort. I need to have the world back around me. Thought has made into two what is originally and always one. As long as I am in the thought mode, the ego mode, as long as I am dwelling in a state of imbalanced consciousness and seeing the world from a standpoint of self-partiality, I am needy. I am driven to action, to reaching across the projected gap of space into the opposite realm, the realm of "natural resources," and acquiring the wherewithal to rebuild the world. For that is what I am doing—rebuilding the world. But in the image of thought and self. This new world will not look like the original. My ethic is one of never-ending competitive acquisitiveness. Me first and you second, as Krishnamurti idiomatically put it. From the centerless, relational view of the wider awareness—that is, from the point of view of nature—this is pathological.

I think it obvious that the tipping of the balance toward thought and self is the engine of history. This shared pathology is the inclusive problem of human life. I hesitate to use a word like pathology, because after all we ought to like ourselves, at least moderately, but the facts of daily life say pathology. The British economist E. F. Schumacher put the case succinctly: "If greed were not the master of modern man—ably assisted by envy—how could it be that the frenzy of economism does not abate as higher 'standards of living' are attained, and that it is precisely the richest societies which pursue their economic advantage with the greatest ruthlessness?"[6] Schumacher describes here the outward manifestations of the inward vicious cycle. It is the endlessness of the ego's security project, founded in the illogic and imbalance of the ego's epistemology, that makes so much of modern life what it is. We can no longer just dip our Sierra cups into any little stream we pass, backpacking; we can't sunbathe; we are watching the topsoil of the world be blown and washed away; oranges reportedly have been found that contain no vitamin C. We have people in Congress trying to destroy the Endangered Species Act of 1973, one of the most significant ethical moves in all of human history. And I could go on. All our perversity and contradiction trace back to the itch and fear that characterize the islanded ego, and that urge forward its furious, alienated activity.

HAVE WE OVERDONE IT?

But there are signs that we are finally getting tired of all this. So many critics and scholars have recently worked the territory of paradigm change—I think of Carolyn Merchant, Gregory Bateson, Theodore Roszak, Fritjof Capra, Paul

Shepard, Dolores LaChapelle, William Barrett, Paul Hawken, and again E. F. Schumacher, among many others—that we might, looking at their stacks of books, even posit a coming revision of Western civilization's dominant paradigm. At the philosophical level we might be readying ourselves to enter a post-Cartesian, postdualistic world. There are signs even in English departments. The common denominator of ecocriticism, feminist criticism, multicultural criticism, and all forms of poststructuralist criticism, is resistance to the linear and separatist habit of mind, and a new openness to relational awareness.

If we perceive relationally, we see that both aspects of the human-consciousness polarity have a legitimate, evolution-earned status. We have been gone, as it were, identified with just one side of ourselves for a time, and now we are noticing the totality again. We are conceiving that health is to be found in wholeness.

The neglected side of consciousness—heart, right brain, Nihsvabhava aware-ness, and so on—does not project a separate subjective identity. Inclusive configu-ration, participative system, is the field of this side of ourselves, and thus a metaphysically needy self-hood does not arise. Being is sufficient. "My pony became quiet at last and I know not how long I sat and looked and listened, con-sciousness merged in the general ecstasy of that April morning," wrote the natu-ralist Roy Bedicheck. Young Bedicheck was not looking at natural resources; he was breathing inside the real, living, natural world, experiencing ecological com-munity. The ethic is one of coexistence. Everything, out to the farthest edge of the universe exists in total symbiosis.

But of course we have both capabilities: linear-sequential thought and config-urative awareness. And what can unify them? D. H. Lawrence wrote a poem called "The Third Thing," which includes these lines: "Water is H2O, hydrogen two parts, oxygen one, but there is also a third thing, that makes it water and nobody knows what that is."[7] I would propose that the third thing is simply the overarching wildness of the world, the nature of nature, the wildness that is in us also, working to unify and to heal. Under this view, nothing is more natural than wholeness.

So I think we should resist the notion that the profound experience of place found in Bedicheck's writings, or Austin's, or John Muir's, or Henry David Thoreau's, is something unusual. We just happen to live in a culture whose reli-gion is the bottom line, and thus we are taught that when these people talk about nature intensely, they are mystics, representing a very minor and occasional play-time of the mind. We are taught to value Gifford Pinchot's utilitarian forestry over Muir's sense of the awesome sacredness of living trees, and to think that these two men are an either-or choice. The egoistic side of consciousness sees the world as distinction and opposition.

That is one of the reasons Wallace Stegner is so valuable. No one can casually put him down as a mystic; he is too clearly rational in his argument and analysis. He uses numbers tellingly, and he knows his history: "In the six mountain states, the Bureau of Reclamation has 5,500,000 acres reserved for dam and canal sites. . . . Then there are the 4,500,000 acres set aside for 'use without impairment' in the National Park system. There are 3,500,000 acres in game and bird refuges run by the Fish & Wildlife Service. The Bureau of Indian Affairs has 188,000 acres, apart from the Indian reservations themselves, which are not federal but tribal land."[8] Now we have the proportions, so that if we talk about those acres we will all be on the same page, with the big map behind the page. It wasn't just knowing the numbers, it was seeing how everything fit together. He saw and could convey the big picture. What gave his words power was that he had the sense of place through the pores. The map of adult understanding, and the feel of young, wide-awake learning. At age eleven, a prairie child as he called himself, on the bank of Henry's Fork of the Snake, the "soft animal" of his body first began to love a new kind of country:

> My imagination was not stretched by the wonder of the parted waters, the Yellowstone rising only a few miles eastward to flow out toward the Missouri, the Mississippi, the Gulf, while this bright pounding stream was starting through its thousand miles of canyons to the Columbia and the Pacific.
>
> All I knew was that it was pure delight to be where the land lifted in peaks and plunged in canyons, and to sniff air thin, spray-cooled, full of pine and spruce smells, and to be so close-seeming to the improbably indigo sky. I gave my heart to the mountains the minute I stood beside this river with its spray in my face and watched it thunder into foam, smooth to green glass over sunken rocks, shatter to foam again. I was fascinated by how it sped by and yet was always there; its roar shook both the earth and me.
>
> . . . By such a river it is impossible to believe that one will ever be tired or old. Every sense applauds it.[9]

That is the root allegiance. Knowledge and the numbers come later, and all these are put into the service of the land, the overarching reality that is also and always felt stirring inside. Anyone who has read *All the Little Live Things* will know that Wallace Stegner had no patience with the imbalance toward the non-rational, an imbalance occasionally popular in history. What he embodies is balance, a unity of consciousness. Rationalism and analysis, the work of the head or the left brain, when they are in service of the wild, are very different from rationalism and analysis when they are in service to the needs of the separate self. When rational thought is out on its own rogue quest of ego, it is like what Robinson Jeffers said of a severed hand: "an ugly thing." When it recognizes the higher truth of community and ecology, thought is beautiful, a true flowering of human nature.

PROTECTING WILDERNESS

From the standpoint of such grateful intelligence and such a living sense of place, protecting and restoring wilderness seems only the most natural activity. And Stegner was and is one of the most significant defenders of wilderness we have had. His "Wilderness Letter" of 1960, judging by the frequency of its reprinting alone, has become as scriptural in its way as Aldo Leopold's *A Sand County Almanac*.

But now we are entering a new era of consciousness about wilderness, and we very much need Wallace Stegner's humane calmness to help us see things whole. Historically, wilderness protection has occurred mainly under the dualistic rubric—the Wilderness Act of 1964 explicitly defines humanity as a "visitor who does not remain" in the wilderness—but this frame of reference is breaking down. We are beginning to see wilderness not only as recreation ground for our urban selves but as the home of biological diversity with inherent, evolutionary rights to exist. We are also beginning to conceive of permanent human presence within wilderness, at present, to be sure, only in the preserves where aboriginal or "first nation" people already have established subsistence. We are starting to transcend the dualistic model of the world. Perhaps we will not much longer see ourselves as visitors in nature.

RESTORING WILDERNESS

The beautiful work ahead of us is the restoration of the natural world to a continuing state of wild health. Stephan Hoeller, in a 1991 article, wrote that "the restoration of biological order must be seen as a metaphor for the restoration of the wholeness of consciousness; otherwise we shall miss the deeper meaning of the present crisis of civilization."[10] I agree, but think it's more than a matter of metaphor: Biological order and the wholeness of human consciousness are totally interpenetrant. "Lack one lacks both," in the words of Walt Whitman. "The reason why the world lacks unity, and lies broken and in heaps," wrote Ralph Waldo Emerson in 1836, "is because man is disunited with himself."[11] It is all one system, and the sense of place is the chiefest, most intimate and real way we know this.

The sense of place lets us into the logic of connection. By the logic of connection—the standard of nature—restoration must include in the end everything, every acre. Speaking now of the West, the "native home of hope," as Wallace Stegner put it, we will not much longer be content with fragments of wilderness. We are beginning to open up to the vision of big-scale protection and big-scale restoration. Historically, we have ghettoized wilderness, in effect, and we are beginning to see that the policy doesn't work. Island biogeography shows that Yellowstone, to the grizzly bear or wolf population, is pretty small—not enough. Back in the 1920s and 1930s, Olaus Murie showed that Yellowstone and Jackson Hole weren't big enough, really, for elk—they had, he believed, always gone south, as far as the Red Desert in south-central Wyoming, for the winter. Now there were too many fences in the way, and the herds had to crowd together on the National Elk Refuge and eat hay and get necrotic stomatitis. The ecological sense of connection says there need to be corridors linking large reservoirs of bio-diversity, and there need to be even larger reservoirs. This is the world, the field of life. This is, in a real sense, our being. The ecological sense of connection says the world should be mostly wild, with humanity fitting into it as a good animal citizen.

Let us start with the largest wilderness left below the 60th parallel, in the northeast corner of British Columbia, where no less than fifty "contiguous, virtu-ally untouched watersheds," in the description of Rebecca Solnit somehow have survived. Save it, leave it, don't even hang a radio collar on it. Link it well to Mount Robson, and Banff, and Waterton Lakes, Glacier, Yellowstone, Grand Teton, the Winds, the Snowy Range, Rocky Mountain National Park, the Sangre de Cristos—all the way down the spinal column, a wide swath of living land, the nerve line, our mind-body alive again. And the same for the valleys, all the way: And here we will be called on for serious restoration. And this is just for starters.

Am I talking wildly? I hope so. If we live without vision, without the wider world, we will be doomed to ego's paltry way. Pavement matters profoundly. Noise matters profoundly. The wilderness is so incredibly important because it is not just a metaphor for health, it *is* health. Stephanie Mills, in her remarkable 1995 book, *In Service of the Wild*, writes,

> What restoration could and should be for in us is the transformation of our souls. In addition to what this work may accomplish in the land, I yearn for it as the yoga that will cause us to evolve spiritually, that will restore to us a feeling of awe in something besides our own conceits.[12]

It seems to me that this beautiful, wild system that has created us and that sustains us, deserves nothing less than a beautiful work of redemption and affir-mation. Perhaps we will come to see wholeness as our ordinary and daily activity.

John Muir seemed to see his own fidelity to nature as a very simple and straight-forward matter. "Not like my taking the veil," he wrote, "no solemn abjuration of the world. I only went out for a walk, and finally concluded to stay out till sundown, for going out, I found, was really going in."[13]

NOTES

[1] Mary Austin, *The Land of Journeys' Ending*. Tucson: University of Arizona Press, 1983, p. 40.

[2] Sigmund Freud, *Civilization and Its Discontents*. New York: Norton, 1962, pp. 11–20.

[3] Joseph Wood Krutch, *The Modern Tempter: A Study and a Confession*. New York: Harcourt Brace, 1929.

[4] Merrell R. Davis and William H. Gilman, eds., *The Letters of Herman Melville*. New Haven: Yale University Press, 1960, p.129.

[5] F. C. S. Northrop, *The Meeting of East and West*. New York: Macmillan, 1946.

[6] E. F. Schumacher, *Small Is Beautiful*. New York: Harper & Row, 1973, p. 37.

[7] Vivian de Sola Pinto, ed., *The Complete Poetry of D. H. Lawrence*. New York: Viking, 1971, p. 515.

[8] Wallace Stegner, *The Sound of Mountain Water*. Lincoln: University of Nebraska Press, 1985, pp. 33–34.

[9] Ibid., pp. 41–42.

[10] Quoted in Stephanie Mills, *In Service of the Wild*. Boston: Beacon Press, 1995, p. 25.

[11] Ralph Waldo Emerson, *The Complete Essays and Other Writings of Ralph Waldo Emerson*. New York: Modern Library, 1950, p. 41.

[12] Mills, *In Service of the Wild*, p. 25.

[13] Linnie Marsh Wolfe, ed., *John of the Mountains: The Unpublished Journals of John Muir*. Madison: University of Wisconsin Press, 1979, p. 439.

Chapter 3

IN SEARCH OF A WESTERN ETHIC
Lessons from Public Land
and Natural Resource Policy

Robert B. Keiter

The recent headlines are telling: "The River Wild—Grand Flush Pours New Life into a Grand Canyon"; "Jekyll & Hyde Tales Won't Keep Wolf Out of Yellowstone"; "Court Reaffirms U.S. Ownership and Management of Public Lands"; and "Ranchers Descend on Capitol to Lobby for Senate Grazing Bill." At one level, the articles accompanying the headlines are simply about traditional western topics: water and dams, wolves, local control, and livestock grazing. At another level, though, the accompanying articles tell a different story—one of change and fear as the West readies itself to move into the 21st century. In the Grand Canyon article, Secretary of the Interior Bruce Babbitt observes that the canyon flooding heralds "a new era in the way we live on the American landscape." And in the livestock article, a Wyoming sheep rancher states, "Basically, this bill is our livelihood. We don't know from one year to the next what our future is going to be."

Without question, each of the articles addresses an important and controversial dimension of western public land and natural resource policy. Each article contains elements of change and constancy—a recurrent theme embedded within contemporary public discourse about the West. Each article provides important insights into the evolving nature of the human relationship with the western environment. And each article confirms one critically important dimension of any western ethic—that place and people matter.

In trying to identify an ethic to define the West, public land and natural resource policy represents an appropriate focal point. Wallace Stegner identified two defining characteristics of the West: its aridity and the presence of large tracts of public lands. These simple geographic and political facts give the region its distinctive character, and also account in large part for the unique and organic quality of so many of its laws and policies. An excursion through the past 150 years of western natural resource law offers strong evidence that the region is still in the process of being defined, and that the human role in the western landscape is still unsettled. The present generation—like those before it—is still struggling to transform its collective knowledge and values into an ethical norm and legal imperative. Stegner, of course, already observed this fact: "Physically and socially, the West does not remain the same from decade to decade. . . . If anything, it changes faster."[1]

It may seem strange to look primarily to federal legal policies to define a western ethic, but a national presence is a major, undeniable fact of life in the West. The West has always been linked to the coasts, whether for marketing its cattle or minerals, or by offering a fresh start to another wave of migrants, or through hosting an annual influx of tourists. Although basic public land policies have always been finalized in Washington, the process has involved a complex interplay between national and local forces, and a keen appreciation for the diverse local settings where these policies will be applied. As reflected in the original 1872 Mining Law and the ongoing reform efforts that have now spanned several decades, the West has always played a major role in formulating these policies and their implementation. Although the West may appear to be a monolithic entity, it has always consisted of an amalgam of people and beliefs, which is as true today as it was a century ago. Natural resource policy, then, is a fair reflection of the West's fundamental beliefs and its collective values.

A HISTORICAL SURVEY: FROM DISPOSAL TO PRESERVATION

Roughly speaking, western public land and natural resource policy has passed through three distinct periods. These are: (1) the 1862–91 period of disposal, characterized by the federal policy of giving away public land and resources to encourage settlement; (2) the 1891–1935 period of reservation and withdrawal, characterized by the federal government's decision to retain and manage parts of the public domain and its resources; and (3) the post-1935 period of permanent retention and management, which ultimately confirmed a long-term and active federal presence in the western states. By my estimation, we are now in transition to a fourth era in public land and natural resource policy—one that is characterized by ecological concerns and public involvement. It portends further changes and the emergence of yet another ethic.

Following acquisition and original exploration of the frontier West, the U.S. government adopted a policy of disposal designed to transfer public land and resources to private ownership to promote western settlement and development. Largely ignoring John Wesley Powell's call—in his *Report on the Lands of the Arid Region of the United States*—for scientifically based policies and cooperative local endeavors geared to the West's dry climate, Congress was content to rely upon an individualistic laissez faire approach to promote western settlement.[2] Federal and state disposal policy was manifested in such laws as the Homestead Act of 1862, Desert Lands Act of 1877, the General Mining Law of 1872, and the prior appropriation doctrine governing access to the region's precious water resources. The general idea was to make the West's abundant land and resources available for the taking on a first-in-time basis. As Wallace Stegner explained it, "The laws that grew up in the [West] . . . were essentially the justification of appropriation, which was itself essentially tolerated trespass."[3]

In addition, federal subsidies in the form of generous land grants were dangled before private entrepreneurs to spur railroad construction across the western expanses. The new railroads in turn brought even more people and speculators to the new frontier. Despite the inevitable, often colorful episodes of fraud and chicanery that accompanied this federal largesse, the related policies of disposal and subsidization were generally successful and soon turned the West into a habitable setting.

During this same period, a few farsighted individuals recognized the uniqueness and vulnerability of special places like Yellowstone and Yosemite. They succeeded in convincing Congress to begin setting aside the region's scenic wonders as national parks—the first time ever that a nation legally removed such large chunks of land from development. John Muir and his newly created Sierra Club became principal proponents of the national park movement and helped ensure that preservation would become an important part of public land policy. Many westerners, though, viewed this new preservation movement with suspicion, fearing more federal intervention into local affairs and adverse economic impacts. Shortly after the turn of the century, this budding preservation movement came into direct conflict with the competing philosophy of resource utilization, creating a tension that persists yet today.

By 1890 according to historian Frederick Jackson Turner, the western frontier was closed. Most of the western territories had secured statehood, the Indians were subdued and relegated to reservations, and the nation was moving into the industrial age. The West's land and resources were tired, having been relentlessly exploited by successive waves of explorers, speculators, and settlers. Francis Parkman, author of *The Oregon Trail*, captured the devastated western landscape of the 1890s:

> The buffalo is gone, and all his millions, nothing is left but bones. . . . Those discordant serenaders, the wolves that howled at evening about the traveller's campfire, have succumbed to arsenic and hushed their savage music. . . . The rattlesnakes have grown bashful and retiring. The mountain lion shrinks from the face of man, and even grim "Old Ephraim," the grizzly bear, seeks the seclusion of his dens and caverns.[4]

In addition, the West's forests and watersheds, following a pattern that had earlier played out in the Northeast and Midwest, were in real danger from uncontrolled timber harvesting.

Confronted with this devastation and with substantial support from westerners themselves, Congress shifted gears and adopted new policies to reserve and withdraw parts of the public domain from unbridled exploitation. In 1891 Congress gave the president authority to designate forest reserves, and Presidents Harrison and Cleveland promptly invoked this power and placed over 17 million acres in the nation's first forest reserves.[5] With passage of the Organic Act of 1897, the Forest Service was created to administer the new forest reserves and the national forest system was established.[6] As the first chief of this new agency, Gifford Pinchot advocated and successfully established the notion of scientific management of natural resources to achieve utilitarian objectives. Although Pinchot's philosophy also gave priority to community needs, his new forest rangers met substantial local resistance when they began imposing permit requirements on western ranchers and loggers. But the Supreme Court, in two landmark 1911 decisions, tersely affirmed the new Forest Service's regulatory authority over its lands, and thus effectively legitimized Pinchot's wise-use policies. This philosophy has since been transposed into the multiple-use doctrine and still governs national forest and BLM public lands.

Elsewhere the federal government and the states sought to slow disposition of the West's public resources and to move toward planned resource management. In 1916 Congress established the National Park Service and charged it with administering a national park system, thus signaling a long-term federal commitment to preserving select portions of the nation's natural heritage. Faced with severely depleted wildlife stocks, President Theodore Roosevelt designated the nation's first wildlife refuge at Pelican Island in 1903, and the states began establishing game and fish management agencies to protect and rebuild big game herds. In 1909 the President, utilizing an inherent executive withdrawal power, withdrew public lands in California and Wyoming to retain the nation's critical oil reserves in federal hands. The Supreme Court sustained this use of executive power, and Congress responded by amending the General Mining Law to remove energy minerals from its coverage.[7] To promote planned resource development in the West, Congress passed the Newlands Act of 1902, and thus committed the federal government to fund reclamation projects to make water available for regional development. The resulting water projects, which eventually reshaped the West's extensive river systems, reflected the prevailing view that human ingenuity, supplemented with generous doses of federal money, could engineer the western landscape into a fertile new homeland.[8]

The rest of the public domain—often referred to as "the lands no one wanted"—remained available for homesteading until the mid-1930s. Then, faced with the Dust Bowl crisis and a severely depleted western range, Congress passed the Taylor Grazing Act of 1934, which effectively halted further homestead entry and signaled the beginning of a third major shift in federal public land policy. Forty years later, what was implicit in the Taylor Grazing Act became explicit with passage of the Federal Land Policy and Management Act of 1976 (FLPMA). This legislation formally ended the policy of disposition by adopting a new policy of permanent federal retention and active management of the remaining public domain. The BLM joined the Forest Service as a statutory multiple-use agency with regulatory authority implemented through comprehensive planning procedures.

Then, beginning in 1960 and continuing through the mid-1970s, Congress passed a plethora of laws that fundamentally reshaped federal resource management policy. These included: (1) the Multiple Use–Sustained Yield Act of 1960, which legitimized the Forest Service's long-standing commitment to multiple-use management principles[9]; (2) the Wilderness Act of 1964, which formally established wilderness as a legitimate use of public lands and removed large blocks of national forestlands from future development[10]; (3) the Wild & Scenic Rivers Act of 1968, which similarly reserved stretches of rivers from further development—a matter of real consequence in the water hungry West[11]; and (4) the National Forest Management Act of 1976 (or NFMA), which mandated comprehensive, interdisciplinary planning on the national forests and imposed significant, science-based constraints—including a biological diversity conservation obligation—on the Forest Service's timber harvesting program.[12]

Also the time of environmental awakening, Congress responded by passing major pieces of environmental protection legislation that continue to impact public land management. These laws include: (1) the National Environmental Policy Act (or NEPA), which has provided a vehicle for public involvement in agency decisions and a basis for judicial review of these decisions[13]; (2) the Endangered Species Act, which has extended federal regulatory power into the area of wildlife policy by protecting all species threatened with extinction, regardless of consumptive worth[14]; and (3) the Clean Water and Clean Air Acts, both of which impose federal regulatory controls to protect against pollution of these important resources.[15]

A CONTEMPORARY ASSESSMENT: ECOLOGICAL AWAKENING

Without question, these recent statutory changes have had a major impact on public land and natural resource policy. First, they imposed new federal preservation policies on the public domain, and new environmental protection responsibilities on federal land managers as well as state and local governments and private landowners. Second, they opened public land and natural resource decision processes to broad public involvement as well as judicial oversight; this has diminished the influence of the traditional public land constituencies and made the courts a major new institutional factor. Third, by expressly injecting environmental considerations into the land management equation, they legitimized application of biological and ecological sciences in agency decision processes, which has gradually expanded federal managerial responsibilities. In short, these laws have laid the groundwork for the transition to a new, fourth era in natural resource policy.

These same laws, however, have also triggered an intense and powerful back-lash. In the political arena, ranchers and other traditional public land users have challenged expanded assertions of federal authority through such vehicles as the Sagebrush Rebellion movement, the War on the West rhetoric, and county supremacy land use ordinances. Western politicians have sought to frame the issue as who governs the West: Washington, the states, or the region's myriad local communities. At the behest of these same politicians, several important leg-islative proposals have been submitted to the 104th Congress, including Endangered Species Act amendments, an overhaul of the NFMA, Senator Domenici's livestock grazing bill, takings legislation, and a return of the public lands to the states. Congress already has authorized intensified salvage logging on the national forests and also removed application of most environmental laws, which has prevented meaningful judicial review. In addition, these same forces have sought and won, at the Supreme Court level and elsewhere, enhanced judi-cial protection of property rights against regulatory takings. Although the Supreme Court rulings have little direct impact on the western public domain, the threat of takings litigation hangs over natural resource managers, particularly in the area of endangered species and wetlands protection.

While Congress has not adopted any major new public land laws over the past twenty years, several important developments portend further changes in natural resource policy. These new initiatives represent an effort to remedy the legacies of past policies, and a response to compelling new scientific insights, as well as economic and cultural changes. To address acid runoff and other residues from past mining operations, several major clean-up efforts have been launched. To address the extirpation of major predators from the western landscape, the U.S. Fish & Wildlife Service has initiated a controversial wolf reintroduction pro-gram in Yellowstone National Park and central Idaho. In the arena of water policy, to address the ecological impacts associated with the network of dams that block many western rivers, multiple agencies have begun cooperating in several locations: to restore native salmon runs in the Pacific Northwest, to simulate flood conditions in the Grand Canyon, and to plan the actual removal of two dams on the Elwha River inside Olympic National Park. The Bureau of Reclamation, which played such a major role in reengineering the West's rivers, is in the process of remaking itself into a water management (rather than water development) agency. At the state level, most western states have now adopted in-stream flow laws, which leaves some water in place and thus represents a major shift in traditional western water law doctrine. And recognizing that past fire suppression policies have eliminated an important ecological renewal force from the West's forests (and perhaps contributed to what has been described as a major forest health problem), the federal land management agencies have committed themselves to reintroducing fire on the public domain. In total, these assorted initiatives suggest a growing recognition that the hitherto distinctive preservation and multiple-use policies are in fact linked; the successful implementation of either policy requires a broad understanding of ecological processes and cooperative management protocols that ensure the integrity of the resource base itself.

The philosophical roots of this revised approach to natural resource management can be traced to Aldo Leopold, whose *A Sand County Almanac* essays have become a true classic in conservation literature and policy. In his "Round River" essay, Leopold makes the important ecological point that all things are hooked together by observing that "[t]o keep every cog and wheel is the first precaution of intelligent thinking."[16] In his seminal "The Land Ethic" essay, Leopold then lays out a new ecological vision of natural resource stewardship:

> [A] land ethic changes the role of Homo sapiens from conqueror of the land-community to plain member and citizen of it. It implies respect for his fellow-members, and also respect for the community as such. . . . The "key-log" which must be moved to release the evolutionary process for an ethic is simply this: quit thinking about decent land-use as solely an economic problem. Examine each question in terms of what is ethically and aesthetically right, as well as what is economically expedient. A thing is right when it tends to preserve the integrity, stability, and beauty of the biotic community. It is wrong when it tends otherwise.[17]

Or, as Wallace Stegner succinctly characterized Leopold's view, "[The] earth is a community to which we belong, and to which, in consequence, we owe a duty."[18]

LOOKING AHEAD: THE EMERGENCE OF ECOSYSTEM MANAGEMENT

What form is Leopold's land ethic taking, and what does it portend for the West's future? According to recent government policy documents, Leopold's land ethic has been translated into the concept of ecosystem management, which has been embraced by all of the federal land management agencies, as well as several state natural resource management agencies. Ecosystem management employs the insights and understandings of the ecological sciences to manage the public domain as a holistic, integrated entity in order to ensure its ecological integrity and a sustainable resource base. This entails a commitment to maintaining native biological diversity patterns and interrelated ecological processes, the use of inter-jurisdictional coordination to transcend conventional boundaries, and an adaptive management strategy to accommodate new scientific and social developments. As important, it also acknowledges a critical human role: It encompasses a commitment to involving the interested public in defining resource management objectives and in making management decisions, through inclusive public participation processes and coordinated partnership arrangements.[19]

In short, ecosystem management reflects a renewed and expanded commitment to place and people—the two elements that have always driven western natural resource policy and that are at the core of any western ethic. What is different, however, is that ecosystem management endorses an expanded conception (or sense) of place; all elements of place—biological, human, inanimate, and aesthetic—are important and must be factored into the management equation. Moreover, ecosystem management recognizes that these elements exist in a dynamic, changing environment, not as part of a static landscape. At the same time, ecosystem management endorses an expanded conception of the role people play in formulating natural resource policy. This means that everyone with an interest in the ecosystem is entitled to a place at the table, to participate in defining basic policies for its future. And because ecological, social, and economic conditions vary substantially from one location to another, it also means important decisions regarding how these basic policies are implemented must directly involve those who are affected locally and take full account of their interests, knowledge, and sensitivities.[20]

The ultimate impact of this shift toward ecosystem management can only be dimly perceived. Some likely effects include a diminishing of the significance of conventional boundary lines, a greater willingness to allow natural processes to occur with minimal human intervention, serious ecological restoration efforts (as already reflected in the wolf recovery program and the Grand Canyon flood), and expanded interjurisdictional coordination efforts. In addition, traditional public land constituencies may see their influence wane as other interests claim a seat at the table (as already is beginning to occur with creation of the State Resource Advisory Councils as part of the BLM's range reform program), long-standing access rights and prerogatives to public resources may be called into question to accommodate important competing ecological and other interests, and environmental concerns may begin to displace production targets in measuring managerial success. To be sure, serious ecological management and restoration efforts will require local involvement, commitment, and support, so these policies must be linked directly to the economic and social health of western communities. A major concern, which already has surfaced in several locations, is a mounting interest in avoiding further fragmentation of the landscape through the sale and subdivision of ranch properties. More distantly, this shift toward an ecological perspective may force a redefinition of property rights, as the public comes to expect property owners to bear some responsibility for safeguarding the nation's biological heritage.[21]

What better place than the American West to attempt such a major reconception of the human relationship with nature? With the West's open spaces and expansive public lands, there is still an opportunity to think big and to create on a large scale. Western settlement and development was itself something of a grand experiment, designed to accommodate the necessities of the time with the physical setting itself. We created laws, policies, and institutions that were intentionally crafted to subdue nature and to transform the harsh landscape into a civilized society. It was bold, visionary, and hard work; it required substantial cooperation at all levels; and it was regularly subject to revision. A similar commitment to thinking expansively and working cooperatively will be required to maintain and restore the West's natural heritage.

With this task at hand, Wallace Stegner's observations on John Wesley Powell's career take on added force. Powell too had a visionary perspective, and he was committed to using scientific rigor to devise functional land and resource policies for the then unsettled West. Yet, according to Stegner, Powell also recognized that his ideas were only "working syntheses" subject to being changed and discarded. In the final analysis, any proposed western ethic will—at best—be merely a working synthesis, one that will be improved upon as our knowledge grows and our values change. After all, an ethic is nothing more—or less—than the collective conscience of the society that produced it. Thus, because the relationship between people and place still counts in the West, it is time to engage in a civil dialogue—applying our own powers of reason and science—to reaffirm and reorder our shared commitment to this special place. We owe at least that much to the generations that will follow.

NOTES

[1] Wallace Stegner, *The Sound of Mountain Water* (Lincoln, Neb.: Univ. of Nebraska Press, 1987), p. 10.

[2] Wallace Stegner, *Beyond the Hundredth Meridian: John Wesley Powell and the Second Opening of the West* (Lincoln, Neb.: University of Nebraska Press, 1953).

[3] Wallace Stegner, "Foreword." In *Wilderness at the Edge: A Citizen Proposal to Protect Utah's Canyons and Deserts* (Salt Lake City: The Utah Wilderness Coalition, 1990).

[4] Francis Parkman (1892), quoted in Peter Matthiessen, *Wildlife in America* (New York: Viking 1959), p.183.

[5] Samuel T. Dana and Sally K. Fairfax, *Forest and Range Policy: Its Development in the United States* (New York: McGraw Hill, 2nd edition, 1980), pp. 56–58.

[6] Idem at pp. 61–63.

[7] *United States v. Midwest Oil Co.*, 276 U.S. 459 (1915). See John Leshy, *The Mining Law: A Study in Perpetual Motion* (Washington, D.C.: Resources for the Future, 1987).

[8] Marc Reisner, *Cadillac Desert: The American West and Its Disappearing Water* (New York: Viking, 1986).

[9] U.S.Code, Vol. 16, secs. 528–31. See George C. Coggins, "Of Succotash Syndromes and Vacuous Platitudes: The Meaning of 'Multiple Use, Sustained Yield' for Public Land Management" (Part I), 53 *University of Colorado Law Review* 229 (1982).

[10] U.S.Code, Vol. 16, secs. 1131–36. See D. Rohlf and D. Honnold, "Managing the Balances of Nature: The Legal Framework of Wilderness Management," 15 *Ecology Law Quarterly* 249 (1988).

[11] U.S.Code, Vol. 16, secs. 1271–87. See Sally K. Fairfax, Barbara T. Andrews, and Andrew P. Buchsbaum, "Federalism and the Wild and Scenic Rivers Act: Now You See It, Now You Don't," 59 *Washington Law Review* 417 (1984).

[12] U.S.Code, Vol. 16, sec.1600–14. See Charles Wilkinson and Michael Anderson, "Land and Resource Planning in the National Forests," 64 *Oregon Law Review* 1 (1985).

[13] U.S.Code, Vol. 42, secs. 4321–61. See generally Special Focus, Articles and Essays: "NEPA at Twenty," 25 *Land & Water Law Review* 1 (1990); "Symposium on NEPA at Twenty: The Past, Present and Future of the National Environmental Policy Act," 20 *Environmental Law* 447 (1990).

[14] U.S.Code, Vol. 16, secs. 1531–43. See George C. Coggins and Irma S. Russell, "Beyond Shooting Snail Darters in Pork Barrels: Endangered Species and Land Use in America," 70 *Georgia Law Journal* 1433 (1982).

[15] U.S.Code, Vol. 33, secs. 1251–1387 (water); U.S.Code, Vol. 42, secs. 7401–7671q (air). See William Rodgers, Environmental Law (St. Paul: West Publishing Co., 2nd edition, 1996).

[16] Aldo Leopold, *A Sand County Almanac* (New York: Oxford Univ. Press, 1966), p.190.

[17] Idem at pp. 240, 262.

[18] Wallace Stegner, *Wilderness At the Edge*, supra note 3, at p.4.

[19] Interagency Ecosystem Management Task Force, *The Ecosystem Approach: Healthy Ecosystems and Sustainable Economics*, Vol. 1—Overview (Washington, D.C., 1995), p. 3; Society of American Foresters, "Task Force Report on Sustaining Long-Term Forest Health and Productivity" (Bethesda, Md., 1993); Norman L. Christensen, et al., "The Report of the Ecological Society of America Committee on the Scientific Basis for Ecosystem Management," 6(3), *Ecological Applications* 665–91 (1996).

[20] The Keystone Center, "The Keystone National Policy Dialogue on Ecosystem Management" (Keystone, Colo., 1996).

[21] Eric Freyfogle, "Ownership and Ecology," 43 *Case Western Reserve Law Review* 1269 (1993).

PART II

A COMPELLING UNITY

INTEGRATING PEOPLE AND ECOSYSTEMS

T hese essays examine how the relationship between people and the western landscape is playing out on the ground. In his writings on the American West, Wallace Stegner frequently spoke in terms of unity—at one point noting "the single compelling unity" of western geography, and at another admonishing westerners toward a unity of purpose through "cooperation not rugged individualism." On a daily basis, the West is still wrestling with the concept of unity: how to manage its lands and resources in a manner sensitive to ecological connections, how to achieve consensus among its diverse citizenry. In her evocative opening essay, Idaho State BLM director Martha Hahn shares hard-earned lessons from her considerable experience managing and advocating for public lands, arguing that a broad public understanding of diverse perspectives, a concerted commitment to working together, and an inclusive sense of place offer the basic tools for achieving "a sustainable relationship between people and the earth." Western writer Teresa Jordan, having herself been raised in a Wyoming ranching family, describes her recent experiences as a newcomer to rural Nevada to illustrate how small western communities can appreciate—even embrace—completely new experiences and ideas; then she reviews the myriad challenges confronting a diverse, citizen-based management group responsible for cooperatively restoring the ecological and economic health of the Tipton ranch and its public land grazing leases. Writer, essayist, and novelist Rick Bass describes his personal experiences with the Forest Service in the Yaak Valley of northwestern Montana in order to mount a challenge to the concept of ecosystem management, lamenting the agency's indifference to the need for wilderness preservation and its arrogance in assuming that intensive logging in roadless areas can simulate critical ecological processes. Collectively the essays reveal both the potential and pitfalls that lurk as the West struggles to pay meaningful attention to vital ecological concerns and to pursue new, consensus-based solutions to its knotty resource allocation issues.

Chapter 4

TWO RIVERS
The View from a Federal Land Manager
Martha Hahn

"It's funny you should remember such different things than we remember. Everything means something different to everybody, I guess." She laughed, and the boy thought her eyes looked very odd and bright. "It makes me feel as if I don't know you at all," she said. She brushed her face with the handful of leaves and looked at the father, gathering up odds and ends and putting them in the picnic box. "I wonder what each of us will remember about today?"[1]

The excerpt above is from one of Wallace Stegner's short stories, "Two Rivers," in which a young family experiences a healing of sort after spending a day on a picnic in the mountains. Better minds than mine probably have analyzed and dissected the story, but one literary device stands out, the use of contrasts. In the story, there are many: the brown, flat plain where the family lives and the high green meadows of the mountains; the feeling of despair in the young boy as he awakens at the beginning of the story and the feeling of exuberance as his family finally arrives high in the mountains; and most prominently, the boy's memories of two rivers in a faraway place that joined in the same channel, one born in the mountains, running clear and cold, the other a valley river, warm and slower.

Three themes emerge in this story that apply to the human dimension of natural resource management and have day-to-day relevance to federal land managers: perspective, concert, and place.

PERSPECTIVE: SEEING ALL SIDES

About her son's recollection of the two rivers, the mother in "Two Rivers" says, "Everything means something different to everybody, I guess. It makes me feel as if I don't know you at all." Although Stegner certainly did not have a land management agency in mind when he wrote those lines, they have application in our daily existence. When we as individuals look at public land, we look at its values, we look at its beauty, we look at its natural resources, and maybe we even look at it through the eyes of a younger generation.

Managing land for many uses is a difficult task precisely because of the different meanings that each of us applies. Imagine a parcel of public land—maybe in Idaho, Utah, or Colorado—with a stream flowing through and good grass growing; a healthy riparian area with a two-track road crossing it. Now, what do you see? The mountain bikers are already on their Marins or Gary Fishers, seeing just where the trail takes them. Ranchers are thinking in terms of AUMs and the number of cattle that could run on this particular plot of land. Anglers have their fishing rods out and are lashing a royal coachman to the tippet. Wildlife enthusiasts are looking for tracks and ticking off in their minds the kinds of animals that could live here: deer, blue grouse, maybe some elk. Miners, photographers, writers, and hikers—they all have their own view of our patch of land. Everything does mean something different to everybody and though we form a community of people who care about the land, I'm convinced we do not know each other well. This, I believe, is at the root of many of our conflicts in the West today. We leap to stereotype. We leap toward disagreement. We leap to our worst suspicions. And we fail to not only understand someone else's perspective but also often deny the fact that there are other worthy perspectives. We leap to contrast, like the two rivers described in the Stegner story, one flowing warm, the other cold.

But in the story, the two rivers eventually share a common channel. We know what the symbolism means. Somewhere farther downstream, they intermingle, they interchange and they become the same river. In the terms of our world today, an understanding of perspectives takes place.

A nice allegory, but how do we make it happen in our real-world setting? How do we get to the point that our rivers flow in the same direction, join, and course toward a common destination?

CONCERT: WORKING TOGETHER

No one approach will guarantee success, but past experience suggests that understanding other perspectives and working in concert—which according to Webster is to settle or adjust by conferring—can result in meaningful change and progress.

A few years back, serving as a BLM area manager in Kanab, Utah, I was responsible for some land not unlike the imaginary piece of ground I described earlier. The area seemed to mean something different to everybody. And nobody wanted to budge.

We established a work group, composed of recreationists, wildlife advocates, ranchers, and others. We met regularly over two years. It was a long, difficult process, but slowly we came to understand different perspectives, and through concert, came to an agreement about the way that land should be managed. Not everyone was 100 percent comfortable with the decisions, but everyone could live with them. That was a major achievement, but probably not the single most important accomplishment.

What I find memorable about that process, even with the passing of almost nine years, is that the people involved soon came to respect one another and actually became friends. Toward the end of the project, the whole group took a hike. I watched the eighty-three-year-old rancher and the thirty-year-old conservationist trekking across a sand dune together; clearly they had learned the principles of sharing perspective and working in concert well.

As we confront different federal and local views, and the accompanying tension that is a part of the West, let us agree to be open-minded. Let us try to see the other points of view and gain an appreciation for differing perspective. Let us agree that we need to find common ground and a unifying theme: the continued health and productivity of the land. If we work in concert to achieve our goal, the two rivers will eventually run as one.

The spirit of concert implies more than mere cooperation. It moves to a unity of purpose that is deeper than cooperation. At this, the cynics may raise an eyebrow. Wallace Stegner used to enjoy citing Bernard DeVoto's notion that the only real individualists in the West would end up on one end of a rope, the other end of which was in the hands of a bunch of cooperators. Given our record in the West, one may indeed be pessimistic when talking about westerners and cooperation, much less concert.

Yet we have places where concert flourishes in land management. In Idaho, a coalition representing wide interests serves as a model for management of the Henry's Fork of the Snake River. In Oregon the Trout Creek Mountains shine as an example of differing interests working toward mutually agreeable management of an area. Lemhi County, in east-central Idaho, was at one time considered one of the most volatile hotbeds of antifederal sentiment. Now, a cooperative approach to management among federal agencies, the county, and dozens of other interests, marks that place as one of the West's most progressive areas.

These bright spots in the western landscape did not just appear spontaneously. It took hard work to bring about the setting for success and a continuing commitment to resolve difficulties along the way. But the unifying theme of local and federal cooperation in management of natural resources overcame the obstacles, as well as the stereotyping and the mistrust.

These and other examples of concert are the future of the West, not wise-use movements, wholesale transfer of land from one entity to another, or rule by edict or regulation. If two rivers are to run together, federal land managers must focus on working with people at least as much as they do on managing resources.

Effective managers must be more than technical marvels, they must know how to manage social relationships to achieve concert. They must know how to reach consensus, work with groups of all different backgrounds and views, and find areas of common agreement. They must be communicators who know how to talk with the people living in Murphy, Idaho, as well as those residing in Salt Lake City.

Dr. James Kennedy, of Utah State University, recently wrote about the social side of resource management in a paper presented to the Society of Range Management. In his thought-provoking presentation, he stated:

> [S]ince so many of the social values that are relevant to us natural resource and environmental managers are in conflict, we might consider our basic professional role as social-political conflict managers.
> . . . Relationship managers? Sounds like a description of personnel managers, marriage counselors, or other psychologically based professions. Yes, it does, but we share more with these disciplines than our natural resource management professions have been able to recognize and embrace. . . . We are (and always have been) human and rangeland relationship managers. We had better recognize this and become better at it.[2]

Of course, having a sound understanding of resource management principles is still important. But given today's scalding political waters and the intensity of feeling, we need people in the federal sector—and in the local communities, too—who can confront adversarial situations and emerge with the beginnings of respect from all parties. We need people who can forge unity by working concertedly.

When I worked for the Grand Canyon Trust, we became involved in an issue dealing with the power rates, economics, and interim flows associated with the Glen Canyon Dam. The problem centered on producing power while still maintaining a flow from the dam that protected downstream resources. At one point the Western Area Power Administration representative, the government's power distributor, asked conservation groups to meet and study figures and other information that would support his position that more power could be generated without damaging resources. He said WAPA needed to demonstrate, only on paper, the amount of power that could be generated, or it would not be invited to participate in forthcoming power allocation decisions. This level of generation would never be reached, he assured us, but WAPA needed to show it could be reached, or the government would not have a voice in the distribution process.

The dialogue was vitally important to the Western Area Power Administration, but to some people his appeal sounded like a call for propaganda. Their response was essentially, "Don't waste our time."

Yet what was he really asking? Wasn't it something like: "We want to present you with some information. This is very important to us and the people we represent. There may be a chance here for everyone to win. Are you willing to discuss it?"

With healthy skepticism, I nonetheless approached the other organizations on a one-on-one basis and tried to show the merits of at least listening. Most of them grudgingly agreed to hear out "the enemy."

We took other positive steps. We hired a consultant, an expert in water law and power rates, to help us understand this complex problem. He pointed out that the way the power was being distributed was a form of collusion, and therefore illegal. In the end, we talked together, and discovered new information. While the issues were not totally resolved, we made important progress, progress that never would have been gained had we accepted the first thumbing-of-the-nose reaction displayed by a half-dozen of the groups involved. In short, we came closer to discovering the truth of the situation through listening and cooperation, rather than litigation and collusion. We valued other perspectives, and we worked in concert.

Becoming the same river is not a matter of losing our identification. Our river will have its pools and eddies, boulders and rapids. It may never reach complete calm, but as long as we are flowing in the same general direction, we will end up in a destination suitable for everyone. We will not be in the condition observed by the mother on a high mountain ridge, "It makes me feel as if I don't know you at all." We will know each other, respect each other, and understand each other, which is the start of perspective and concert. None of that runs contrary to the grain of western attitudes.

SENSE OF PLACE: IDENTITY AND RESPONSIBILITY

Whose place is the public land? The answer seems rather simple: It's a place that belongs to us all. But the question, direct as it seems, has been convoluted and clouded by foes of the public land.

Wallace Stegner had strong views and feelings about the system of public land ownership in the United States. We miss his voice but his thoughts and wisdom on the topic are well known. In an essay called "Striking the Rock," he wrote: "One of the things Westerners should ponder, but generally do not, is their relation to and attitude toward the federal presence."

> Though I have been involved in controversies with some of them, the last thing I would want to see is their dissolution and a return to the policy of disposal, for that would be the end of the West as I have known and loved it. Neither state ownership nor private ownership—which state ownership would soon become—could offer anywhere near the usually disinterested stewardship that these imperfect and embattled federal bureaus do, while at the same time making western space available to millions. They have been the strongest impediment to the careless ruin of what remains of the public domain, and they will be necessary as far ahead as I, at least, can see.[3]

So our system of public land management is not perfect. Is that reason to abandon it for uncertainty? Is that reason to try another system that may be less efficient and disallow almost unfettered use of tens of millions of acres? Stegner persuasively says no, it would be the end of the West as we know and love it.

Our public lands are important. They provide something for everyone, whether it is the sense of renewal and exhilaration that many feel when visiting public land, or the resources that support livelihoods for thousands of families. Western lands are also vast repositories of wildlife and fish resources, and though many of these populations are battered, public land is still the best hope we have for ensuring their existence. ublic land is the last best place to recreate and renew in hundreds of different ways. Its existence alone is a value beyond measure.

I remember hearing about an easterner who was explaining her love of wide, western open spaces. "But have you ever visited the West?" the listener asked. "No," said the easterner, "but it makes me feel better to just know it is all there." And as we face our daily responsibilities, do we not feel better knowing that the aspens will bud soon in the Schell Creek Mountains of Nevada, that waterfowl are landing in the Montana pothole country, or that the deserts of Arizona and southern Utah are taking on their fine sheen of pale green?

In short, we have a public land system in place that works reasonably well. We should not spend precious time and resources wrangling about ownership. We all own it now. What system could be better? The stakes in talking about changing jurisdiction are incredibly high, and the payoff, if any, is unknown. As Stegner said, we stand to lose this place we love.

In addition to asking who owns public land we'd be well served asking who is claimed by it. Stegner knew firsthand about the links between land and place. "I was born on wheels . . . ," he wrote in an essay called "The Sense of Place." "I know about the excitement of newness and possibility, but I also know the dissatisfaction and hunger that result from placelessness. Some towns that we lived in were never real to me. They were only the raw material of places, as I was the raw material of a person. Neither place nor I had a chance of being anything unless we could live together for a while. . . ."[4]

Unfortunately, the history of the West has denied many people the chance of living together for long periods. Cycles of boom and bust, towns coming and going, people packing up and moving on for the next surefire opportunity or lives of sunbaked bliss, have all contributed to the lack of sense of place that might otherwise characterize much of the West. I am still surprised at the temporariness I feel when driving through Elko and Phoenix, St. George, and Las Vegas: outlet malls tucked between the sagebrush and interstates.

I know I may offend some, particularly those who have lived in unbroken generational links in Richfield, Utah, or Glasgow, Montana. But for every one of those folks, there are 10,000 others who have shifted again and again. The West is a place of change, and was once, at least, the geography of hope. But as Stegner noted, it's an area known as much for its mirages as its realization of dreams. Without the roots, sinking deep and strong into one place, we risk not understanding who we are and how our decisions may affect the land's future. In the worst case, people find themselves simply unable to care.

A few years ago, when I worked with the Grand Canyon Trust, I had an interesting conversation with a man named Bill Redd, a San Juan County commissioner and native of southern Utah. During a symposium at the conference we were attending he said, "I don't understand the environmentalists. I don't know why they want to come into our country and make it their own. They all come from somewhere and that's their home, not here."

My response was straightforward. I told him that I was jealous, and that he was fortunate to be in and from a place that he loved so much. I said to him, "You have a place. That is who you are. You know who you are because of the country, and the country is you. Most people don't have that sense of place and they feel an emptiness and a lack of identity because of it." Maybe I got a little passionate about it. I told him that although I was from California, my identity was in the Four Corners area. That is the place I felt I belonged.

Bill looked at me and then said, "Can we adopt you?"

In short, a sense of place is important, not only to those who have strong ties to an area, but to those who want to develop strong ties to a place. And with a sense of place comes a sense of ethic and responsibility. As Stegner wrote:

> Plunging into the future through a landscape that had no history, we did both the country and ourselves some harm along with some good. Neither the country nor the society we built out of it can be healthy until we stop raiding and running, and learn to be quiet part of the time, and acquire the sense not of ownership but of belonging.
> "The land was ours before we were the land's," says Robert Frost's poem. "Only in the act of submission is the sense of place realized and a sustainable relationship between people and earth established."[5]

Stegner knew that submission to place is difficult. It is not as if we can say "Stay where you are, rural dwellers. Portland and Phoenix and Denver have nothing for you. Stay where you are, and develop a sense of place." It is equally difficult to stem the flow of emigrants from larger cities to rural areas. Maybe the best we can do is recognize the desire for a sense of place in others, whether they are coming or going or not sure at all, and try to understand what deep roots and a finely woven culture mean, and overlay it all into how we live and treat the land. Did Robert Frost have the cold deserts of the Great Basin in mind when he wrote the poem? No. But that does not make his insight less valuable. A sense of place must be realized before a sustainable relationship between people and earth is established. It must be established or at least recognized and accounted for, not only by new and old residents, but also by land managers. It is good preventive medicine. Where wounds have occurred, such recognition will help us all to heal and forge ahead.

I am reminded of another story by Wallace Stegner, set in the same rough-hewn region as "Two Rivers," the high-line country of northern Montana. "Carrion Spring" tells of a newly married couple who barely manage to endure a rough Montana winter on a ranch. For the woman one winter is enough; she is strong but ready to return to town, friends, and family. For her husband the decision is not as clear. He is a man of the land. He wishes to remain and harbors a dream of buying the broken and ruined ranch. It is the first spring day when they are able to travel the muddy wagon road. As the husband drives the wagon toward the small town where his wife will climb aboard a train to return—perhaps temporarily, perhaps not—to her hometown, they stop to eat on a windy benchland overlooking the prairie, a thawing river, the slough.

> He sighed. He lay back and closed his eyes. After about three minutes he said, "Boy what a day, though. I won't get through on the patrol trail goin' back. The ice'll be breakin' up before tonight, at this rate. Did you hear it crackin' and poppin' a minute ago?"
> "I didn't hear it."
> "Listen."
> They were still. She heard the soft wind move in the prairie wool, and beyond it, filling the background, the hushed and hollow noise of the floodwater, sight of drowned willows, suck of whirlpools, splash and guggle as cutbanks caved, and the steady push and swash and ripple of moving water. Into the soft rush of sound came a muffled report like a tree cracking, or a shot a long way off. "Is that it?" she said. "Is that the ice letting loose?"[6]

Waters and channels. Flows and destinations. It is time for the ice to let loose, time for a thaw among all. It is time for the two rivers to become one. At stake is the West, the land we know and love, a place that we call home, a place that we belong to and that belongs to us.

NOTES

[1] Wallace Stegner, "Two Rivers." In *Collected Stories of Wallace Stegner* (New York: Random House, 1990).

[2] J. J. Kennedy, B. L. Fox, and T. D. Osen. "Changing Social Values and Images of Public Rangeland Management." In *Rangeland Journal* 17, no.4 (1985): 127-32.

[3] Wallace Stegner, "Stiking the Rock." In *Where the Bluebird Sings to the Lemonade Springs: Living and Writing in the West* (New York: Random House, 1992).

[4] Wallace Stegner, "The Sense of Place." In *Where the Bluebird Sings to the Lemonade Springs: Living and Writing in the West* (New York: Random House, 1992).

[5] See Stegner, "The Sense of Place."

[6] Wallace Stegner, "Carrion Spring." In *Collected Stories of Wallace Stegner* (New York: Random House, 1990).

Chapter 5

THE TRUTH OF THE LAND

Teresa Jordan

We have all heard that the West is at war. Counties fight states and states fight Washington; newcomers fight longtime residents; environmentalists, ranchers, miners, loggers, and Indian tribes fight each other; developers fight anyone who is old and in the way. Some of these enmities are new, but most of them have existed in one form or another for a long time. Like all wars, this one has casualties. A dozen cows are shot in Colorado; a forest ranger barely escapes injury when his car explodes in Nevada; two environmentalists are hanged in effigy in Oregon; a logger dies when his saw hits a spike in Washington. All of these are hate crimes, a vigilante individualism run increasingly amok, and hate spreads like wildfire when the winds are right.

My husband and I live in Starr Valley, a ranch community in Elko County, Nevada. We live in the middle of this conflagration, and yet, on a day-to-day basis, it's easy to forget about the fighting. It's spring. The creeks are high and the willows in bud, the sandhill cranes leap and flirt in our meadows, fresh green grass is poking up everywhere. This is a time of hope when all things seem new and fresh and possible. Today I bring you stories of hope. They come not from spring but rather from the dead of winter. I'll begin with a Christmas story.

Hal and I moved to Starr Valley in 1994 and had lived there about eight months before our first Christmas. As we searched the papers and local bulletin boards for festivities, one event in particular caught our eye. A group of Tibetan monks was scheduled to perform a concert of sacred music in Wells, our nearest town, population 1,250, fifteen miles away. We decided to go. We both knew how hard it could be to attract an audience for an event, and Buddhist monks in Wells, ten days before Christmas . . . well, we thought they'd need all the help they could get.

The night of the concert we stopped first at a potluck dinner in the fellowship hall of the Presbyterian church. The dozen monks joined us to eat braised ribs, green beans, scalloped potatoes, and blackberry pie, and then we moved to the Mormon church for the performance. On the way over, Hal and I voiced our concerns: The Mormon church has the biggest hall in town and nothing is more demoralizing than a lot of empty seats. Except for the truck stops, the church also has the largest parking lot in town, and we were surprised when we pulled in and had trouble finding a place.

The ground was icy with snowpack, and we helped an older woman cross from her car to the sidewalk. She told us that she came originally from Germany; she'd settled in Wells nearly forty years ago. We mentioned that we were surprised at the turnout, and asked what attracted her. "These things don't happen so often around here," she told us. "When they do, I like to take advantage."

The auditorium was crowded, but we found our seats. The lights dimmed and the monks came on stage. They wore long burgundy robes, brilliant saffron shawls, and high fringed hats like bright yellow coxcombs. They carried long horns that reached clear to the floor and curved back up again, as well as a variety of other instruments. When the hall had grown completely silent, the monks with the long horns stepped forward. They blew several deep notes, making sounds that were almost animal, like elephants trumpeting before a charge. Short horns joined in, running up and down the atonal scales like hyenas; the cymbals, bells, and drums broke into a wild cacophony. The monks began to chant. Each one produced a three-note tone from deep in his throat. The tones started low and gradually climbed, sounding like a herd of heavily loaded trucks ascending a steep grade.

Please understand, I mean no disrespect with these descriptions. I want only to capture how foreign this music seemed to us, ranchers and farmers and teachers and truck drivers whose own traditions of sacred music were so different. We grew restive, squirming in our chairs, coughing, clearing our throats. I feared a mass exodus at intermission. But in time our ears grew accustomed to the music. We began to really hear it, to understand its nuances. When the break came, no one left. Instead, long lines formed at the table where the monks sold CDs and prayer scarves to support their monastery. During the second half we sat quietly, transported by the ancient power of sacred traditions we didn't need to fully understand in order to respect. When the performance ended, the applause went on and on.

When the hall had once again grown quiet, a spokesman for the group stepped forward and told us a bit about their lives. They belong to a monastery in exile in India. They have suffered dearly under the Chinese occupation of Tibet that has sacked their monasteries and killed so many of their brethren. They travel around the United States to present what is sacred to them. As we learned that night about the great injustices that had been served upon them, many of us sat in awe to hear no ill will in the spokesman's voice. The monks simply wanted us to know who they were, trusting that once we did we would insist on the most basic of all rights—the right to exist.

When we emerged from the hall it was into a night shimmering with diamonds. The temperature had dropped and frozen the moisture in the air so that it glittered like the star-strewn sky above us. A light skim of ice had glassed the sidewalks and the parking lot. We saw our German friend looking at the slippery walk, and we each took one of her arms. When we asked what she thought of the concert, she chuckled. "Boy," she said, "that was weird." And then she added, quite simply, "I'm glad I came."

I like this story because of what it says about the potential of small communities to embrace something foreign or new, and also because it shows the power of the truly authentic to transcend barriers of language, custom, and belief. I think that night meant so much to me, and I've thought about it so many times since because of a turbulent meeting I had attended just a few days earlier in the central part of the state.

Ever since Hal and I moved to Nevada in 1992—we lived in Elko for a while before we moved to Starr Valley—I have worked with a ranch in the Toiyabe Range around Austin, Nevada, that is managed by a collaborative team. The ranchers, Tony and Jerrie Tipton, run almost entirely on public land. When they took on their allotments eight years ago, the land was in terrible shape. Ground cover was sparse and even though the land had been rested completely for five years when the Tiptons first saw it, the existing grasses were largely decadent and dying. Erosion was high, streambanks were broken down, and springs ran full of silt and mud. Fish, birds, and other wildlife were rare.

Trained in ecosystem-based or holistic ranching, the Tiptons believed they could improve things, but they needed more flexibility than Bureau of Land Management and Forest Service leases allowed. They worked out an agreement with the agencies. If the agencies would waive restrictions on how many cattle the Tiptons ran, where, and for how long, the Tiptons would give the authority over how that flexibility was used to a collaborative team composed of representatives from the BLM and Forest Service, state agencies such as the Nevada Division of Wildlife and the Nevada Division of Forestry, environmental groups such as the Sierra Club and Trout Unlimited, and anyone else who was interested.

The Toiyabe Watershed and Wildlands Management Team formed and developed goals, which are revised each year, for the improvement of the land base that forms the Tipton ranch. The team is open to everyone, and all members have their interests reflected in the goals. Anyone who would like to join the team is welcome. If his or her particular interest is improved trout habitat, say, or the reintroduction of blue grouse, and the goals don't already reflect these concerns, they will be revised to include them. To move toward these goals the team develops and constantly revises a management plan that the Tiptons put into action. The team monitors the ranch closely, measuring everything from ground cover to stream flow to wildlife populations to insect activity. The Memorandums of Understanding from the federal agencies that allow flexibility remain in effect only so long as team members are in agreement—and the monitoring data reflect—that there has been significant improvement. Anyone can derail the process if he or she is unhappy with what is going on and can back up that frustration with evidence from the land.

Shortly after I moved to Nevada, I heard about this group. I attended presentations by team members, I pored over monitoring data and photographic records, and I started visiting the land. I was amazed by what I saw. Ground cover had increased dramatically—in places by more than 500 percent—and the ratio of perennials to annuals had also increased several-fold. Both of these factors contributed to watershed improvement. Streambeds had raised, banks had stabilized, and in several cases ephemeral streams were flowing year round while others that had been dry for decades had started to flow or showed signs that they soon would.

With great excitement I joined the team. Here at last seemed to be a solution for the long-smoldering enmities I watched flare to explosion all around me. Ranchers, environmentalists, and government agents were working together, and both the land and the people were the better for it. Looking back at my early involvement with the team, I was downright infatuated. This is it, I'd thought. This is the answer! But then, that summer, before the monks came to Wells, things fell apart.

To move toward its goals of increasing the health and biodiversity of the land, the team has several tools at its disposal, including rest, fire, grazing, animal impact, technology, and plant succession. Cattle are part of the equation, but they are managed differently than has traditionally been the case, stocking an area more densely but for a much shorter period of time. This allows hooves to till the land, breaking up the soil to retain moisture and allow seedlings to establish, while dung and urine provide fertilizer. Forage plants get eaten once, which revitalizes them, and the cattle are gone before they can eat regrowth, which weakens the plants. This sort of grazing can improve land, increasing the amount of ground cover dramatically and jump-starting succession so that perennials, with their stabilizing and water-storing root systems, succeed over annuals. Although many team members initially opposed cattle, over time we have all come to see them as an effective tool for ecosystem restoration.

For the process to work, however, the cattle must be carefully controlled. In our biological planning session each year, we plot where they will be throughout the summer, in what numbers, and for how long. This works fine in theory, but in the summer of 1994 the cattle failed to listen to our finely wrought plans. The Tiptons had introduced new livestock to the ranch that didn't know the lay of the country. No sooner would the Tiptons move the cattle to a new place than they would head back to the old. Compounding the problem was the fact that after years of red tape the Forest Service had finally succeeded in contracting out a five-mile stretch of fence that the team had deemed necessary to help with cattle control. Unfortunately the contract ran out a half-mile from completion, rendering the fence essentially useless. In midsummer, when some team members from the Nevada Division of Wildlife brought visitors to the ranch to show off what they had billed as a great success, they were embarrassed to find cattle on a stream from which they should have been excluded, and the cows had trashed the place. There were other problems of a similar nature; the Forest Service had issued a letter threatening an end to the Memorandums of Understanding; the Tiptons and others were mad at the Forest Service for not completing the fence; and the wildlife agents were angry that their trust had been abused. Accusations and letters were flying in all directions.

Such was the climate in December when we all headed to Austin for the annual biological planning session. I left home long before dawn, and I remember speeding down the highway in the dark, contemplating what lay ahead. We had hired a facilitator for the meeting. I'd never worked with a facilitator before, but I imagined it as a sort of touchy-feely process. I figured he would start out building empathy among members of the group. Perhaps he would have each of us state the problem, and I set about articulating my view. Or perhaps he'd start by having each of us describe someone else's view of the problem. I tried to imagine how Tony and Jerrie might see it, or how Dayle Flanagan, the forest ranger, might state his case. But then I arrived at the meeting and Steve Rich, the facilitator, didn't invite us to talk about the problem at all. Instead he asked each of us to introduce ourselves, tell why we had joined the team, describe the landscape when we first saw it, and describe it as it was now.

At first many of us were impatient. We didn't need introductions. We already knew each other; some of us knew each other so well we hardly talked—we had too much to accomplish in too short a time. But as we went around the table and listened, each of us reconnected with the authentic passion that had brought us to the team in the first place. We remembered that we were fighting for the simple right of various communities of plants and animals and people to exist. As we heard descriptions of changes in the land and recorded our own observations, we recognized that for all our setbacks we had accomplished incredible things. Many of the people in the room had spent their lives trying to improve the health of western lands, and every person, every single one, said they had never realized the success we had achieved. By the time we had completed the circle, we were no longer at war. We were a team again, trying to figure out a way to make things work. The truth of the land had united us, winning out over opinion and blame.

The Dalai Lama, the spiritual leader of the monks who visited us in Wells, says that war happens when we lose touch with others' humanness. What we know about war is that it makes people suffer, and we know too that the land suffers in return. On the Toiyabe, our task is not of such daunting magnitude as that which faces the Tibetan monks. However much our conflicts are trumpeted as war, we are not yet in exile from our public lands.

When I first started working with the Toiyabe Watershed and Wildlands Management Team, I wanted it to be the answer. It is not *the* answer, but it is *an* answer. Wendell Berry entreats us to think locally and act locally. The dark side of local control of course is local tyranny. The collaborative process can escape tyranny only if it remains open. Our team has members from Utah, California, and Arizona; we'd be happy to have them from much farther away. We are a community truly of the land, of a particular piece of land, which we have each committed to know as intimately as possible, and it is from this base, this place, this locality, that we make our decisions. It is on this land that we measure our failure and success.

Wallace Stegner once quipped that the only true rugged individualists were usually found hanging from a rope, the other end of which was held by a group of cooperating citizens. The will to individualism and the will to cooperation run side-by-side in the American West, but Stegner knew how much the romance of the man alone could make our willingness to listen and work with people unlike ourselves seem like a cop-out. We like to see ourselves as warriors, fighting the righteous fight.

I am not naive. I know that there are manipulators in the world and that greed exists as well as the hunger for control. But too often righteousness leads to fundamentalism, where we identify enemies not as individuals but as entire groups. We deny others' humanness. Hate is born and spreads like wildfire. But winds can change and fires can put themselves out. On the western lands, we know that if fire hasn't burned too fiercely or too long, the grass comes back with new life, eager and strong.

I don't have space here to explain in detail the biological particulars of our work on the Toiyabe, to present photographs or monitoring data. Even if I had, a great many of you would still have doubts. I have doubts myself, for I know how strongly the will to believe can determine what we think we perceive. And so I invite you to see for yourself.

Dan Dagget, in the recent book, *Beyond the Rangeland Conflict*, describes a dozen ranch-based collaborations; there are many others all over the West that deal with a variety of land use issues. All of them need help with the time-consuming jobs of monitoring and decision making. Why not adopt a piece of ground, get to know it intimately, take responsibility for its husbandry?

I think of a Portland, Oregon, friend, Terrence O'Donnell, a gracious man on a cane, who takes care of a particular rose garden in a downtown park. Certainly, we must preserve our wilderness, and the current discussion of wilderness set-aside as a tithe is brilliant and true. But whatever the final percentage, 8 percent or 10 percent or 12, wilderness is an oxymoron if we turn to it to meet the deep human need to participate in natural processes. We will consume it, as we have consumed so much else. But like Terrence, we need to look at our daily communities as natural places, our streets and our inner-city parks and our industrial areas as much as our wide-open spaces, and commit to them, on our knees, the position for monitoring as well as for prayer.

"There can be no purpose more enspiriting than to begin the age of restoration," wrote E. O. Wilson in the closing paragraphs of *The Diversity of Life*, and he continued:

> We should judge every scrap of biodiversity as priceless while we learn to use it and come to understand what it means to humanity. We should not knowingly allow any species or race to go extinct. And let us go beyond mere salvage to begin the restoration of natural environments, in order to enlarge wild populations and stanch the hemorrhaging of biological wealth. . . .

"The stewardship of environment," Wilson reminds us—and I believe that by stewardship he includes the sort of restorative husbandry I have talked about here—"is a domain on the near side of metaphysics where all reflective persons can surely find common ground."

Sometimes when I sit back at a meeting of the Toiyabe group and look around the room, I can't get over how weird it all is: ranchers talking about biodiversity as if their very lives depended on it—which, of course, it does—and environmentalists and agency people talking about cows the same way, all of us moving outside to get down on all fours and look at the ground. It is weird, and yet I'm always glad I came.

Chapter 6

ECOSYSTEM MANAGEMENT, WALLACE STEGNER, AND THE YAAK VALLEY OF NORTHWESTERN MONTANA

Rick Bass

I keep waiting each day to make friends with the Forest Service—not with the individuals, but with the agency itself. The agency harbors, as a rotting log harbors nutrients and hope for the future, some of the country's best and most passionate hydrologists, entomologists, range managers, recreation specialists, ornithologists, wilderness specialists, and big game biologists. But the gears and levers of the agency are still pulled and fitted in Washington, in an agency run by a Congress that in turn is run not by the people but by the corporations that funded their election campaigns.

We all know this. The simplicity of it makes us want to shriek. The inevitability—the brute force, the economic biomass behind this process—also makes us want to shriek. Artists in the West continue to do battle daily with the struggle over how best to combat the madness of this loss, whether to choose to lay down works of beauty—classical art, in the form of song, sculpture, stories, paintings, poems—or to lay down works of essay and activism. Whether to speak directly to the politics of this loss, as the health of our communities and our wild heritage continues to be taken from us—a taking, a theft, that is funded by our own dollars, like some hideous, wounded wolverine caught in a trap, eating its own entrails.

I am speaking about wilderness, of course, or about the lack of wilderness—not just in Montana's Yaak Valley, but in Idaho, and Utah—the failure to protect as wilderness anything beyond rock and ice. Under the rubric of ecosystem management, there are those of us who believe that this is only a new methodology for building more roads into the last roadless areas. The Forest Service chief himself once issued a memo directing his regional foresters that if they are denied entrance to a timber sale in a roadless area because it would violate the law, to not try and make up that lost volume by moving the sale to a roadbed area, but to try to instead substitute it with entrance into a different roadless area.

I'm not going to address ecosystem management directly because I have not yet heard ecosystem management talk about conservation biology, or wilderness cores. It has thus far skirted this issue so completely that I believe its true heart has been revealed: that it is a ploy to further fragment things, rather than begin healing and weaving them back together.

One does not need to belabor the point that in talking about the wilderness system of the West, one is speaking indirectly about the work of Wallace Stegner. Like some team of oxen in a double yoke, he used his talents as both an artist and an activist, all his life, to help give us that which we have now—a community of artists as well as a community of those who love the landscape of the West itself.

Central to the science of conservation biology is the necessity of cornerstone or foundation areas of undisturbed cores of diversity. Forests, or any other ecosystems, are of such radiant health and strength that they not only exist strong and free in the world by themselves, but also pass on their genetic and spiritual vigor to things and places beyond their perimeters.

You don't want to try to figure out how to go into those places and dissect or harm them. You want to move in the opposite direction, as the Forest Service has yet to do, in the Yaak and other places. You want to devise ways to protect these places, turn away from them and walk in the opposite direction.

You want to preserve them, not extinguish them.

While on the topic of harm and injustice and what's wrong with these initial visions of ecosystem management, and what's right and diverse and healthy about Wallace Stegner's vision of wilderness, let me use a specific example: the Yaak Valley of northwestern Montana, resting up against the Idaho and British Columbia borders. It is a straw, a pipeline of genetic diversity, down out of Canada and into the rest of the West. It is also totally unprotected. Over 150,000 acres of roadless cores exist there, still connected or nearly connected in an archipelago of vibrant health. The valley itself is almost 500,000 acres in size, and yet not a single acre of wilderness is protected for future generations.

The valley lies in a seam, a crevice, between the rainforest ecosystems of the Pacific Northwest and the jagged mountains of the northern Rockies. The richness of these two systems combines to create an even more palpable richness. When you sleep in the Yaak for the first time, you have dreams you have never had before; as a writer you think of stories you had never imagined; as a painter you see shadows and colors not earlier noticed; as a hunter you see and feel the different movements, different relationships to each other, of the animals in the forest; as a scientist you think of connections you have not made before. The double richness of the landscape of the Yaak itself is like the mysterious, tempting, rich and troubling territories of the heart in the areas between art and activism.

Woodland caribou utilize this country, as do moose, elk, mule deer and white-tails, mountain goats, bighorn sheep along the Kootenai River. It is a zone, a secret gift of life, of unprecedented speciation and uniqueness in the West. On any given mountain you can find three species of grouse—ruffed, spruce, and blue. There are vegetative assemblages as yet undescribed and unknown—the stuff of literature, dreams, and mystery.

It is a predator's showcase as well, home to a snarling and scrapping, reclusive combination of tooth and claw: wolves, wolverines, lynx, black bears, grizzlies, bobcats, martens, fishers, coyotes, mountain lions, hawks, owls, golden eagles, bald eagles. It is a valley of giants: great blue herons, thousand-year-old cedar trees, and 500- year-old tamaracks; sturgeon, bull trout weighing twenty and twenty-five pounds. It is the most savage and delicate place I've ever seen—a vital organ of the West, a core—and yet it continues to be ignored for wilderness protection.

Perhaps in talking about my valley so much I am not properly addressing Wallace Stegner, and yet I think or feel that somehow I am.

Is it too easy a compromise, too easy a metaphor, to discuss Stegner's work as its own core of community health and wilderness health? In a healthy forest, vertical and horizontal matrices of diversity—by species, age, structure, by everything—are interwoven, and certainly in this regard Stegner's work was the healthiest. In all different dimensions—as a writer of novels, short stories, novellas, and essays; as an activist, a teacher, a father, and a husband—he was exemplary in the truest sense of that word, a bedrock core to provide an example for the rest of that country around him.

I keep trying to figure out how he was so forcefully and powerfully able to maintain a vertical and horizontal strength throughout his working career—publishing in seven decades—for roughly one-third of the United States' history. In the end—in theory, at least—the answer to this question is really no mystery at all. It's like wondering how a forest that has such big trees can also have such rich soil, or how a forest that has a diversity of bird life can also have such a diversity of mammals.

In his essay "The Law of Nature and the Dream of Man," Stegner wrote: "How to write a story, though ignorant or baffled? You take something that is important to you, something you have brooded about. You try to see it as clearly as you can, and to fix it in a transferable equivalent. All you want in the finished print is the clean statement of the lens, which is yourself, on the subject that has been absorbing your attention. Sure, it's autobiography. Sure, it's fiction. Either way if you have done it right, it's true."

Ecosystem management is not yet true. It will not succeed without vital cores—anchor points—of wilderness in each ecosystem. Only a few islands of health exist in the West, and even the health of those is suspect. Agency discussions of ecosystem management avoid acknowledging that there are relationships we can never understand. This convinces me timber managers speak only of managing those few factors they think they understand: more fiber production of one or two species of tree, over the short run, and maybe—again, for a short period—more big-game summertime forage.

We can't control a region's balance of, say, seed-eating versus insect-eating birds, due to factors within that region. The faces of different forest types—particularly in a land as diverse as the Yaak—are still in wild flux, especially compared to our knowledge, or lack of it. Even a 500-year-old larch forest is in relative flux, part of an earth-desired, rock-and-soil-desired cycle of progression and regression, a pulse that is specific to that particular spot on the earth, yet connected to all others. Core samples in the bogs in the interior of that old tamarack forest will reveal the ashes of sagebrush and juniper from only a few thousand years ago. In the wilderness the forest continues to tilt, to change, under its own rules, with all the wonderful accompanying (and invisible) genetic alterations in species and speciation of the forest trees themselves and everything else above and beneath them—birds, plants, mammals, insects, fungus. It keeps changing through the centuries and millennia like the shadows of clouds drifting across one mountain.

Of course there are places where we need to attempt, with respect, to do our awkward best. Ecosystem management acknowledges this, but again, to pummel the dead horse, it does not yet acknowledge the necessity of protecting significant wilderness cores in each and every watershed. It must not shift these wildernesses around, like moving senior citizens from one rest home to another on a Forest Service shuttle bus, but commit these cores, these anchor points, to nature for the duration of mankind's time on earth.

A number that is commonly heard with regard to tithes, both spiritual and biological, is 10 percent. I propose that in fragile or ravaged landscapes such as the Yaak 15 or 20 percent is entirely more appropriate. In some landscapes, 100 percent is appropriate to initiate the healing process, to reestablish health and balance and cycles. A solution in the Yaak, a place wildly out of balance (the insect-killed lodgepole was ignored as timber in the 1980s, with two-thirds of the harvest comprising instead green larch and fir) is still within reach. Wilderness designation of at least the last roadless areas in the Yaak would still leave almost

350,000 acres for the hard-core, high-volume timber yearnings of Congress and the Forest Service, and our own societal hungers. Let the ecosystem managers then tie in their activities to these cores or anchor points, rather than running over and erasing these last fixed points of reason, fixed points of data.

Is chaos theory applicable to insect and fire patterns in lodgepole stands and the soil changes, and forest succession, through the centuries' cycles, on these spots? Should we walk along every streambank following a fire, whether natural or prescribed, and attempt to manage or evaluate, as nature does, whether every burned snag should be left standing for one of the forty-seven species of cavity nesters that use the Kootenai? Should every snag be pushed over at a 45- to 90-degree angle into the stream to help trap ash and other sediment runoff, or pushed over to land parallel to the slope to help hold ash and soil in place on site, or pushed to land upslope to rot in the soil and produce a seedbed for ceanothus or kinnikinick? But wouldn't that then help the seed-eating birds instead of the insect eaters? And wouldn't the insects get out of hand? And then after the insects took over the world, wouldn't that mean more dead trees, hence still more fires? I guess the fires would fry some of the insects but then wouldn't it just start all over again? Maybe we need to rethink this. Maybe we need to do another study.

Even in 1996 Forest Service officials made statements like, "It's comparatively easy for foresters to emulate nature's large severe fires . . . by clearcutting large areas and burning the slash." The truth is we haven't figured it all out, and I don't think we ever will, not to the extent that we can outmanage the wilderness cores that inspire and nurture an ecosystem's health. We can't even make up our minds about whether to burn slash or leave it on the ground, whether to try and aerate the compacted soil of clearcuts or leave it alone to recover in the next millennium on its own.

We're only just beginning to figure out site-specific light management for overstory openings, the mix of photosynthesis versus UV shielding required for different seedlings; what about the understory and the mechanics of soil? Does anyone really think we can manage 2 million or 4 million or 12 million acres of dirt? Wilderness cores are, beyond sources of radiant health, buffers against our trials and errors. In a phrase that would drive Wise Use fundamentalists nuts, wilderness cores forgive us our trespasses into other areas.

The light touches that Stegner could wield with his pen, in his art, cannot of course be wielded by man upon the land. We are too small and the land is far larger than a sheet of paper, and infinitely deeper than the little three-pound electrical impulse generators we know of as the human brain, marvelous as that organ is. The earth is a 65-zillion gigaton brain and we ought to let pieces of it, places of it, function under the grace and power of its own miracle. The Yaak is only one instance of our present failure to do this.

I like to believe that Stegner was aware from a historic standpoint of the healthy influence the cores, the anchors, his work gave the country, not just the migration corridors or interconnectedness of his work to that of his many students, but the corelike nature, the sanctuaries, of his individual books. In the manner of a complex, mature climax forest—a healthy forest—it was in Stegner's era that we evolved from a heritage of a few individuals carrying most of the load of ecological literacy and the duty or obligation to disperse it. In this country's first century and a half, the shifts of duty among these writers was a somewhat linear model remarkably similar to that of the beginnings of a forest—new seedlings and new species concentrating on vertical growth rather than on diversity. Only a handful of names led the way through this period—Thoreau, Emerson, Muir, Austin, Leopold, Carson, Stegner, and relatively few others—whereas now there are hundreds, even thousands of nature writers, blossoming from Stegner's era as if from a nurse log. The core of his work acted as an incubator, a radiant source, of health and diversity in the literature of nature. A critical threshold of literary health was reached, due in large part to his efforts alone, and there is now, in literature if not out on the land, a community of health because of Stegner's and a few others,' cores: his numerous cores and anchor points.

If the last roadless areas of the West are lost—entered and further fragmented rather than reconnected—will this cause the works that have sprung up out of this love of earth, love of country, to somehow lose part or all of their power? Will they become like ghosts, tales of things gone by, like empty insect husks in the autumn?

As much as I love the works of Stegner and other writers whose work is based on these roadless cores, and in the healthy country that lies on the perimeter of these cores, I cannot argue that the power of those works is not at risk. They are so intimately and fully connected to not just the spirit of those places but to the elements, the physical presences of those places. In these sanctuaries there is a blood of vitality that still flows from the land to its literature (and perhaps from the literature back to the land—perhaps the dirt desires stories, as it desires life). The land and the literature are still connected. Harm the land further and a case can be made that it will diminish our literature—both that which has already been gifted to us and that which is still to come.

If ecosystem management continues to avoid committing to the protection of these last undesignated wilderness cores, it is nothing more than another blueprint for extinction and extinguishment. We might just as well not only enter these last roadless areas but also gather up all of Stegner's books and get it over with. Rip the pages out of them, or hire lesser writers to manage them—rewrite, re-create, reshape, and reimagine them.

New York literary folks were sometimes not particularly able to understand Stegner's work, nor were the extractive industry corporations and chamber of commerce flash-in-the-pan boosters always overly fond of it. If they could have outlawed or fragmented him, I think they would have. If they could have ignored him, they would have. If they could have clearcut his work, I think they would have, or even if they could have ecosystem-managed it, they would have. But they couldn't. Nature, like art, desires life. His books and his life have everything to teach us about watershed analysis of ecosystem management and we all need to go back and reread them, and then reread them again, and keep rereading them. And we need to protect the Yaak, and our other last wild and roadless places. We need to guard them as fiercely as we would our libraries or any of our other heritages, against intruders either foreign or domestic.

We need to keep using and saying the word *wilderness*—not replacing it, through time, with lesser phrases—with diluted, and later, vanishing and invisible nonwords such as ecosystem management. We owe it to Stegner and we owe it to ourselves and we owe it to those who will be following after us—both the scientists and the artists.

I want to believe in ecosystem management and I keep waiting to be friends with the Forest Service again. But in the meantime there is still no protected wilderness in the Yaak Valley, nor is the lack of it being discussed enough.

PART III

To
CHERISH
AND RENEW

RESTORATION AS THE NEW ORDER

These essays explore the emerging concept of ecological restoration, both its meaning and ramifications. In one of his last writings, Wallace Stegner observed: "I believe that eventually, perhaps within a generation or two, they will work out some sort of compromise between what must be done to earn a living and what must be done to restore health to the earth, air, and water." Though still quite controversial and often misunderstood, those restoration efforts are now under way as reflected in endangered species reintroduction programs and river system reengineering experiments. University of Montana historian Dan Flores places these contemporary ecological restoration activities in historical context, first describing how the West has been altered by both Native American and early European settlement activities and then explaining why these profound changes should not deter current restoration efforts. After distinguishing restoration from other related resource management goals, ecologist Duncan Patten explains how science can be employed to pursue ecological restoration policies as well as the limitations inherent in any restoration effort. In the final essay, University of California–Davis law professor and botanist Holly Doremus examines the legal concerns likely to arise in response to wildlife restoration programs, and concludes that existing law should not inhibit these efforts.

Chapter 7

MAKING THE WEST WHOLE AGAIN
A Historical Perspective on Restoration

Dan Flores

In his 38th year, less than a decade before death came calling in 1862, the Massachusetts essayist and iconoclast, Henry David Thoreau, fell into the habit of studying the accounts of early settlers who had left descriptions of New England as it had appeared to them 200 years earlier. Compared with the America they had found, Thoreau realized, his experience in the woods was analogous to listening to a symphony played without most of the instruments. As he further considered, what became his essay "To Know an Entire Heaven and an Entire Earth," Thoreau finally decided that his forebears on the continent had acted as demigods who had impoverished his world by, in effect, plucking from the heavens many of the best and brightest stars.[1]

Only a few years later and a continent farther west, the Crow leader Plenty Coups, spoke of his great vision atop the Crazy Mountains wherein he witnessed in his mind's eye the replacement of buffalo with speckled cattle. Plenty Coups summarized the Indian perspective on that change with this cryptic remark: "After this, nothing happened."[2] Even western pioneers who experienced the change were shocked by it all. As L. A. Huffman, the famous Montana photographer, recalled when he first came west in the 1870s: "This Yellowstone-Big Horn country was then unpenned of wire, and unspoiled. . . . One looked about and said, `This is the last West.' It was not so. There was no more West after that. It was a dream and a forgetting, a chapter forever closed."[3]

From any perspective, that great world of sunlight and grass, with its endless forests, clear streams and Eden-like abundance amid a fresh, prismatic natural shine, now seems cometary in our experience as a people. It was built across a three-century brilliance to its provocative and compelling western phase, then winked out suddenly, and apparently forever. Being born literary, Native American, or a sensitive pioneer was and is no requisite to mourning the loss of a world like that, a wilder life on a wilder continent. Most people interested in the natural world on the eve of the 21st century have experienced the feeling that, as Thoreau put it, "I am that citizen whom I pity."[4]

Looking out my windows at the American West from a Rocky Mountain valley in Montana, I can identify with both Thoreau's pathos and Huffman's lament. Less clearly I can see what Plenty Coups meant when he said that after the historic period began for the whites, history ended for the Crows. Stepping out my door, I`m enveloped by a classic western landscape that at first glance seems very little different from what the Salish and Kutenai saw here. The mountain valley and its sagebrush foothills have not gone anywhere, and neither—in places—have the fescues and bluebunch wheatgrasses, or the cottonwood and aspen groves along the river. But like everyone alive in this time, I in fact inhabit an impoverished nature, an impoverishment made emblematic by the erasure of many of the great animals that once lived here. The bison herds that the early British traders describe frequenting this valley two centuries ago are entirely gone now.

In the mind's eye, picture the process of the bison erasure: considerable herds right to the end, but more and more sporadic in their appearances; the last time or two it was almost magical, seeming rather like echoes of a past world than tangible beasts of the present. Soon the foothills no longer smelled like them, and their tracks no longer appeared along the creeks. Two winters' worth of snow melted their droppings into the soil, and magpies eventually hauled off all the lingering tufts of hair still snagged on the sagebrush. Their wallows gradually filled in with vegetation and disappeared. Their trails, which through the centuries had significantly shaped the very topography of the West, were appropriated by cattle, or deepened into gullies, or drifted in and became unrecognizable. Today the only physical evidence that the great animals were ever here is the infrequent skull or scapula eroding out of a streambank. That—and similar accounts of the Snake River brigades and the oral memories of the Native peoples—are about all that remain to testify that a century ago the Bitterroot Valley lay at the Rocky Mountain heart of a great, biologically diverse and rich continent.

On the cusp of the 21st century, those who know something of the history of the West—particularly a kind of western history marked by the hard thinking and fine writing that were Wallace Stegner's legacy—recognize that we live in an impoverished West. For most of the past two centuries, the West has been growing smaller before our eyes, and not just because it is now possible to traverse in three days what once took three months. For the past 200 years—actually 400 years if you count the first Spanish colonies planted along the Rio Grande in northern New Mexico—the human inhabitants of the American West have been dismantling and simplifying the place piece by piece.

But beginning 125 years ago, with the preservation of Yellowstone and Yosemite National Parks, and then followed with the Wilderness Preservation System in 1964, the visionaries of our culture have checked the dismantling process by attempting to preserve some select pieces of the natural world as vignettes of what we think the West once was. The national park and wilderness systems in two ways resemble great literature, art, and music. While striving for high expression they rarely obtain it. But nonetheless they serve as cultural land-marks, tangible expressions of something good and noble in the human spirit. Stegner thought of them as a kind of "geography of hope."[5]

In his later years Stegner despaired that the West would continue to serve as any kind of hopeful geography for America or the world.[6] It was being assailed too rapidly, on too many fronts. His one hope in fact was that the West's great deficiency, its relative aridity and finite water sources would ultimately serve to slow the assault and place limits on western growth. But restoring the West was not a topic to which Stegner devoted much attention.

However, many of our conservation visionaries, who originally thought of western resources as a commons to be shared and managed by the federal plan-ners, and who in another phase thought of preserving parts of the West as parks and wilderness systems, have recently turned their attention to the theme of restoring the West. The idea of restoration is as old as the first great book of American conservation history. In his 1864 classic, *Man and Nature*, George Perkins Marsh urged that "[Mankind] is to become a co-worker with nature in the reconstruction of the damaged fabric" of the natural world.[7] If public retention and management of western resources is the great conservation theme of the late 19th century, and if preservation of select pieces of the West is that of the 20th, restoration may well be that of the 21st.

As noble a cause as restoration is, however, the plans and processes of it raise many difficult questions. Preservation ought to have raised similar questions, but actually has only in reflection and then too often only after its shortcomings have become apparent enough to tarnish its image. While I do believe, strongly, that restoration *will* be a major theme in the environmental future of the West, acknowledging some of its problems early on is commonsensical. If we aim to restore the West, we need to know what we are about. And to avoid some of the mistakes and grand controversies that have come to surround preservation, look-ing restoration problems in the eye might not be a bad idea either.

The place to begin is with the premise itself. What exactly do we mean when we speak of "restoring" the West? And what on earth was the West's "original condition"? For a long time in American environmental history, certainly for most of the 20th century, we've thought that we knew the answer to the latter question. Certainly John Muir, gazing awestruck at the soaring gray granite in Yosemite, was convinced that he knew. Since Thoreau, and right down to the time of Aldo Leopold and Wallace Stegner, we were sure we knew what the West was originally. The tradition, as spelled out in the enabling acts of both the National Park Service and the Wilderness Preservation System, has been to seek that baseline condition as described in the earliest journals of European explorers and travelers. Ernest Thompson Seton's famous *Lives of Game Animals* did that three-quarters of a century ago and produced not just anecdotes but extrapolated statistics. If big predators are regarded as a sign of a healthy continental ecology, Seton's wildlife figures for the original West are truly astonishing: 60 to 75 million bison, 30 to 40 million pronghorns, 10 million elk, 10 million mule deer, 1.5 to 2 million sheep spread across the West at the time the first European explorers traversed it. Seton assembled accounts indicating that grizzlies had been so numerous that the rate of encounters in early America ranged from 30 to 40 sightings in a single day in Northern California, to 9 sightings in a month in the Bighorns in 1877, to bears every 50 yards during salmon runs in Idaho.[8]

Relying less on journal descriptions and more on ecological carrying capacities, more recent scholars (commencing with Victor Shelford) have revised many of Seton's figures, yet the imagery of a great natural garden remains. Shelford speaks of an average of 400 whitetail deer, 50 to 200 wild turkeys, 5 black bears, 3 cougars, and 1 to 3 wolves per ten square miles along the edges of the Great Plains in 1500. I have personally calculated that bison herds on the Great Plains, in times of good grass, reached as high as 24 to 28 million.[9] For the country from the Rockies westward, Frederic Wagner estimates 20 to 30 million large mammals aggregate in 1492, including 5 to 10 million bison, 10 to 15 million pronghorns, 1 to 2 million bighorn sheep, 5 million mule deer, and 2 million elk.[10] And in *Mammals of North America*, Hall and Kelson believe that the eastern perimeter of the grizzly's range originally stretched from Mexico's Sierra Madre Mountains across West Texas to eastern Kansas, then due north along the Mississippi to Hudson's Bay.[11] We now think grizzly populations across that vast stretch totaled more than 100,000 animals.[12] Along the Alaskan coast and in the Northwest as far inland as present Idaho, salmon runs featured so many different species that it would take several minutes just to list them, a living mass that surged up the rivers during spawning runs with such need and power that even those who had witnessed bison herds on the plains were stunned to speechlessness.

Of course, this brief litany of diversity and abundance only scratches the surface. Hundreds of cactus and reptile species can be found in the deserts of the Southwest. As Stephen Trimble notes, endemic populations have regularly migrated northward and southward in response to changing climates on almost every mountain range in the Great Basin.[13] So many passenger pigeons made the annual migration flights up from Texas that some scholars believe the Cross Timbers, a 400-mile-long strip of oak woods reaching almost to Kansas, was planted by their droppings and exists today as a mute testimony of their presence.[14] So many prairie dogs existed that a single dog town covering much of the Texas Panhandle is believed to have harbored more than 400 million of them.[15] Old-growth giants, such as firs, redwoods, and sequoias, reached up and down the Pacific Northwest and the Sierra; parklands of fat, yellow-bellied ponderosas stretched from the San Francisco Range in Arizona to the Flathead Valley in Montana. And great seas of tallgrass prairie lay across most of the basins and benches and foothills everywhere in the West—switchgrass, bluebunch, mid-height gramas, bluestems, fescues, and buffalograss. Meriwether Lewis described the velvety buffalograss, as it appeared in North Dakota in the spring of 1805, as resembling nothing else quite so much as a huge "bowling green in fine order."[16]

But the West of 200 to 400 years ago has now been eaten away and diminished. To illustrate, from among too many examples, there are today not 25 million bison but only a quarter million, not 100,000 grizzlies but fewer than 1,000, and not billions of passenger pigeons but only stuffed ones in a diorama in Philadelphia.[17]

For parishioners of the environment, the West-That-Was has long been worshiped as the holiest of the holies. Aldo Leopold enshrined the idea in essays like his 1933 piece "The Virgin Southwest," and since then we have made it sacred and deeply internalized an ideology of its meaning. Leopold of course also called the America that the earliest European explorers saw "wilderness." The Romantic Age and America's cultural need had already made the primeval continent into a metaphor for the Divine, if not actually God, as then the best and freshest example of His handiwork. In seminal essays like "Pioneers and Gullies," Leopold coupled that idea with a conviction that the presence of humans, or at least Northern European humans, could only detract from or despoil the perfection of that wilderness.[18] The emphasis on that despoliation has become the defining idea in how we think about American environmental history.

Now, however, the word *wilderness* (as well as *nature*) has come under assault from historian William Cronon and other academic deconstructionists.[19] Although I am one who demures from Cronon's conclusions, I do feel obligated to point out (because the evidence is too overpowering to do otherwise) that wilderness is certainly the wrong word for what early America was. It is the wrong word because it is Eurocentric and it obscures more than it reveals. What it obscures is that the garden does not have to be free of the human touch to still be a garden.

At the time of contact between Europe and the Americas, at least 350 generations (probably more) of men and women had been living in and transforming North America in a span of well over 100 centuries. Thus, based on recent Pre-Columbian population estimates, the supposed "virgin" American landscape—over the past 500 years before Contact—had been home to 150 million people! As geographer William Denevan argued in an article titled "The Pristine Myth," the ecological changes produced by that many people over the full span of occupation means that North America, when Europeans first saw it, was in fact a managed landscape, much of its look and ecology the product of the human presence.[20] Indians had cleared forests, drained swamps, and engineered significant water diversions and highway systems. They had built public works in the form of earthen mounds that for two centuries were larger construction projects than anything the Europeans attempted in America.

Indians had also engaged in environmental modifications that, in our Eurocentric guilt, we tend to associate only with industrial societies. Their ancestors had played at least some role in the extinctions of the Pleistocene megafauna, ecologically the most significant transformation to occur in the West since humans have been here.[21] Indian farmers had introduced dozens of domesticated exotic plants to the West, and moved several native species around from one location to another. And the fire ecology they practiced had altered successional patterns and even floral and faunal ranges significantly.[22] In Utah, half a century ago, ecologists like Walter Cottam and John Wakefield argued that the waving grasses that drew the Mormon pioneers to the benches of the Wasatch Front were relict populations maintained by Indian fires; that they so quickly gave way to chenopods and spreading junipers was the result of substituting one land use scheme for another.[23]

Thus, the great diversity of North America was the creation not only of eons of evolution, geology and climate, but equally of thousands of years of the Indian hand. Those thronging herds of animals and grasses were a legacy of simplification, and the animals that did survive were mostly Eurasian adventives.[24] In fact, North America lost 73 percent of its large fauna 10,000 years ago, including most of the animals like horses and camels that actually evolved here. That the West looked and functioned ecologically the way it did 400 years ago had everything to do with the fact that Indians managed it with fire as a great gathering and hunting continent, that tribal wars and hunting based on maximum take for least effort kept intertribal buffer zones full of animals, that taboos kept some aspects of nature (beavers among the Blackfeet, for example)[25] sacrosanct, and that no clear distinctions were drawn between humans and certain humanlike animals, which meant big predators like grizzlies or wolves were not pursued or eradicated.[26] And finally, we have to face squarely the fact that America was populated by no more than about 10 million people (north of Mexico) at the time of Contact—approximately one-thirtieth the present population of the United States and Canada.[27] Even so, Denevan figures it took the European settlers more than 250 years to produce as much ecological alteration in America as existed on the continent at the time of Contact.[28]

To further complicate matters, Denevan and geographer Martyn Bowden believe that much of the natural diversity and richness in our literary accounts actually reflects a continent that was in ecological rebound as a result of Indian depopulation from European disease.[29] (Bowden, of course, also calls the pristine wilderness idea "the grand invented tradition of American nature as a whole . . . a succession of imagined environments.") For example, bison, which were never seen in the Southeast by a DeSoto expedition that infected the numerous tribes of the region with disease, were widely reported there over the next century or more, until Indian populations rebounded, whereupon bison once again vanished from the region.[30] Several recent paleobiologists, most notably Charles Kay, believe that populations of many western ungulate species remained suppressed for more than 7,000 years before being briefly released, by human disease epidemics, in the 17th and 18th centuries.[31]

While these arguments may never persuade us to drop the word *wilderness* for "Indian-Managed America" or "Continent Undergoing Ecological Rebound," these insights are obviously problematic for restoration ecology. Even if I succeed in eradicating the CRP-planted Asiatic wheatgrass and the exotic spotted knapweed that have mostly supplanted the native fescues and bluebunch on my twenty-five acres of Bitterroot Valley prairie, and even if I turned a buffalo loose on it, I may have restored only a snapshot of time and place. In other words, I may not re-create the face of nature as pristine superorganism, but merely another of the kinds of landscapes that humans and history have produced. At least since 1990, with the publication of Daniel Botkin's *Discordant Harmonies*, environmentalists have been asked to reassess what they mean when seeking to re-create wilderness.[32]

But after much hard thought, I have decided that I simply don't care if the image of America that we hold in our heads does not really deserve to be called wild. After all, most of the things humans hold dear and value are cultural constructions. Few readers of the Bible think that its accounts of the creation are anything but metaphorical, yet that knowledge apparently does not dim the power of the book. I feel the same about wilderness and ecological endeavors aimed at restoring North America to its previous or baseline condition. The United States exists in historical context. For Americans, value in nature lies firmly rooted just there. To give credit where it is due, I personally prefer the term "Indian America" when imagining that baseline nature of five centuries ago. But acknowledging that what I value springs not so much from God as from evolutionary history, with humanity's hand firmly on the tiller for several thousand years, should not diminish the luster.

But we should be candid about this revisionist thinking, because we have to be clear about which West we are trying to replicate. The Pre-Contact West? The Post-Contact West? A pieced-together Pleistocene West? Or the best West we can imagine? I have a real soft spot for a restored West with wild mustangs in it; that's a very specific snapshot in time, even if you argue—taking the long view— that horses really are a native taxa. And once we decide which West we ought to restore, we will likely as not face (in fact we already have) plenty of questions. How can we expect to restore Indian fire ecology to an America speckled with houses and latticed with roads that act as firebreaks? How do we replicate a continent managed for hunting and gathering with a population thirty times larger? Restoring a West that entirely lacked industrial development is unlikely for an industrialized society as interested as ours continues to be in metals, coal, wood, and hydroelectric power. And even after returning wolves and building in livestock losses, there are further nuances: In the age of mass media, how accepting are we going to be that lions or grizzlies returned to the Bitterroots are going to munch the odd jogger on a recurring basis?

Although there are far too many specific problems to list, a few examples might give us an inkling of the range. For one, what we have often destroyed are not just species but ecosystems. We certainly do not know enough yet to be able to reassemble whole ecosystems. Recent research indicates, for example, that the prairie dog communities on the Great Plains supported more than 150 different species.[33] And the prairie dog community may be simple compared to restoring salmon runs on the tributaries of the Columbia. As those of us who have supported bison restoration learned when the Poppers called for a Buffalo Commons, not everyone is going to be happy with our visions.[34] I still believe a Buffalo Commons may be the best use for certain parts of the Great Plains. But Reed Noss, editor of the *Conservation Biology* and *Wild Earth* journals, thinks that to support a viable population of 100,000 large ungulates like bison, along with their carnivores, it would take an area of approximately 10 million acres.[35] None of the great parks that we created during the heyday of the preservation movement is nearly that large. In bison restoration on the Great Plains, therefore, lies the 21st century's restoration challenge—one equivalent to creation of Yellowstone or passage of the Wilderness Act.

Finally, if practical on-the-ground democracy has been one of the defining triumphs of conservation and preservation, then we have to beg the question: Who gets to be in charge of restoration in the next century? No doubt some restorations—wolves and fire to the public lands; bison to the plains; Western grasslands after a century of plowing, grazing abuse, and brush spread; and salmon to the Columbia—are obviously of national interest and scope. But many restoration projects are purely local and often occur on private land, which involves the shortest feedback loop of all. Arresting weed spread, for example, has an enormous private land dimension.[36] Across the West, the spread of exotic weeds, one of the largely unintended aspects of European biological imperialism, is creating biological wastelands at a dizzying rate. On the public lands, roughly 4,600 acres of wildlife habitat are being lost to weeds every day. And on private land the rate of spread (and corresponding loss of native species) is horrifying. In

Montana a 1988 study found that in three years of invasion, the exotic spotted knapweed is capable of knocking six of twenty-one native plants in mountain meadows into the "rare" category. A knapweed-infested foothill prairie eventually will lose 95 percent of its native grasses. And between 1989 and 1993, knapweed spread from 4.5 million acres in Montana to cover nearly 12 million acres.[37]

Finally, I wonder whether in our efforts to restore the West we may not confront an issue that will bewilder all our inspiration and striving. I seem to have shaken hands with it already. Fifteen years ago, in the Texas Panhandle, with literary descriptions and 19th-century photographs in hand, I set about using fire to restore to native prairie a little twelve-acre ranchette then enveloped in a mesquite thicket almost impossible to walk through. Two or three good burns and the grasses were back: The little blue gramas waving about like thousands of little quarter-notes stabbed into the ground, the side-oats gramas growing heavy with seedheads that resembled rows of feathers on a lance. It was beautiful.

Then the weather started changing. The period from 1500 to 1850 that we associate with classic American wilderness description was in fact a time of climate anomaly, the "little ice age." It was great for grass as well as big animals. But present global warming has a tendency in the Southwest to produce droughts broken by almost unprecedented gullywashers, so that annual rainfall is up while soil moisture is dropping.[38] On my place, this has favored desert species, which means fifteen years later that I am watching the cactus and the kangaroo rats march onto ground those Indian era photos show was a waving empire of grass.

Just another small instance of what we are likely to face at every level of restoration in the 21st century. And a further demonstration of that old maxim of history: What happens next is going to be awfully interesting.

NOTES

[1] Henry David Thoreau, "To Know an Entire Heaven and an Entire Earth," in Thoreau, *Writings* (6 vols.; Boston: Harvard University Press, 1953): V, pp. 181–84.

[2] Plenty Coups, "Vision in the Crazy Mountains," in Frank Bergon. ed., *The Wilderness Reader* (New York: Mentor, 1980), pp. 223–29.

[3] Mark Brown and W. R. Felton, *Before Barbed Wire: L. A. Huffman, Photographer on Horseback* (New York: Bramhall House, 1956), p. 5.

[4] Thoreau, "To Know an Entire Heaven and an Entire Earth."

[5] Wallace Stegner, "The Wilderness Letter," in Bergon, *The Wilderness Reader*, pp. 328–33.

[6] See, particularly, his interviews with Richard Etulain, in Stegner and Etulain, *Conversations with Wallace Stegner on Western History and Literature* (Salt Lake City: University of Utah Press, revised edition, 1983), especially the "After Ten Years" essay in the revised edition, pp. ix–xxix.

[7] See George Perkins Marsh, *The Earth as Modified By Human Action. A New Edition of Man and Nature* (New York: Arno and The New York Times, reprint of the 1874 edition). See especially pp. 48–55.

[8] Ernest Thompson Seton, *Lives of Game Animals* (Boston: Charles T. Branford, Co., 1953): I, part 1, pp. 258–65; II, part 1, p. 21; IV, part 2, pp. 447–48. Donald Worster, "Other People, Other Lives," in Worster, *An Unsettled Country: Changing Landscapes of the American West* (Albuquerque: University of New Mexico Press, 1994), pp. 66–71; Tim Clark and Denise Casey, *Tales of the Grizzly: Thirty-nine Stories of Grizzly Bear Encounters in the Wilderness* (Moose, Wyoming: Homestead Publishing, 1991): xiii; R. Edward Grumbine, *Ghost Bears: Exploring the Biodiversity Crisis* (Washington, DC: Island Press, 1992), p. 67.

[9] Victor Shelford, *The Ecology of North America* (1963): 28–29; Dan Flores, "Bison Ecology and Bison Diplomacy: The Southern Plains from 1800 to 1850," *Journal of American History* (September 1991), pp.165–85.

[10] Frederic Wagner, "Livestock Grazing and the Livestock Industry," *Wildlife in America*, Howard Brokaw, ed. (Washington D. C.: Council on Environmental Quality, 1978), pp. 133–35.

[11] E. Raymond Hall and Keith Kelson, *The Mammals of North America*, map p. 870.

[12] Seton, *Lives of Game Animals*, 2, part I, p. 21.

[13] Stephen Trimble, *The Sagebrush Ocean: A Natural History of the Great Basin* (Reno and Las Vegas: University of Nevada Press, 1989).

[14] Richard Phelan, *Texas Wild: The Land, Plants, and Animals of the Lone Star State* (New York: Excaliber Books, 1976), pp. 123–452.

[15] Vernon Bailey, *Biological Survey of Texas* (Washington, DC: Government Printing Office, 1905).

[16] Moulton, Gary, ed., *The Journals of the Lewis and Clark Expedition* (10 vols.; Lincoln: University of Nebraska Press, 1984–): III.

[17] See Grumbine, *Ghost Bears;* Ernest Callenbach, *Bring Back the Buffalo: A Sustainable Future for America's Great Plains* (Washington, DC: Island Press, 1996), p. 118.

[18] Aldo Leopold, "The Virgin Southeast" [1933] and "Pioneers and Gullies" [1924], in *The River of the Mother of God and Other Essays by Aldo Leopold*, Susan Flader and J. Baird Callicott, eds. (Madison: University of Wisconsin, 1991), pp. 106–13, 173–80.

[19] See especially Cronon's introductory pair of essays, "In Search of Nature" and "The Trouble with Wilderness," in William Cronon, ed., *Uncommon Ground: Toward Reinventing Nature* (New York: W. W. Norton & Co., 1995), pp. 23–90.

[20] William Denevan, "The Pristine Myth: The Landscapes of the Americas in 1492," *Annals of the Association of American Geographers* 82 (September 1992), pp. 369–85.

[21] Paul Martin, "Prehistoric Overkill: The Global Model," in Paul Martin and Richard Klein, eds., *Quaternary Extinctions* (Tucson: University of Arizona Press, 1985), pp. 354–403; N. Owen-Smith, "Pleistocene Extinctions: The Pivotal Role of Megaherbivores," *Paleobiology* 13 (1987), pp. 351–62.

[22] In several articles, among them "Indian Fires as an Ecological Influence in the Northern Rockies," *Journal of Forestry* 80 (1982), pp. 641–53, Steven Barrett has shown how even at high elevations in the Rockies, fire frequency accelerated dramatically some 10 millennia ago, when Indians began inhabiting the region.

[23] Walter Cottam, "An Ecological Study of the Flora of Utah Lake" (Ph.D. dissertation, University of Chicago, 1926); John Wakefield, "A Study of the Plant Ecology of Salt Lake and Utah Valleys Before the Mormon Immigration" (MA thesis, Brigham Young University, 1933).

[24] See Martin, "Prehistoric Overkill."

[25] Grace Morgan, "Beaver Ecology/Beaver Mythology" (Ph.D. thesis, University of Alberta, 1991). Her argument is that the aversion to killing beavers, judging by their paucity in the archeological record, is ancient, and sprang from the foot nomad background of the Plains people such as

Blackfeet, Gros Ventres, and Plains Assiniboine. These people found that beaver populations conserve and stabilize surface water in select habitats, usually large tributaries, on the plains.

26 See as an example of the literature, Nancy Williams and Eugene Hunn, eds., *Resource Managers: North American and Australian Hunter-Gatherers* (Boulder, Colo.: Westview Press, 1982).

27 For a good, recent guide to the past 30 years of revisionist literature on estimates of Pre-Contact Native American populations—which emerged after scholars recognized the profound effects of Virgin Soil Epidemics—see Wilbur Jacobs' essay, "The Tip of an Iceberg: Pre-Columbian Indian Demography and Some Implications for Revisionism," in Jacobs, *The Fatal Confrontation: Historical Studies of American Indians, Environment, and Historians* (Albuquerque: University of New Mexico Press, 1996), pp. 77–89. The critical works in the field have been Henry Dobyns, *Their Number Become Thinned* (Knoxville: University of Tennessee Press, 1983), and Dobyns's "Estimating Aboriginal American Population: An Appraisal of Techniques with a New Hemispheric Estimate," *Current Anthropology* 7 (1966), pp. 395–416, wherein Dobyns estimates 90 to 112.5 million people for the hemisphere before 1492 and 9.8 to 12.25 million north of Mexico.

28 Denevan, "The Pristine Myth."

29 Martyn Bowden, "The Invention of American Tradition," *Journal of Historical Geography* 18 (January 1992), pp. 3–26.

30 Earhard Rostlund, "The Geographical Range of the Historic Bison in the Southeast," *Annals of the Association of American Geographers* 50 (December 1970), pp. 395–407.

31 Kay's book, *Aboriginal Overkill*, is soon to be released from Oxford University Press. See also, J. Wayne Burkhardt, "Herbivory in the Intermountain West," in Burkhardt, et al., eds., *Herbivory in the Intermountain West: An Overview of Evolutionary History, Historic Cultural Impacts and Lessons from the Past* (Walla Walla, Wash.: Interior Columbia Basin Ecosystem Management Project, 1994); W. A. Laycock, "Stable States and Thresholds of Range Condition on North American Rangelands: A Viewpoint," *Journal of Range Management* 44 (1991), pp. 427–33.

32 Daniel Botkin, *Discordant Harmonies: A New Ecology for the 21st Century* (New York: Oxford University Press, 1990).

33 Conserving Prairie Dog Ecosystems on the Northern Plains (Bozeman, Mont.: Predator Project, 1997).

34 That "unhappiness" is ably documented in Anne Matthews, *Where the Buffalo Roam: The Storm Over The Revolutionary Plan to Restore America's Great Plains* (New York: Grove Press, 1992).

35 Ernest Callenbach, *Bring Back the Buffalo! A Sustainable Future for America's Great Plains* (Washington: Island Press, 1995).

36 USDA, *America's Private Land: A Geography of Hope* (Washington: Government Printing Office, 1997).

37 Ted Williams, "Killer Weeds," *Audubon* 99 (March–April 1997), pp. 24–31; Sherm Ewing, *The Range* (Missoula, Mont.: Mountain Press, 1990), pp. 228–29.

38 Gerald North, et al., "The Changing Climate of Texas," in Gerald North, Jurgen Schmandt, and Judith Clarkson, eds., *The Impact of Global Warming on Texas* (Austin: University of Texas Press, 1995), pp. 24–49.

Chapter 8

RESTORATION AS THE ORDER OF THE 21ST CENTURY
An Ecologist's Perspective
Duncan T. Patten

INTRODUCTION

The word *restoration* has many meanings in many disciplines. We restore an old building, we restore our health, or we restore a forest or a grassland. What do we mean by these actions? Have we re-created an entity or condition that is exactly like something that existed some time in the past, or have we only created something that generally resembles that entity or condition from the past? Because there is lingering confusion about the word *restoration*, we have tried to define it, and in the process added another set of words to the lexicon: re-create, rehabilitate, reestablish, redevelop, reclaim. Each of these terms has a subtle difference in meaning, yet each conveys a sense of accomplishment.

A National Research Council committee sought to clarify these concepts in examining restoration of aquatic ecosystems.[1] The committee defined restoration as "the return of an ecosystem to a close approximation of its condition prior to disturbance" and "the reestablishment of predisturbance aquatic functions and related physical, chemical, and biological characteristics." The committee explained that restoration was "different from habitat creation, reclamation, and rehabilitation," because "it is a holistic process not achieved through isolated manipulation of individual elements."

This discussion of the meaning of restoration is not meant to set boundaries around a widely appreciated process, but rather to note the many perceptions of what restoration entails. We might add that "we know restoration when we see it," but that statement would reflect one's own discipline or background. This examination of restoration is presented from the perspective of an ecologist who has studied different western ecosystems and thought intensely about how we might restore the many ecosystems that have been purposely or inadvertently lost or altered by human activity.

PRE-COLUMBIAN WESTERN ECOSYSTEMS

In the early 1800s, explorers from eastern North America initiated an accelerated alteration of western ecosystems. Previously these ecosystems were occasionally modified by indigenous peoples through fire, small irrigation projects, and limited timber cutting. Only when these populations stayed in one locale for long times did their impact have ecological consequences; these areas usually returned to near-original states upon the demise or migration of the people. On the western plains, fire was often used to drive bison and other grazing animals. These fires may have altered the extensive grasslands of the West, but fire was also a normal disturbance phenomenon, suggesting that human use of fire may not have disrupted natural ecological processes. On the other hand, extensive irrigation by the Hohokam and other tribes of the Southwest may have altered soils, increasing salinity and causing the land to be nonarable. Today some areas along the Gila River in Arizona have salt-tolerant vegetation growing on soils where irrigation and farming were abandoned more than 800 years ago.

Although it is often difficult to assign a primeval label to areas that appear never to have been disturbed, we can use the word *pristine* for those areas that have little or no evidence of disturbance by modern man (i.e., post-1800s in the West). This means that these areas still maintain their original biological communities and ecological processes, and show no evidence of nonnative vegetation or significant human disturbance. This describes conditions discovered by Lewis and Clark as they passed through what is now Montana, and probably depicts conditions found by early Spanish explorers in the Southwest.

Fire and flood were important controlling factors that determined ecosystem composition. Grasslands and forests burned regularly and usually in small patches, but fires were periodically extensive (i.e., decadally for grasslands and 100 to 300 years for forests). Riparian areas depended on floods to maintain streamside forests and to prevent upland plant invasion, but devastating floods that removed most riparian vegetation occurred only every 50 to 100 years. Most forests would be described as old-growth in today's vernacular. Trees were multi-aged, with many dead snags, downed timber, and forest openings covered with younger trees. In fact the forest consisted of patches from different successional stages; some were postfire forest types, whereas others were hundreds of years older with totally different climax species.

Today, however, few examples of pristine ecosystems remain in the West. Most grasslands have been converted to farmland or grazing land, and most forests have been modified through harvest. But in some wilderness areas and national parks, near-pristine ecosystems can be found. Yet because of various resource management activities, even these areas are limited and rapidly changing.

ALTERATION OF WESTERN ECOSYSTEMS

Western ecosystems did not change rapidly as a result of western expansion, but gradually with increasing population and resource exploitation. Beaver trapping was probably the first major impact; it altered hydrological conditions that maintained wetlands and riparian areas. The loss of the beaver caused water tables to decline. Cover was lost as wetland plants dependent on a shallow water table diminished. And with greater influx of pioneers, land and water resources were increasingly modified, culminating in a West with little unaltered terrain.

Land Use

The discovery of high-grade ore bodies in the mountains caused intensive impacts on small areas where people flocked to gain instant wealth. Although abandoned long ago, remnants of these developments have long-term effects on land and water quality. Some western streams, for example, are highly acidic due to leachate from old mine tailings. More extensive land exploitation can be traced to domestic livestock grazing, whereas farming was limited to providing food for early settlers and miners. Once the settlers discovered that western grasslands were productive grain farms, they converted them to farmland, or used them as rangeland for thousands of domestic livestock.

At the same time, timber harvesting had moved from the eastern states to the mountains of the West. Although extensive timber production in the Rocky Mountain states developed later than in other areas of the West, it is now one of many land use activities that have permanently altered western watersheds, crisscrossing mountains with low-grade roads, clearcutting forests, reducing habitat diversity, increasing erosion, and reducing stream water quality. Forest management includes reducing fires that might destroy the economic potential of western forests. Forest fire abatement programs have eliminated one of the processes that helped create and maintain the ecosystems discovered by early explorers. Crop production in the grasslands did essentially the same for that ecosystem.

Water Management

Development of the West was dependent on an ensured supply of water, which is vital to farming, mining, urban expansion, and industry. Western hydrology typically is highly variable, wet periods followed by droughts. To maintain a water supply and to produce electricity, most western rivers have been harnessed by dams throughout their length. Consequently, there are few free-flowing rivers in the West.

Stream flows have been managed for nonecological purposes, which has greatly altered riverine ecosystems. Riparian vegetation is dependent on flood disturbances and high spring flows for recruiting and maintaining a riparian community across the floodplain. Many aquatic ecosystem components need seasonal fluctuations to develop during parts of their life cycles. In addition, many western streams have been altered through the introduction of nonnative species. Riparian areas have been invaded by nonnative plants more adapted to controlled hydrological conditions. Nonnative fishes have been intentionally introduced for recreation and accidentally from other sources.

Rivers controlled by dams are no longer recharged with new sediment during high flows, because the sediment is held in upstream impoundments. The loss of sediment, reduction of riparian vegetation, loss of beavers, and creation of controlled flows have all led to channel down-cutting. This condition, which is exacerbated by grazing in riparian areas, tends to lower the water table, thus causing a further reduction in riparian vegetation.

Gravel extraction in western rivers has also altered the hydrology. Gravel mining produces deep pits that lower the water table and may alter the path of the river. These conditions directly affect recruitment and survival of riparian vegetation.

Land use and water management function synergistically. For example, increased runoff from timber cutting in the watershed causes changes in seasonal stream flow magnitudes. Consequently, we now realize that we must "manage" the whole watershed to better maintain all ecosystems for production and sustainability.

EVOLUTION OF ECOLOGICAL SCIENCE

Ecological science did not develop until the late 19th century, when biogeographers sought explanations for the existence of many of the world's species. Since then it has expanded and provided critical insights for understanding populations, communities, ecosystems, and landscape functions and characteristics. As ecology has increased our understanding of complex relationships among organisms and their environment, it has created a discipline that is well-suited to developing guidelines for restoring degraded or altered ecosystems.[2] What drives these systems? How do the components respond to external variables? How do internal components interact with each other? How does one ecosystem influence another? Answers to these and related questions should provide us with the foundation of ecosystem management.

EARLY CONCERN FOR THREATENED ECOSYSTEMS

Public concern over lost or degraded ecosystems is not just a latter 20th-century development. Although resource exploitation was the leading principle of land development during western expansion, concern over the impacts of exploitation arose in the 1920s and 1930s. By then, ecologists had formed the Ecological Society of America and established a committee to address the rapid decline of natural ecosystems in the United States. In 1951 members of this committee formed The Nature Conservancy, which has become a leading organization for identifying and preserving habitat for threatened or endangered species. Its efforts have focused on buying ecologically important lands and restoring original habitats. Through these efforts, The Nature Conservancy has developed extensive information on restoration techniques, including reasons for successes or failures. The Wilderness Society also was formed during the 1920s with the goal of identifying and protecting North America's rapidly disappearing wildlands. These organizations helped to draft and pass the Wilderness Act.

Since the 1960s, many other groups have become involved in saving threatened ecosystems. Some of these groups have the same goals as The Nature Conservancy, others function like the Wilderness Society, as watch dogs of federal and state agencies.

ROLE OF THE ECOLOGIST: ACTIVIST AND SCIENTIST

The ecologists who helped found The Nature Conservancy were functioning as environmental activists—a role not often associated with a scientific discipline. This role is most commonly associated with environmentalists and other advocates of resource protection or preservation. Not many ecologists, however, are willing to wear both an activist and scientist hat. Yet few individuals are better qualified than a fully trained ecologist, with extensive experience in understanding ecosystem function and structure, to be an advocate on issues concerning the loss or degradation of ecosystems, animal or plant populations, or even whole watersheds.[3] Nevertheless, some ecologists, often working with nonadvocacy-oriented colleagues, are willing to give guidance to resource managers, landowners, decision makers, and the public about the "what, where, and how" of ecosystem degradation and restoration.

UNDERSTANDING ECOSYSTEM PROCESSES

Ecosystems are more complex than biological populations or communities. Ecosystems include the interactions among the biotic and abiotic components of a system, as well as those that influence the system from outside. Many of these components function within the system in a cyclic nature, such as nitrogen, carbon, or water cycles. Some components such as energy flow through the system, but also include both biotic and abiotic aspects. Understanding the processes that control or influence these cycles of elements or flows of energy is a critical part of taking an ecosystem apart and putting it back together. This understanding is essential background to any restoration activity.

Some simple energy flow processes or elemental cycles can be studied in the laboratory, which provides a foundation to understand the "real-world" system. We then take this information to the field, where we design research to test our knowledge base (i.e., hypothesis testing), run experiments, and monitor the system. From this process we will eventually learn how the system responds to external variables (including parameters that we cannot control) and how internal processes evolve under these conditions. By applying our research to pristine ecosystems, we can acquire a fundamental database for guiding restoration activities and for developing evaluation procedures (i.e., measuring success or failure in reestablishing certain ecosystem processes).

UNDERSTANDING ECOSYSTEM COMPOSITION, STRUCTURE, AND FUNCTION: USE OF REFERENCE AREAS

Besides ecosystem processes, we must also understand the composition, structure, and function of the system if we want to restore it. This understanding should be of a system considered representative of "pristine" conditions. Reference areas should therefore be identified and preserved for this purpose. Although it is unlikely that many truly pristine locations exist, reference areas that come close to this condition, based on expert opinions and extensive data searches, should be located and set aside.

Reference areas will generally be found within wilderness areas, preserves, and national or state parks. Some, however, have been managed for purposes other than "preservation," or have been mismanaged and are no longer "pristine." Yellowstone National Park, for example, contains a few areas at higher elevations that could qualify as reference areas, but much of the park is degraded from excessive ungulate populations or human activities. Reference areas can and should be found as soon as possible, because ever expanding resource needs will continue to put pressure on them.

At these reference sites, the information sought should focus on composition, structure, and function of biotic communities, particularly "ecosystem services." This information should include, for example, how the ecosystem contributes to animal habitats, runoff control, and water quality and recharge.

RESTORATION OF FUNCTIONAL SYSTEMS

Restoration can occur only after baseline information about the site and similar reference sites is compared. Then, the level of restoration success can be estimated. If the site still has many of the components found at the reference sites, or other sites that are known to be fully functional, then the potential for success is high. However, if restoration requires modification or replacement of many essential ecosystem components,then the potential for success is questionable.

All ecosystems cannot be restored. As noted earlier, restoration is intended to return an ecosystem as close as possible to predisturbance conditions. Obviously, closeness is dependent upon the starting point, as well as the ability to modify both external and internal variables. But the goal of restoration must be a realistic one; if a less than pristine level of restoration is not acceptable, then restoration should not proceed.

Regulated rivers, for example, offer restoration opportunities that are limited by our ability to modify dam operations. Dam operations can be modified to regain "normative attributes" of the riverine ecosystem, such as water temperature and flow regimes.[4] In March 1996, an experimental flood was introduced into the Grand Canyon to test the potential for re-creating riverine ecosystem processes that had been significantly altered by dams for hydropower production and water storage. The experimental flood successfully restored elevated sediment deposits throughout the canyon and scoured backwater habitat for native fishes. However, similar attempts to re-create natural processes within other ecosystem types, such as fire in grasslands, have met with mixed success.

ACCEPTANCE OF CHANGE: THE NONRESTORATION ALTERNATIVE

Restoration is not possible for every altered or degraded ecosystem, but we can try to mimic natural processes to return the system to some level of "naturalness." Although dams have greatly altered both downstream and upstream riverine ecosystems, most dams will not be removed. Nevertheless, dam operations are increasingly being adjusted for controlled releases to mimic the effects of downstream floods and thus "restore" some natural processes. Large open-pit mines, abandoned for lack of valuable ore, may never be restored, but these sites might be modified to allow native plants to reinvade and other ecosystems to gain a foothold. As another alternative to full restoration, productive farm- and forestlands might be left in a sustainable state rather than attempting to rehabilitate or restore them.

Throughout the world, an increased human presence has disseminated species far beyond their normal ranges. In some cases, species were introduced for economic or ecological reasons; in other cases, they were inadvertently introduced. Nonnative species, once naturalized, become part of the functional ecosystem. These species often replace less durable native species and may play a functional role in the ecosystem equivalent to the lost native species. Because most naturalized nonnative species cannot be easily removed, changes attributable to them must be accepted and built into restoration procedures.

Although the resulting ecosystem with nonnative components may never achieve a near-predisturbance level, it may still contribute required ecosystem services and promote long-term sustainability. In the Southwest, for example, saltcedar (tamarisk) has invaded most regulated and grazed riparian ecosystems. Saltcedar is nearly impossible to eliminate, and it often affords habitat for threatened species. By creating conditions suitable for its recruitment and maintenance and by accepting its functional role in the riparian ecosystems, we must also accept its presence as part of western riparian vegetation. Other examples of plant

and animal species similar to saltcedar abound. Russian olive, originally introduced as an ornamental, is now a well-established component of many central
and northern Rocky Mountain riparian communities. Striped bass, originally
introduced as a game fish in many western rivers, lakes and reservoirs, is now a
dominant fish in these systems but may contribute to the extirpation of native
fishes.

HUMAN WILLINGNESS TO CHANGE

The human use of ecosystems is often incompatible with restoration goals.
Historically, western ecosystems have been used economically. More recently,
those who wish to protect an area from more drastic modification have advocated recreational use, which also has an economic component. But if restoration
means returning an ecosystem to a near-predisturbance state, then all human disturbance must be removed. If the human disturbance cannot be removed, then
reclamation or rehabilitation should be the goal rather than restoration. In areas
where disturbances such as nonnative species are not removable, or where dams
cannot be feasibly removed, something less than restoration must be an acceptable alternative.

A long-term goal, however, should be to alter human attitudes about those
factors that prevent full restoration. Humans attitudes must be changed to elevate
"natural" ecosystems to a priority level at least equal to economical considerations. In fact, ecologically sustainable economic systems require reestablishing
systems that possess more natural components and functions than those that are
managed strictly for resource production. Thus, human attitudes and actions
must be altered in order to create sustainable systems and restore ecosystems to
near-pristine conditions.

The late 20th century has witnessed substantial changes in resource management attitudes. These changes, largely triggered by public and scientific pressure,
reflect the realization that natural processes may have a greater potential for
longevity than human-altered processes. By emphasizing the long-term sustainability of ecosystems over resource extraction and short-term profits, restoration
activities may secure necessary support from decision makers, the public, and the
scientific community.

NOTES

[1] National Research Council, *Restoration of Aquatic Ecosystems* (Washington, D.C.: National Academy Press, 1992).

[2] O. Ravera, ed., *Terrestrial and Aquatic Ecosystems: Perturbation and Recovery* (New York: Ellis Horwood Publ., 1991).

[3] A. D. Bradshaw, "What Has the Ecologist to Offer?" In *Terrestrial and Aquatic Ecosystems: Perturbation and Recovery,* O. Ravera, ed. (New York: Ellis Horwood Publ., 1991).

[4] J. A. Stanford, J. W. Ward, W. J. Liss, C. A. Frissell, R. N. Williams, J. A. Lichatowich, and C. C. Coutant, "A General Protocol for Restoration of Regulated Rivers," *12 Regulated Rivers: Research and Management* (1996) pp. 391–413.

Chapter 9

PRIVATE PROPERTY INTERESTS, WILDLIFE RESTORATION, AND COMPETING VISIONS OF A WESTERN EDEN

Holly Doremus

Recent years have produced a few hopeful signs for those seeking to restore ecological integrity to the western United States. In January 1995, gray wolves brought from Canada raced into the snow of the central Idaho wilderness, returning after a fifty-year absence. Late in 1996, condors soared above the sun-washed Vermilion Cliffs of northern Arizona for the first time in nearly a century.[1]

Not all observers were pleased, however. Property owners in the northern Rockies and Southwest, respectively, fiercely opposed each of these reintroductions. Each dramatic homecoming occurred against a backdrop of stylized battles in dignified courtrooms. But the battles weren't limited to those bloodless courtroom confrontations. About two weeks after the Idaho wolf release, one of the wolves was found shot to death near the body of a dead calf. Two years later the bullet-riddled body of another reintroduced wolf was dumped in a river near Yellowstone Park.[2]

Of course disputes between property interests and environmentalists are neither new nor unexpected. Environmental regulation can have heavy financial consequences. Restrictions imposed on timber harvesting to protect dwindling species, such as the northern spotted owl, can cost landowners as much as $40,000 per acre. But money does not fully explain the furor of the battles over wildlife restoration. Offers of compensation for damages have not silenced opposition to wolf releases or bison restoration. One explanation for the continued resistance is that the significance of these struggles is not limited to their financial consequences. These are battles for control of the relationship between humankind and nature, pitting the individual against the government, local interests against national ones, and rural residents against urbanites. Appropriately, they are fought primarily in the West, home to most of the country's remaining wildlands, heir to a fierce tradition of rugged individualism and self-determination, and currently the site of a wrenching transition from rural to urban domination.

Combatants on both sides of these battles are striving to construct or maintain what they imagine to be a western paradise. Their utopian visions, however, are diametrically opposed. On one side the environmentalists of the new West seek a paradise where nature represents an awesome presence, an intricate and beautiful dance to be admired and respected in its own right. These advocates of wild nature measure choices against the standards articulated by Aldo Leopold: Things are morally right if they tend to preserve the integrity and beauty of nature; they are morally wrong if they tend otherwise. On the other side are the ranchers, loggers, and miners of the old West, seeking to preserve the western utopia their forebears created through arduous labor and single-minded determination. Their Eden is a garden in which nature has been tamed, stripped of its wildness in order to maximize its utility as the servant of humankind.

Efforts to restore wildlife species to areas they once called home present this struggle over the dominant vision of paradise in a particularly acute form. Although their financial impacts on property owners often seem relatively small, restoration efforts carry great symbolic weight. When the government undertakes such efforts, it is choosing moral sides, affirming the naturalist's vision of paradise, and the primacy of wild nature over human control. As such, restoration projects offer a useful lens through which to view this larger conflict.

RESTORATION IN HISTORICAL PERSPECTIVE

Wildlife restoration, in the narrow sense of returning species to their historic range, has a long history in the United States. The second half of the 19th century was a time of rapid liquidation of game and fur species; although the buffalo slaughter may be best remembered, many other species were hunted, trapped, or driven by development to near extinction. When the toll on these species became apparent, state and federal governments began systematically seeking to prevent further declines and to restore the remaining populations.

One early restoration project brought the beaver back to the Adirondacks of upstate New York. At the time of European settlement, roughly 60 million beaver were spread across the continent. By 1900, though, extensive trapping had reduced that number to about 100,000. In an effort to restore the commercially valuable beaver, New York became the first state to experiment with beaver reintroduction. Beginning in 1904, state game officials live-trapped beaver in their remaining strongholds and moved them to unoccupied but suitable habitat.[3]

Predictably, the relocated beaver set right to work gnawing down trees. Just as predictably, vociferous objections from impacted landowners followed. The Barretts owned a woodland abutting Eagle Creek, one of the sites chosen by the state for beaver release. The beaver severely damaged the Barretts' trees, which in turn greatly reduced the land's value as a potential building site. The Barretts sued, claiming that the state must pay for the damage. In a decision that foreshadowed the future for property owners aggrieved by restoration efforts, they lost.[4]

Those early restoration efforts, although they certainly imposed financial costs on landowners like the Barretts, did not carry the symbolic freight of today's programs. They concentrated on species with significant utilitarian value, typically as the source of commercial products or the object of recreational hunting. They sought to increase wildlife populations in order to facilitate continued exploitation. Such projects did not challenge popular views about the primacy of humankind over nature or conflict with the desires of most local landowners. Consequently, they typically enjoyed widespread popular support. The Depression-era restoration of beaver, a valuable income commodity, to rural America was one highly popular example.[5]

PRIVATE PROPERTY AND ENDANGERED SPECIES

Many of today's restoration efforts have a different focus, one far more likely to arouse local opposition. They seek to bring wild nature back for its own sake, and for its aesthetic and symbolic value, rather than for its economic resource value. The architects of the gray wolf restoration program in the northern Rockies and the condor program in the desert Southwest, for example, do not envision those programs primarily as a source of trophies for future hunters. Rather, they see wolves and condors as essential elements of the natural world, and their restoration as a way to heal an old wound. Restoration projects of this type endorse the Leopoldian vision of paradise, and inevitably call into question the competing vision upon which many rural western communities were founded.

The rhetorical salvos launched in the battle over wolf reintroduction illustrate the extent to which this fundamental clash of values underlies the dispute. Ranchers, whose predecessors only recently brought nature to heel in the region through a concerted effort to eradicate wolves and other predators, are appalled at the idea of reversing that course. They stress the importance of choosing "man's way" over nature's. Environmentalists use many of the same words, but urge precisely the opposite choice. They talk of an obligation to make amends for past mistakes,[6] and describe wolves as the ultimate symbol of wilderness.[7]

Inevitably, private property rights have become the focus of many restoration battles. The legal institution of property in the United States has come to symbolize the search not only for human dominion over nature, but for personal dominion over individual slices of nature. The early English commentator Blackstone described property as "that sole and despotic dominion which one man claims and exercises over the external things of the world, in total exclusion of the right of any other individual in the universe."[8] Although that absolutist description has never been an accurate statement of American property law, many Americans, particularly in the rural West, subscribe to the mythic image of property it embodies. That image dovetails with their view of paradise as a place where rugged individuals control their own destiny and that of their land.

However, the urge to heal wounded nature also enjoys widespread public support. Its influence is felt in a variety of state and federal laws. The federal Endangered Species Act (ESA)[9] is perhaps the strongest expression of these preservationist urges, as well as the one that throws the longest shadow over private land in the West. The ESA is best known for its two strong prohibitory provisions, one forbidding federal actions likely to jeopardize the continued existence of a listed species and the other barring any actions, private or governmental, that kill or harm listed species. The reach of the ESA, however, potentially extends well beyond these stopgap measures, which are designed to impose a last barrier between listed species and extinction. The law's ultimate purpose is to return listed species to surer ground, bringing them to the point where they no longer need legal protection.[10]

To that end, the ESA directs the government to prepare a recovery plan, a blueprint to guide recovery efforts, for each listed species. By the time species reach the protected list, many are severely depleted. Recovery of those species will often require relocation or reintroduction to areas beyond their current range. Not surprisingly, a 1993 study of recovery plans found that fully 70 percent called for transplanting individuals from one wild population to another area, and 64 percent incorporated captive breeding, presumably with the eventual goal of reintroduction.[11]

Reintroduction efforts create or threaten a variety of conflicts with private property interests. Wolves and other predators may prey on privately owned livestock. Herbivores may be feared as a source of communicable livestock diseases. Wild herbivores may also trample crops, knock over fences, and compete with livestock for forage. Undoubtedly, the most feared threat is that land use restrictions will eventually be imposed on surrounding landowners.[12]

WHY THE TAKINGS CLAUSE DOES NOT APPLY

Like the Barretts, property owners opposed to reintroduction programs often appeal to the "takings clause" of the federal constitution, which requires the government to provide compensation when it takes property for public use.[13] And like the Barretts, those property owners typically do not prevail. Notwithstanding Blackstone's absolutist description of property, the government is not required to pay for every encroachment on private property interests. Although the takings clause protects more than just economic value, it does not protect against the symbolic loss of control these landowners must endure.

As currently interpreted by the United States Supreme Court, the takings clause requires compensation, at a minimum, for two classes of government actions: physical invasions and regulations that deny an owner all economically viable use. Wildlife reintroduction programs will rarely fall in either category.

The prototypical physical taking is the acquisition of a right-of-way for a road across private property. The government becomes the owner of the roadway, taking from the prior owner the rights to possess, control the use of, and exclude others from that property. Compensation is always required for physical takings, no matter how minimal the financial impact, how small the area occupied, or how strong the government interest it advances. Requiring compensation in these circumstances vindicates the owner's interests in possession, use, and control, all of which are important incidents of ownership. But there is more to the special treatment accorded physical takings. Physical invasion of an owner's land, the Supreme Court has observed, "literally adds insult to injury," completely shattering the owner's symbolic and psychological as well as physical control of the property.[14]

Claims that damage caused by protected wildlife amounts to a physical taking have a long but unsuccessful history. Property owners who have watched helplessly as elk ate their forage or bears feasted on their sheep, prohibited by government regulations from killing or driving off the marauders, understandably tend to view these incidents as equivalent to physical confiscation of their property. Their interests in possession and control of their crops and livestock have plainly been infringed. Nonetheless, state and federal courts have consistently rejected the argument that the government bears responsibility for that invasion.

Probably the best known of this line of cases is *Christy v. Hodel*. Christy, a Montana rancher, fatally shot a grizzly bear that was attacking his sheep. Because the bear enjoyed the protection of the ESA, the government levied a civil penalty against Christy. He challenged that penalty, arguing that enforcement of the ESA under the circumstances unconstitutionally deprived him of his property without compensation. The Ninth Circuit rejected that claim. Although it conceded that the bear had physically taken Christy's sheep, the court refused to attribute that taking to the government. Essentially, the decision equates losses of livestock to wildlife predation with losses to fire, floods, or other natural disasters. The government, the court concluded, need not insure landowners against such losses.

Because the marauding grizzly bear found its way to Christy's ranch without government intervention, the court in that case did not have to decide whether the government would be liable for damage by wildlife it introduced to the vicinity. Other courts, however, have rejected the notion that reintroduction or relocation of wildlife makes the government liable for any resulting damage. In the Barrett case mentioned earlier, for example, New York's highest court refused to hold the government responsible for harm caused by transplanted beavers. The California Court of Appeal reached a similar result in 1993, rejecting government liability for crop and fence damage caused by relocated Tule elk. So long as the government does not directly place protected creatures on private property without the owner's consent—something it has yet to attempt—claims of physical takings are likely to fail.

Nor are landowners likely to succeed, absent similarly unusual circumstances, with claims that wildlife restoration denies them all economically beneficial use of their property. Although Christy lost all use of the sheep consumed by grizzlies, that type of loss is not sufficient to create a categorical regulatory taking. The relevant test is whether the regulated parcel as a whole retains any economic viability. As long as the government does not prohibit ranching in grizzly territory or farming within historic Tule elk range, this type of taking has not occurred.

If the challenged government action does not fall into either of these per se taking categories, compensation may still be required in some circumstances. The Supreme Court has suggested that, absent physical invasion or deprivation of all economically beneficial use, any regulation that substantially advances a legitimate state interest will survive a takings challenge. If that is indeed the test, wildlife reintroduction programs will nearly always pass muster. Wildlife conservation has long been recognized as a legitimate state interest. Because wildlife restoration efforts are expensive and often politically controversial, they are not undertaken lightly. Few reintroductions will be so carelessly designed or executed that they will fail to substantially advance the legitimate government interest in conservation.

In a footnote in *Lucas v. South Carolina Coastal Council*, a majority of the Supreme Court hinted that the Court might entertain a regulatory takings challenge even if all economically viable use were not taken and the government action were not wholly irrational or illegitimate. The federal courts of appeals have split on whether to take up that veiled suggestion. If appropriate at all, scrutiny of such regulations would take the form of an ad hoc, fact-specific inquiry, with the burden on the landowner to show that the challenged regulation forced her to bear burdens that properly belong to the general public. Important factors to consider would include the economic impact of the regulation, the extent to which it interfered with reasonable investment-backed expectations, and the character of the government intrusion, that is, whether the government action more closely resembled a physical invasion or an adjustment of "the benefits and burdens of economic life."[15]

Although it is obviously difficult to make a generic prediction about the outcome of such an ad hoc test, it seems likely that most existing wildlife reintroduction programs would survive. The economic impact of such programs is often relatively small, is shared among all landowners in the vicinity of the release, and may be counterbalanced by widespread economic gains to the region. In the Yellowstone area, for example, wolf reintroduction was expected to produce livestock losses on the order of $5,000 to $50,000 per year, but annual economic benefits from increased tourism in the region were projected at about $25 million. The impact on reasonable investment-backed expectations is difficult to evaluate. On the one hand, ranchers might argue that the government's role in funding, encouraging, and even carrying out past wolf eradication efforts led them to expect that wolves would never return to plague their ranches. On the other hand, environmentalists might draw on the long tradition of government regulation of wildlife conservation to argue that no landowner could reasonably expect complete freedom from wildlife damage. Finally, as already explained, courts have been reluctant to view wildlife protection regulations as a kind of physical invasion, which means the third factor is likely to weigh in favor of the government.

INTO THE POLITICAL ARENA

Typically, then, constitutional claims raised by property owners will fail. Given the nature of the dispute, that outcome is perfectly appropriate. The political process rather than the constitution is the usual forum for resolving disputes about both the nature of the earthly paradise society should seek, and the steps the government might take to reach it. Nor does removing this issue from the constitutional arena give government the ability to run roughshod over the interests of either landowners or environmentalists. There is a great deal of sympathy in the political community for each of the competing visions of paradise: for the rugged individualist triumphing over nature on the one hand, and for nature as an increasingly essential wild counterpoint to civilization on the other. The result is a series of compromises through which neither vision of paradise will be fully achieved, but perhaps the two can coexist.

Government reintroduction programs under the ESA vividly illustrate these compromises. The ESA seeks to preserve wild nature, but the agency regulations implementing reintroduction efforts provide numerous protections for impacted property owners. The government must, for example, consult with affected landowners before undertaking any release of a listed species. Reintroduced populations are generally designated as "nonessential," and therefore not entitled to the full protection of the ESA. Special protective regulations are drafted for each introduced population, in consultation and, insofar as possible, agreement with affected landowners. The regulations often require that the government physically remove the transplanted creatures if they stray onto private land, and in some cases even allow property owners to kill wildlife they find attacking their livestock.[16]

These compromises have eased political tensions and reduced conflicts between landowners and introduced wildlife. Livestock losses to wolves in the northern Rockies, for example, have been considerably lower than anticipated. At the same time, of course, these concessions to property owners both increase the costs of restoration programs and decrease the extent to which they move the West toward the wild vision of paradise.

The compromise position embodied in the ESA and other laws deserves continued scrutiny from all sides. Wildlife restoration efforts are one context in which we must grope our way toward the compromise Wallace Stegner envisioned between humans and nature, between economic health and the health of the earth. We cannot give up the image of nature as servant; none of us can walk through the world without leaving any trace. We are unlikely ever to return to the days when 25 million bison roamed the plains, and grizzlies could be found from northern California to Kansas. We are equally unlikely to give up our ingrained, and very human, urge to transform and control the landscapes we inhabit. But we have also come to recognize the intricate and fragile beauty, as well as the awesome power, of uncontrolled nature. Most of us, I think, seek both kinds of paradise. If we craft our compromises with that in mind, perhaps we can create a place in the West for condors and wolves as well as for humans.

NOTES

[1] Tom Kenworthy, "Condors Soar Again Over Grand Canyon," *The Washington Post*, December 13, 1996, at A1.

[2] "Wolf Death in Yellowstone Prompts Posting of Reward," *The Oregonian*, Feb. 9, 1997, at A19.

[3] Edward P. Hill, "Beaver Restoration." In *Restoring America's Wildlife 1937–1987* (Kallman et al., eds. 1987).

[4] *Barrett v. State*, 220 N.Y. 423, 116 N.E. 99 (1917).

[5] Hill, *supra* n. 3, at 282.

[6] L. David Mech, "A New Era for Carnivore Conservation," 24 *Wildlife Society Bulletin* 397 (1996); see also Ed Timms, "Revival of the Species," *The Dallas Morning News*, Mar. 18, 1996, at A1 (quoting the head of a group seeking reintroduction of wolves to Colorado as saying that returning wolves is "making nature the way it should be . . . putting Humpty Dumpty back together again"); Rick Bass, *The Ninemile Wolves,* p. 35 (1992), quoting Renee Askins of the Wolf Fund as explaining that reintroducing wolves to Yellowstone "is an act of making room, of giving up the notion of bigger, better, more, to hold onto complete, balanced, whole. It is an act of giving back, a realigning, a recognition that we make ecological and ethical mistakes and learn from them . . . [It] is a symbolic act, just as exterminating the wolves from the West was a symbolic act."

[7] Roger Schlickeisen of Defenders of Wildlife has been quoted as saying that the howl of the wolf "is synonymous with the call of the wild. Putting wolves back into Yellowstone is like putting the 'wild' back into the wilderness." Quoted in Oliver A. Houck, "Why Do We Protect Endangered Species, and What Does That Say About Whether Restrictions on Private Property to Protect Them Constitute 'Takings'?" 80 *Iowa Law Review* 297, 300 n. 15 (1995). *The New York Times*, among others, agrees. See "Wolves at Our Door" (editorial), *The New York Times*, November 24, 1996, at D14.

[8] Blackstone, *Commentaries on the Laws of England*, Book II, Chap. 1, p. 2 (15th ed. 1809).

9 16 U.S. Code secs. 1531–1544.

10 See 16 U.S. Code sec. 1531(b) (purposes of the ESA include providing means to conserve listed species); idem sec. 1532(3) (the term "conserve" means "the use of all methods and procedures which are necessary to bring any endangered or threatened species to the point at which the measures provided pursuant to this chapter are no longer necessary").

11 Timothy H. Tear, J. Michael Scott, Patricia H. Hayward, Brad Griffith, "Status and Prospects for Success of the Endangered Species Act: A Look at Recovery Plans," 262 *Science 976* (1993).

12 See Loren Webb, "Residents Tear into Condor-Release Proposal," *The Salt Lake Tribune*, January 26, 1996, at B8; Richard P. Reading and Stephen R. Kellert, "Attitudes Toward a Proposed Reintroduction of Black-Footed Ferrets (Mustela nigripes)," 7 *Conservation Biology* 569, 573 (1993).

13 U.S. constitutional amendment V. The takings clause does not by its terms provide a means for property owners to prevent government action; as long as the government is prepared to pay compensation, it can take any property for which it has a public use in mind. The compensation requirement, however, can act exert a powerful inhibiting force on financially strapped governments.

14 *Loretto v. Teleprompter Manhattan CATV Corp.*, 458 U.S. 419, 436 (1982).

15 *Penn Central Transportation Co. v. New York City*, 438 U.S. 104, 124 (1978).

16 The special rules developed for each release prior to 1996 are described in Mimi S. Wolok, "Experimenting With Experimental Populations," 26 *Environmental Law Report* 10018 (1996). In the case of the Arizona condor release, the Fish & Wildlife Service went so far as to sign an agreement promising to recapture the condors should they ever become "essential" to the species, thereby threatening serious land use restrictions. Jim Woolf, "Landuse Debate: Condor Compromise Shows Talk Works Better Than Fighting," *The Salt Lake Tribune*, December 24, 1996, at A1.

PART IV

The
EDGE
of VISION

SUSTAINABILITY, WILDERNESS,
AND THE COLORADO PLATEAU

The lengthy and bitterly contentious debate over wilderness preservation on the Colorado Plateau has focused on congressional wilderness designation for Utah's Bureau of Land Management (BLM) public lands. It has pitted environmentalists who advocate expansive wilderness designations against many of the region's rural residents who resist any wilderness allocation, fearing its potential impact on traditional natural resource–based economic activities. Wallace Stegner was an enthusiastic wilderness proponent: In 1960 he penned his famous "Wilderness Letter," which argued that "[w]e need wilderness preserved—as much of it as is still left, and as many kinds—because it was the challenge against which our character as a people was formed." Over thirty years later, while sympathizing with local opponents who feared federal wilderness designations, he reiterated his wilderness convictions by supporting the Utah environmental community's expansive wilderness proposal, observing that "wild nature [is] precious in itself—beautiful, quiet, spiritually refreshing, priceless as a genetic bank and laboratory, priceless either as relief or even as pure idea to those who suffer from the ugliness, noise, crowding, stress, and self-destructive greed of industrial life." In September 1996 President Bill Clinton weighed directly into this debate when he used the Antiquities Act of 1906 to create the new Grand Staircase–Escalante National Monument to preserve unique biological, archaeological, geological, and paleontological resources on 1.7 million acres of largely undeveloped BLM land in southern Utah.

In the two essays that follow, the Utah wilderness preservation controversy is subjected to critical scrutiny from two quite different long-term perspectives. In the opening essay, University of Colorado professor Charles Wilkinson, a prominent natural-resource law scholar and accomplished writer, reviews the history of the Utah wilderness debate against the backdrop of development on the Colorado Plateau, concluding that a substantial wilderness designation is appropriate to safeguard these unique lands and will not harm southern Utah's existing communities. Writing from an economist's perspective, Brad Barber and Aaron Clark, with the Utah State Governor's Office of Planning and Budget, examine current economic trends in southern Utah counties and conclude that environmental protection should ultimately enhance the region's gradually diversifying economy; they also conclude that the debate over wilderness designation and economic sustainability should be addressed through existing cooperative planning initiatives. Although the Utah BLM wilderness debate may currently be stalled between rigid competing positions, the essays suggest that wilderness protection is not incompatible with regional economic trends, which are increasingly attaching tangible value to the region's natural splendor. And they suggest that the new national monument planning process will afford an opportunity to demonstrate how important preservation goals can be realized without sacrificing local economic opportunities.

Chapter 10

FILLING UP THE EYE AND OVERFLOWING THE SOUL
Sustainability, Wilderness, Remoteness, and the Colorado Plateau

Charles Wilkinson

The Colorado Plateau lies across the crest of the Wasatch from Salt Lake City, reaching to the foothills of the Colorado Rockies, bounded on the south by the edge of Arizona's Mogollon Rim and reaching north to the Uintahs. It's young, the product of an upthrust 25 million years ago or less,[1] and it's desert, so that wind and especially water have worked on the frail soils to make all manner of canyons, monuments, mesas, and colors. Eighty million acres, a little larger than Arizona, it's Indian country, nearly a third of it, and almost all of the rest is public land. The LDS Church founded many communities and made much of the plateau into Mormon country also.

Even with all the pressures on it, the Colorado Plateau is kin to the River of No Return country in the central core of Idaho and the North Slope of Alaska. It remains, especially in its interior, one of America's few large and spectacular areas that can give us the rare and strong surge of deep remoteness. Distant, rugged, and dry, at once forlorn and glorious, this is a separate place, a place with its own distinctive landscape, history, and future. Nobody ever put it better than Wallace Stegner: This is a land of places that "fill the eye and overflow the soul."[2]

My task is to address the subject of wilderness and sustainability on the Colorado Plateau. The day may come when sustainability will be organic in our society, more than a code or an ethic, just something we do. But we are far from that, and the Colorado Plateau is a place where you can see, in spite of the wild land and remoteness that remain, just how fast and hard humans can move, how we can overwhelm the land.

Not so long ago the Colorado Plateau lay beyond our consciousness. By the end of World War II, only about seventy-five people had gone down the Colorado River through the Grand Canyon since John Wesley Powell, an average of one per year. There were just two stretches of paved road between Flagstaff and Green River, Utah, and none between there and Green River, Wyoming. Nobody lived on the plateau, except Indians, who didn't much matter to most of society, and some Mormons, to whom a big energy buildup could be made to sound a lot like a bee-hive. On the outside nobody cared about the plateau except a few scattered rock hounds, archaeologists, desert-rat geologists, and aficionados of Navajo blankets.

A sleeping giant lay to the west on the Pacific shore. Others wanting to become giants—and quick—were located in southern Nevada, on the Wasatch Front, below the Mogollon Rim, and beyond the Continental Divide. The cities quickly fell into lockstep with each other and, too, with the Department of Interior, which administered most of the land on behalf of the United States or the tribes, who were supposedly entitled to a trust relationship.

Within twenty years, in what may have been the most intensive exercise of peacetime industrial might ever undertaken, hundreds—perhaps thousands, depending on how you count—of projects were built. The big dams. The coal mines. The power plants. The transmission lines. The highways. The oil and gas fields. The water pipelines and tunnels. The oil, gas, and coal slurry pipelines. The uranium mines and mills and dumps.

The times were perfect. There were essentially no laws, not even a National Environmental Policy Act to let in some sunshine. No budget constraints, no concern about subsidies. Big money to be made all around. And no oversight. No oversight of the health, environmental, and budget costs of this unprecedented development. And also no oversight of the lawyer for the Hopi who also worked for Peabody Coal in the leasing of the Hopi Black Mesa coal, the linchpin for the whole sprawling 1968 compromise that built the Central Arizona Project, Navajo Generating Station, and a slew of other water and energy projects. There was nobody—at least no one who mattered—to object. With the urban centers using the Colorado Plateau as their main engine, the population of the Southwest shot from 6 million people in 1945 to 28 million today.

People rightly point to Glen Canyon Dam as the symbol for the Big Buildup of the postwar era. Glen Canyon Dam, though, only marked the opening of a very long story that has played out on the plateau. What excesses we can breed. Of course, the Big Buildup is not somehow over. Numerous examples persist yet today. Los Angeles and Phoenix export their waste 800 and 600 miles into the northeastern part of the plateau: Their power plants in the cities of Hayden and Craig, Colorado, pump their acid rain into the high country at the head of the Yampa watershed, country we claim is wild by law.[3]

And now, in the twists of irony, shifting preferences, determination, and technological might that help comprise our relationship to the natural world, we invade the Colorado Plateau out of reverence rather than contempt. Where better to take off on a mountain bike? Where better to learn of deep human history than a place where master builders like the Anasazi left durable structures in a desert land where wood does not rot? Where better to learn of the earth's far deeper history, where the work of the ages, up to 1.7 billion years' worth, is laid bare before us?

This largesse of natural and human history entices no fewer than 25 million visitors a year to the plateau's national parks alone. This 25 million visitor figure is up from 15 million visitors in 1980. It represents industrial tourism, just as Edward Abbey warned. And they—we—are everywhere. At least the power and water rushes played out in specific projects at identifiable sites.

I believe in sustainability as a good set of ideas for approaching daunting modern problems, such as those fostered by the industrial buildup and recreational assault on the plateau. I believe it can help create the overarching ethical and policy framework. People say it is a vague idea, and so it is. It is young. Freedom and equality were young once, too, and also were once abstractions. Yet today they maintain their broad symbolic force. And over time they have matured into specific programs, such as voting rights acts, the right to peaceful protest, and fair housing laws.[4]

I think of sustainability as a young concept comparable in many ways to freedom and equality. Each of those ideas blossomed when our society realized we had a serious problem. Now we are beginning to understand how serious a problem we have with the ability of the natural world to stand up against the excesses we inflict through our might. You see it in many places. The Colorado Plateau is a notable one.

In these, the early days of acknowledging sustainability and applying it, we are jostling over the phrase "sustainable development." Some people hear the first of these words, others hear the second.

In my judgment, sustainability will not fully mature until we listen to the ideas and implications of the word sustainable. I don't fear for our capacity to achieve development. We are not in danger of losing our will or ability to develop.

The heart of sustainability, as I think of it, is intergenerational equity. Our generation has received an environmental, economic, and cultural legacy, and we should pass it on to the next generation intact or, better yet, even more robust.[5] But we cannot reach intergenerational equity until we acknowledge two things: that we have a serious problem and that we need to take individual actions to resolve it.

Sustainability is not an idealistic state. We will reach it. Our current curves of population growth and consumption absolutely will level off and decline, will they not? The only questions are when and on what terms, and whether we do it ourselves, or the earth does it for us, almost certainly on less acceptable terms. Sustainability is a natural law that will take hold, whether or not we choose it. I think Wally Stegner would call it a matter of civility toward the natural world and toward those of our own kind who will follow us.

Our first job therefore is to develop an understanding of the things we mean to sustain. To do this, we must choose more than the traditional measuring sticks—megawatts, board feet, acre feet, animal unit months, visitor days, and so forth. Although maintaining economic well-being is an important aspect of sustainability, I want to focus on sustaining the natural legacy, because the scale and pace of development's impact on the plateau have been so extreme. In addition, I'm satisfied that sustaining the plateau's natural legacy is fully consistent with economic objectives and the needs of tribal, Mormon, and other communities of the plateau.[6]

One objective is biodiversity, now widely accepted as a goal of sustainability. Let us be clear, however, that on the Colorado Plateau we have other highly specific, tightly defined things that we mean to sustain. We mean to sustain the long, sacred vistas from Muley Point, Black Mesa, Kaiparowits, the North Rim, the South Rim, the east flank of Boulder Mountain, the LaSals, and Dead Horse Point. We mean to sustain the archaeology—sacred, private places we can take our daughters and sons to visit. We mean to sustain the geological wonders. And last, we mean to sustain not just wilderness but remoteness, healthy distant country where there may be some roads but where a person can be immersed in farness. One of the highest values of the plateau is exactly that it is still hard to get to, still hard to traverse, still remote.

At Yellowstone we have employed the device of ecosystem management, as a method that we can use to achieve sustainability. Thus, sustainability can be seen as a concrete, working policy. At Yellowstone the things we have decided to sustain are evidenced by such programs as grizzly bear recovery; bison, moose, cutthroat trout, and elk management; fire policy; coordination of information on campsite vacancies throughout the ecosystem; limitations on roading for logging and mining; and now, wolf reintroduction. Some of these overlap, all are being changed and modified to reflect new data, but we have defined the qualities we are trying to sustain, and the ways we are going about it, in Yellowstone.[7]

Yet, inherent in the idea of sustainability is the notion that there is no template. Sustainability on the Colorado Plateau must be fundamentally different than at Yellowstone because the place is different. Yellowstone's lodgepoles are the plateau's piñon-juniper; Yellowstone's geysers the plateau's exposed geology; Yellowstone's grizzlies the plateau's humpback chub; Yellowstone's fires the plateau's flash floods. And the Colorado Plateau has a whole set of unique opportunities and challenges—the Anasazi, the modern tribes, Glen Canyon Dam, Lake Powell, the Four Corners Power Plant.

There is no sustainability plan in place for the plateau. Like Yellowstone, though, it is a logical candidate: The plateau is a geologic province with many unifying natural, economic, and social characteristics. Perhaps a comprehensive approach, in which all federal, tribal, state, and local governments and interest groups participate, will emerge—and it is important that it does emerge. Surely we need to recognize officially the plateau's uniqueness and the high value of this place, and assess the total impact of all of our activities.

We have, however, already applied sustainability over a key natural area within the Colorado Plateau—the Grand Canyon. Here, we have developed approaches, which can and will be improved upon, to move toward sustainability. Much has been accomplished in recent years. The attempt to protect endemic fish species through the Endangered Species Act. The attempts to protect the fish, the riparian areas, and recreational campsites through the Grand Canyon Protection Act, evidenced by the big flush of 1996. The effort to return the clarity to the air through the EPA regulations for the Navajo Generating Station and through the work of the Grand Canyon Visibility Transport Commission. The beginning efforts, which will stiffen, to preserve archaeological sites. The efforts to limit overflights. The new Grand Canyon General Management Plan, which deals with issues of overcrowding and tourism in a serious way. The implicit, but still firm, decision to sustain and preserve the living river and deep canyon walls and all their world history by never, despite all the many proposals, plugging Grand Canyon with any dam.[8]

These and other efforts at the Grand Canyon are overlapping, though many of them have been taken independently. They are not the neat, single plan an efficiency expert might wish. But they represent public decisions to sustain a natural area. Taken as a whole, the actions at the Grand Canyon constitute an important model of sustainability. While recognizing that the whole of the pateau is not a national park, we need to apply the ideas and determination we've shown at the Grand Canyon throughout the plateau.

Wilderness holds a special place in the search for sustainability. It promotes biodiversity. Aldo Leopold, who loved wild land absolutely, saw it as a critical measuring device, a way to test how degraded more developed land systems have become. Wilderness gives us solitude and fires our imaginations, each of us in a different way. Our wilderness laws have their faults and limitations, but official wilderness is the best way we now have to preserve the tart, savory taste of wild backcountry and remoteness. The original Wilderness Act of 1964 included no land on the Colorado Plateau. It did, however, direct the National Park Service to study all of its roadless areas and make recommendations for congressional protection. Except for 19,000 acres of declared wilderness in Colorado, the recommendations for the plateau's parks are still pending. The numbers are substantial. Grand Canyon and Canyonlands now have over 1.5 million acres of recommended wilderness between them. John Leshy, in his study of plateau lands for the Grand Canyon Trust, estimates that the plateau's parks have 2.1 million acres of potential wilderness. Most of those lands are managed like wilderness areas, with the significant exception of the Colorado River corridor through the Grand Canyon, where motorized boats are allowed. Eventually one can expect that Congress will add most of the 2.1 million acres in Leshy's estimate to the wilderness system.[9]

Needless to say, the less controversial wildlands in the national parks have taken a backseat to the byzantine and bizarre controversy over Utah's BLM backcountry.

In 1976 Congress directed the BLM to study the wilderness potential of all roadless areas under the agency's control. In 1979 the BLM released its inventory—not its actual recommendations for wilderness, just a listing of the areas to be studied. Within weeks, a group of Grand County commissioners and Main Street businessmen from Moab had climbed on a county bulldozer and, to much hoopla, proceeded to clear out the stone barricade the BLM erected to keep Negro Bill Canyon roadless. Similar festivities were performed at nearby Mill Creek Canyon on July 4, with the added touch—these were patriots, after all—of American flags draped over the bulldozers.[10]

Almost impossibly the situation has gone downhill from there. The BLM wilderness study process was badly botched. Counties, in order to prevent the establishment of roadless areas, filed hundreds of road claims under R.S. 2477, a law passed the year after the Civil War ended. Congress finally repealed R.S. 2477 in 1976, but it grandfathered in existing roads. The counties took this to mean any scrape on a slab of slickrock made by a long-ago solitary hardrock miner's rig, five head of cattle, or, apparently, the sandals of an Anasazi clan heading south to worship at Chaco Canyon.[11]

Over the past two years, the Utah congressional delegation has championed the most extreme wilderness bill ever introduced. The bill, with its minimal acreage designations and extreme release language and water rights provisions, has met its demise on the House and Senate floors. Sen. Bill Bradley and his numerous congressional allies led a determined opposition. This day, at least, seems to have been carried by the people Senator Bradley spoke for—a majority of Americans and, for that matter, of Utahns.[12]

My own guess, however, is that when the final histories are written, the critical event for Utah wilderness will be understood to have taken place in 1990. At that time, the Southern Utah Wilderness Alliance served as a driving force behind a remarkable document, *Wilderness at the Edge*. Thirty-five Utah conservation organizations—calling themselves the Utah Wilderness Coalition—conducted their own inventory and made wilderness recommendations totaling 5.7 million acres of BLM land. The supporting research, although it was mostly a volunteer effort, was head-and-shoulders above the work done by the BLM, which recommended less than one-third of the acreage in the conservationists' proposal.[13]

Wilderness at the Edge is likely, over time, to prevail. The reasons are several: The demographics in Utah are steadily changing; Utah wilderness has become a national issue; and the citizen proposal is a serious, responsible approach toward classification of BLM land in Utah. Put all of the acreage recommended by Wilderness at the Edge in wilderness, and southern Utah's economy will benefit, not suffer. And the glory lands, and the legacy of the Old People, will be protected, as they should be.

But *Wilderness at the Edge* had something else going for it: an introduction written by our greatest conservationist, Wally Stegner. When Wally typed his "Wilderness Letter" in 1960, he was writing of the plateau's wildlands, which he loved so. He had them foremost in mind when he wrote that "something will have gone out of us as a people if we ever let the remaining wilderness be destroyed."[14] Wally's later introduction to the Utah citizen's proposal will also always hold a prominent place, even in the crowded upper reaches of his legacy. He told the story of southern Utah, and told it straight and fair.

Wally Stegner said this of Negro Bill Canyon and the hangings in effigy of Clive Kincaid and Robert Redford:

> That violence is an expression of desperation, the frontier dying hard, the reaction of people pushed to the edge of their tolerance by forces they do not understand. I sympathize with their feelings; I also think they are profoundly wrong. . . .[15]

And he concluded this way:

> The Utah deserts and plateaus and canyons are not a country of big returns, but a country of spiritual healing, incomparable for contemplation, meditation, solitude, quiet, awe, peace of mind and body. We were born of wilderness, and we respond to it more than we sometimes realize. We depend upon it increasingly for relief from the termite life we have created. Factories, power plants, resorts, we can make anywhere. Wilderness, once we have given it up, is beyond our reconstruction.[16]

So let us follow Wally's lead in perhaps the most deeply held public position he ever took. Let us acknowledge finally that 5.7 million acres is a sensible, conservative position. Put them all in. All of them: Negro Bill, Comb Ridge, Cedar Mesa and all of its canyons, the San Rafael Swell, Kaiparowits, the whole

Escalante drainage, the Henry Mountains, all of them, and all of the many others, too. All of the national park wilderness study areas. And all of the wild country in the new Grand Staircase–Escalante National Monument, too. Put them all in. We will make a strong stand for sustainability. We will be a far better and richer people if we do. We would have fulfilled deep-running duties to the whole world, and earlier worlds, and worlds still to come.

In sum, if we are going to be serious about sustaining the Colorado Plateau, we must move beyond wilderness per se and decide to sustain the plateau's remoteness. This is why road policy, at the Burr Trail and many other places, is so critical. We should put a hold on roads and road widenings on the plateau, not out of antipathy for any local economy, but out of a need to sustain our dwindling remoteness. We should not even repair rickety old bridges, not even the one over the San Juan River at Mexican Hat. And we should phase in visitation ceilings at the national parks, and slacken the pressure on roads all across the plateau.

We need to be much clearer that remoteness ought now to be a policy objective on the Colorado Plateau. Once, in the early 20th century, we thought in terms of recreation in a generalized sense. Then we created a new kind of value, a separate resource, and called it wilderness. Later, in the 1980s, we recognized that the terms *timber*, and even *forest*, were inadequate and we recognized old growth as a separate value, or resource, to be sustained.

Now, as racing events press in on us, we can appreciate the full distinctiveness of the Colorado Plateau and how one of its rare values is its remoteness. We ought to build the courage to act on it. There are specific tests that we can apply: whether the corridor along the Vermilion Cliffs can remain sufficiently remote to rejuvenate a population of creaky-winged California condors, and whether the North Rim will continue to be wild enough to receive the call of the wolf.

At those places, and all across the plateau, we should commit to work from one premise: sustain the big openness, the long, vacant spaces. Otherwise, something will go out of us as a people. We must remember: This land fills the eye and overflows the soul.

NOTES

[1] Donald L. Baars, *The Colorado Plateau: A Geologic History* (Albuquerque: University of New Mexico Press, 1982), pp. 203–20.

[2] Wallace Stegner, *The Sound of Mountain Water* (New York: Dutton, 1980; reprint ed., Lincoln: University of Nebraska Press, 1985), p. 18.

[3] Dan Ely et al., "Certifying Visibility Impairment in the Mount Zirkel Wilderness Area—

Technical Background Document." Colorado Department of Health, Environmental Protection Agency, U.S. Department of Agriculture Forest Service (June 30, 1993); "Colorado Utility Settles CAA Action for $140 Million in Upgrades and Fines," Energy Report, May 27, 1996 (available in LEXIS, News Library, Curnws file); Mark Obmascik, "Acidity in Snow a Record," *The Denver Post*, 28 January 1995, A1.

[4] On "sustainability," see Kai N. Lee, *Compass and Gyroscope: Integrating Science and Politics for the Environment* (Washington, D.C.: Island Press, 1993).

[5] On "intergenerational equity," see Edith Brown Weiss, "In Fairness to Future Generations," *Environment* 34 (April 1990), p. 6.

[6] See infra Chapter 8.

[7] Robert B. Keiter and Mark S. Boyce, eds., *The Greater Yellowstone Ecosystem: Redefining America's Wilderness Heritage* (New Haven: Yale University Press, 1991).

[8] Dale Russakoff, "Fears Linger Over a Grand Canyon Dam," *The Washington Post*, 24 July 1983, A15; Roderick Nash, *Wilderness and The American Mind* (New Haven: Yale University Press, 1982 3d edition), pp. 234–37.

[9] John Leshy, *The Future of the Colorado Plateau*, Appendix J; Jon Roush, "30 Years of Wilderness," *Wilderness* 58 (September 22, 1994), p. 58; Kim Crumbo, "Wilderness Management at Grand Canyon—Waiting for Godot?" *International Journal of Wilderness* 2 (May 1996), pp. 19–23.

[10] Raymond Wheeler, "Boom! Boom! Boom! War on the Colorado Plateau," in Ed Marston, ed., *Reopening the Western Frontier* (Washington, D.C.: Island Press, 1989), p. 16; Interview with Bill Hedden and Jose Knighton, Negro Bill Canyon, Utah, May 18, 1994.

[11] R. Blain Andrus, "Access to Private and Public Lands Under R.S. 2477," 31 *Public Land and Resources Digest 145* (1994).

[12] Wayne Owens, "Is Preservation of Utah's Remaining Wilderness in Utah's Best Interest?" in Samuel I. Zeveloff and Cyrus M. McKell, *Wilderness Issues in the Arid Lands of the Western United States* (Albuquerque: University of New Mexico Press, 1992), pp. 13–34; Margaret Kriz, "The Wild Card," *The National Journal*, 13 (January 1996), p. 65.

[13] *Wilderness at the Edge: A Citizen Proposal to Protect Utah's Canyons and Deserts* (Salt Lake City: Utah Wilderness Coalition, 1990).

[14] Stegner, *The Sound of Mountain Water*, p. 146.

[15] *Wilderness at the Edge*, p. 7.

[16] Idem, p. 8.

Chapter 11

RECONCILING ENVIRONMENTAL PRESERVATION AND ECONOMIC SUSTAINABILITY ON UTAH'S COLORADO PLATEAU
The State's Perspective

Brad T. Barber and Aaron P. Clark

INTRODUCTION

The unparalleled natural beauty of Utah's portion of the Colorado Plateau is a global, national, state, and local treasure. Home to some of the earth's most magnificent landscapes and pristine ecosystems, the physiographic region spanning the eastern, central, and southern portions of Utah truly is, as Wallace Stegner once observed "a country of spiritual healing, incomparable for contemplation, meditation, solitude, quiet, awe, peace of mind and body." It is an unfortunate irony that a land offering so many unique opportunities for tranquillity and renewal, a natural setting lending itself to what is best in the human spirit, is the stage of such pronounced and deeply rooted contention: Utah's acrimonious Bureau of Land Management (BLM) wilderness designation debate.

Traditionally the primary argument made by Utah's rural citizens against preservation—be it wilderness, endangered species, or clean air and water—has been economic. Whether accurate or not, the perception exists in rural Utah, as in many of the West's rural regions, that preservation is tantamount to lost jobs and unrealized economic potential. This perception is exacerbated on Utah's plateau, where local economies are heavily dependent on mining, grazing, and other activities requiring access to federal lands. Any attempt to preserve public lands by perceived "outsiders"—either the federal government or environmental interests—is interpreted by plateau residents as a direct and lucid threat to livelihood, living standards, and liberty.

To explore how environmental preservation and economic sustainability might be reconciled on the Colorado Plateau, this paper presents the state of Utah's views on four elements central to this debate: (1) the role played by the public in Utah's wilderness designation process; (2) the economic transformation presently reshaping many of Utah's Colorado Plateau communities; (3) the state's rural economic resettlement and diversification policies, including implementation of the ecoregion concept in planning for the new national movement; and (4) the state's position regarding the preservation of Utah's open lands.

UTAH WILDERNESS DESIGNATION: A DIVISIVE PUBLIC PROCESS

The related questions of whether and how much BLM land should be set aside as wilderness in Utah have undergone extensive examination through the state's public comment process. Only Congress, however, can legislatively designate a wilderness area. In 1991 the BLM submitted a report to Congress that recommended a final Utah wilderness designation of 1.9 million acres that met every wilderness classification requirement with little or no conflict. In January 1995, the state's elected officials began soliciting public input on a final wilderness bill. Fully appreciating the issue's volatility, state and federal officials sought to provide the citizenry ample opportunity for comment.

Approximately forty public meetings were held throughout Utah, including five regional public hearings and two additional meetings in Salt Lake City and Provo. Moreover, the governor's office received over 3,030 written responses to the wilderness issue.[1] From the public testimony of 551 people, 457 individuals indicated support for wilderness designation whereas 94 were in opposition. Roughly 43 percent supported 5.7 million acres of wilderness proposed by H.R. 1500, 3 percent supported Representative Orton's proposal of approximately 1.2 million acres, 3 percent supported the Utah Wilderness Association's proposal of roughly 3 million acres, 4 percent supported rural county recommendations of little more than 1 million acres, and 18 percent, though supporting wilderness, did not designate a specific proposal or recommend a number of acres to be designated. Approximately 29 percent of the comments received favored no wilderness designation.[2]

In short, public comment and opinion polls indicate that there is great divisiveness over how much wilderness should be designated in Utah. Most rural citizens, who live where these lands are located, strongly oppose any federal regulation that might limit local access to and economic development of BLM lands. Yet many citizens in the state's urban areas support the federal designation of 5.7 million acres of BLM wilderness. By revealing these divisions, the public process has effectively blocked resolution of the wilderness debate.

The inability to reach solid consensus over the wilderness issue stems from differing convictions about the land and from the lack of a meaningful, conciliatory dialogue between the debate's participants. Polarization and mistrust have intensified on Utah's plateau as misconceptions spread concerning permissible uses in and around designated wilderness areas. Many of Utah's plateau residents remain firmly convinced that designated wilderness would result in substantial job losses in their communities, particularly in those jobs tied to extractive industries. Moreover, these same people often assume that once public lands have been designated as wilderness, all the economic benefits they offer will be forever lost.

On the other side of the wilderness debate are those who seem to have limited empathy for the concerns of rural Utahns. Most people who favor 5.7 million acres of wilderness do not live in communities surrounding proposed wilderness areas and are not in danger of suffering any direct economic consequences from expanded wilderness. The notion of protecting the wild and scenic lands they use for recreation and escape often takes precedence over the economic considerations of Utah's rural citizenry.

THE TRANSFORMATION OF
UTAH'S COLORADO PLATEAU ECONOMY

The apprehension expressed by Utah's rural residents toward wilderness designation generally stems from concern over the future of their Colorado Plateau communities. In their view the region will be economically devastated if its public lands are deemed off-limits to natural resource development. Since statehood, Utah's rural plateau communities have drawn upon the region's abundant energy and mineral resources as well as its timber and grazing lands for most employment and income. Over recent decades, however, "national and global changes in technology, the changing role of materials, energy, technical knowledge and information services in the industrial economy, and foreign competition have all meant a steady diminution of traditional resource-based economic activity."[3]

Plateau communities have historically endured the effects of boom and bust economies tied to fluctuations in domestic and global energy markets. Many communities have experienced the rewards and sudden turbulence of rapid growth, as well as the disappointments and hardships of failing economies. Local jobs for graduating high school seniors throughout the region were relatively plentiful when natural resource commodities were in great demand. But when these markets became volatile and the demand for domestic energy commodities decreased, both existing workers and new entrants to the regional labor force were compelled to look outside the region for a steady income. The modernization and subsequent restructuring of extractive industries in the aftermath of the energy crises of the 1970s and 1980s further compromised job security on Utah's plateau. The region's once dominant mining industry has undergone sweeping structural changes toward more efficient mechanization, leading to increases in productivity but reductions in labor requirements.

In short, rural Utah has constantly struggled for economic stability; permanent hometown employment and income-generating opportunities have been rare. But despite local economic decline, Utah's plateau communities might overcome this difficulty with a systematic, coordinated, and long-term effort to foster steady economic growth and development for the 21st century. Increasingly the region's community leaders see economic diversification as a means to minimize the cyclical booms and busts that have plagued them. Realizing that lower levels of diversification increase a community's vulnerability to swift economic changes, farsighted rural leaders have made economic diversification and labor force development primary objectives in promoting sustainable community and economic development.

To reveal the structural transformation occurring in many of Utah's plateau communities, changes in the region's economic specialization can be measured over time. One measure of economic specialization is the location quotient (LQ). The LQ measures industrial economic specialization for a given geographical area (e.g., county, state, etc.) relative to the nation. An LQ equal to 1.0 denotes that a region has the same proportion of its employment in a given industry as does the nation. In San Juan County, for example, an LQ of 23.0 for the mining industry would indicate that mining's employment share is 23 times greater there than in the nation as a whole.

On the Colorado Plateau, the 1980–95 LQ trends for the four Utah Multi-County Districts (MCDs)[4] reveal that resource extraction, while still a dominating component of the region's economy, is giving way to other growing sectors, such as service and amenity-based industry and government. Throughout the region, specialization in both mining employment and income have declined dramatically since 1980, though mining remains an important sector of specialization. Farming and ranching, also a highly specialized sector of the region's economy, showed increasing specialization during the 1980s, followed by periods of decreasing specialization from 1990 to 1995. Many of the region's highest-paying nonprofessional jobs are still provided by the mining industry, thus many plateau residents see mining-related jobs as their best employment alternative. They view service industry jobs associated with an increased tourism industry as unacceptable if it means lower pay.

The employment share of the service and trade sectors, though on the rise in the region's economy, is still dwarfed in terms of economic specialization by the traditional resource-based industries. However, substantial proportional increases in the employment share of the service and trade sectors are occurring throughout the region, most notably in the Southwest and Southeast MCDs. Nevertheless, as a whole, Utah's plateau economy remains far less concentrated in service and trade sector employment than is true for the rest of the state and the nation.

Government continues to be a major economic specialization sector throughout the region. Government employment's share has increased in all regional MCDs, except the Southwest, where it has markedly declined from 1980 to 1995. Government's high employment share is explained by the large role federal, state, and local governments play in resource management and in providing services to a dispersed population.

In sum, measures of specialization from 1980 to 1995 indicate that Utah's

Colorado Plateau economy is gradually evolving into one less dependent on traditional natural resource–based industries. Tourism and recreation-related industries comprise a growing percentage of the area's economy, most notably in the Southwest and Southeast MCDs. The number of people visiting the five national parks throughout Utah's plateau region demonstrates this growth: Visitor days at the national parks increased by 132 percent between 1980 and 1993, from 2,320,500 annual recreational visits to 5,391,800.[5] Thus, the Colorado Plateau's land, open space, and other natural resources continue to play a fundamental role in sustaining the region's economy. And as recreation, tourism, and other amenity-based industries continue to grow and redefine the economy, its foundation will increasingly depend on the quality of the region's environment and communities.[6]

RURAL RESETTLEMENT AND THE ECOREGION CONCEPT

For the majority of Utah's plateau communities, the transition from an agriculture and mining economic base to one based on services, government, and trade is proving difficult. Many regional communities are suffering from problems related to the natural setting and local economic conditions. These problems include concern over increasing recreation use, the appropriate level of wilderness designation in the region, funding shortages linked to inadequate local tax structures, multiple jurisdictions that hamper formation of a common regional vision, and often difficult personal economic conditions. Noting these problems, the governor has identified and prioritized three related land use, environmental, and economic strategies: (1) promoting the economic resettlement of rural Utah; (2) studying the ecoregion concept; and (3) funding revenue sources for tourism development. The first two issues will be further examined below.

Economic Resettlement in Rural Utah

Under the governor's vision, the first step for the economic resettlement of rural Utah is based on adequate planning for economic growth, and land and infrastructure development. Planning should then be followed by incentives that are coupled with the development of rural job skills. Moreover, economic resettlement should, to the extent possible, facilitate a symbiotic relationship between economic growth and the natural environment.

The rural economic resettlement legislation that was passed during Utah's 1996 general legislative session elicited broad support among Utah's rural leaders. The legislation is intended to create designations, modeled after existing enterprise zones, which target incentives toward Utah businesses, rather than out-of-state businesses. These zones will offer state tax and other incentives to Utah businesses that expand or relocate their operations to qualifying rural locations.

By providing incentives to Utah companies, resettlement zones may keep jobs from leaving the state, can help reduce urban congestion along the Wasatch Front, and can provide much needed stimulus for Colorado Plateau economies and residents.

The creation of good jobs, filled by skilled and capable rural workers, is central to the concept of economic resettlement in rural Utah. However, the rural labor pools of many plateau communities do not yet have the skills required by certain businesses, nor do all rural citizens have convenient access to needed educational and job transition training facilities. Thus, rural leaders see labor force development as vitally important to rural workers and potential employers.

The rural economic resettlement concept seeks to capitalize on the phenomenal success of Utah's urban economy by enabling plateau communities to tap into the state's dynamic urban markets. Past efforts by rural Utah to recruit out-of-state businesses have been largely unsuccessful. But many Utah firms, unlike out-of-state firms, are already familiar with the rural areas of the state, and often have family, property, or recreational ties to Utah's rural communities.

Recent research suggests that newly created businesses in Utah's plateau region can provide a wide range of subcontracting services to businesses located along the Wasatch Front—services currently being contracted to firms outside of the state. This potential appears especially great for Wasatch Front businesses engaged in manufacturing recreational and outdoor equipment. Peter Metcalf, CEO of Black Diamond, Ltd., a successful manufacturer of specialized climbing and skiing gear headquartered in Salt Lake City, is excited about the prospect of using subcontractors in rural southern Utah, where his company's products are seeing increased use. He also expressed interest in the region's "nature hook" marketing potential, referring to the marketing possibilities of being connected to the preservation movement.[7]

The Ecoregion Concept

The ecoregion concept is another encouraging dimension of the state's rural economic resettlement policy. The ecoregion concept is an innovative, sustainable development strategy for Utah's plateau region that is designed to preserve and enhance its natural and human components by protecting the natural environment while developing tourism resources to enhance its economic base. The ecoregion initiative seeks to define a common management vision among private landowners, business, and local, state, and federal land managers to preserve the region's natural setting, while simultaneously providing sustainable economic benefits to a more diversified regional economy.

In this context, sustainability means managing resources within larger ecosystems, to protect them for long-term consumptive and nonconsumptive uses, and to reduce or eliminate boom-bust cycles. Diversification implies that local economies should not be heavily dependent upon one industry, but must diversify into many, possibly smaller, industries tied to the sustainable use of the region's resources.

Under the ecoregion development concept, Utah's rural plateau communities would gain sustainable economic benefits by developing destination tourism attractions. These attractions, funded by a consortium of governmental and private interests, would incorporate natural and human environmental themes. The concept is based on a marketable development philosophy, and includes activities and capital facilities. Financial options and marketing strategies are also considered, as are employment opportunities for rural workers and environmental management.

A more diversified and sustainable local economy, economic resettlement opportunities, and cooperative consensus-building planning efforts should help to overcome the widespread mistrust and uncertainty that exist in the region's rural communities. There are more than a dozen examples of federal, state, regional, and local planning efforts taking place on Utah's plateau, each working to find common solutions to the region's unique problems. These include the Washington County Habitat Conservation Advisory Committee; Southern Utah Independent Forest Products Association; Local Government Comprehensive Planning Project; Southwestern Utah Planning Authorities Council; Natural Resources Coordinating Committee; Emery County Wild Lands Futures Project; Virgin River Coordinating Committee; Snake Creek Preservation Project; BLM Resource Advisory Council; BLM Joint Planning Discussions; Four Corners Heritage Council; Southern Corridor Task Force; Canyon Country Partnership; and Colorado Plateau Forum. Each effort represents a new way of doing business and a new type of partnership. Although there is room for improvement, each effort is helping to overcome differences, develop working relationships, and build trust among different plateau factions.

Applying Ecoregion Concepts to the Grand Staircase–Escalante National Monument

On September 18, 1996, when President Clinton designated the 1.7 million acre Grand Staircase-Escalante National Monument on Utah's Colorado Plateau, he provided federal, state, and local officials an unexpected opportunity to test the ecoregion concept. Given the secrecy surrounding the monument designation, the challenge is for the diverse constituencies concerned about the Colorado Plateau's future to join to create a new model for environmental management and intergovernmental planning.

The seeds for this new land management model were planted several years earlier when federal, state, and local land managers jointly authored the *Canyons of the Escalante: A National Ecoregion* concept paper. The paper outlined a common management vision for the area that preserved the natural setting while simultaneously providing real and sustainable local economic benefits. Governor Leavitt has drawn upon these concepts to define his vision for the new monument. He has also directed state and local leaders to participate as full partners in the planning process, despite the flawed process preceding the monument's designation.

Relevant economic data and trends establish two important facts that exist across the region. First, many jobs in the communities adjacent to the monument are tied to the public lands, including agriculture, tourism, and resource extraction jobs. Second, the economies surrounding the monument are struggling. For these reasons monument management planning is of paramount importance to the local communities. The monument plan must therefore focus on developing real economic opportunities for local residents to build a more healthy, diversified, and sustainable economy. Several promising opportunities should be explored such as value-added sustainable timber and wood products; environmentally sensitive ranching with higher-value beef and other products; high-value destination tourism developments; employment of local guides and outfitters; promotion of industries that use local materials, products, and labor; and development of recreation equipment and other industries that capitalize on the unique local landscape.

From the state's perspective, the Grand Staircase–Escalante National Monument should be a showcase for cooperative and innovative regional planning and management. It should preserve the area's resources while providing benefits to the surrounding communities as well as the state and the nation. The monument plan should be sensitive to the area's unique demographic and economic circumstances. Among other things, monument planning and management should strengthen intergovernmental relationships, maximize local economic benefits, increase economic diversity, capture revenues to cover local services, and enhance the local quality of life. If successful, this cooperative process can be a model for future state and federal partnerships in other multi-jurisdictional contexts.

To implement this vision, extensive coordination will be required. Since the monument designation, the state of Utah, local governmental entities, and the federal government have worked together to define a cooperative three-year planning process. Several important steps have been taken to promote full intergovernmental cooperation. First, the state has assigned five people to work full-time on the Monument Planning Team as fully integrated members of the planning staff. Second, the state is forming a Subcabinet Advisory Group to support the state-appointed members of the planning team by providing an interface between state agencies and the planning team. Third, the state, in partnership with local governments in Kane and Garfield Counties, has developed a Community and Economic Development Strategy Committee focusing on the land adjacent to the monument and other planning issues that directly affect the surrounding communities. In combination, these initiatives should ensure that local economic concerns are integrated into management of the new monument.

PRESERVING UTAH'S OPEN LANDS: A COLLABORATIVE VENTURE

The natural beauty that defines the Colorado Plateau and the resources that have sustained its human inhabitants both derive from the natural forces that have shaped this distinct province. Combined geological processes endowed Utah's portion of the plateau with extraordinary landscapes and awe-inspiring views. If a common ground exists within the region, it is the widespread agreement that the plateau's priceless open spaces and long views must be protected for future generations.

The governor, who is committed to protecting Utah's urban and rural open lands, included open space on the state's 1995 Growth Summit agenda. At the summit, both state and local leaders recognized that open space preservation in Utah will—and should—take place at the local level. The participants acknowledged, however, that all levels of government, as well as the private and non-profit sectors, must jointly develop mechanisms to preserve open space and wildlife habitats while protecting individual property rights.

The newly formed Utah Critical Land Conservation Committee embodies this spirit of cooperation. For the first time in Utah, this committee brings together state, local, and federal governments, along with conservation, development, industrial, and agricultural interests, to help local governments preserve their unique open lands. The committee's mission is to preserve important agricultural lands, critical wildlife habitat, watersheds, recreational lands, and other important lands necessary to preserve economically sustainable agricultural production as well as the state's quality of life and cultural heritage. The committee is guided by several principles, including the protection of private property rights, local control over land use decisions, and no-net loss of private land in the state. Significantly, the committee is also committed to creating partnerships to fund open space preservation.

Partnerships to secure funding for open space preservation are particularly critical on Utah's Colorado Plateau. Although Utah's plateau lands are mostly managed by federal or state government, most of the development-prone land is privately owned. Many of these privately owned lands constitute important parts of the plateau ecosystem that must also be protected. To preserve these private lands as open spaces, such proven tools as land trusts, conservation easements, and private sector land transactions must be utilized. Working collaboratively with land conservation groups and local citizens, the Utah Critical Land Conservation Committee is prepared to assist locally initiated projects to preserve open space on Utah's plateau region.

Two land conservation organizations—the Utah Open Lands Conservation Association and The Nature Conservancy—have already mounted important efforts to preserve the state's open spaces, wildlife habitats, and ecological diversity. Unique within the state, the Utah Open Lands Conservation Association (Utah Open Lands) has evolved from a local Summit County group to one with a statewide focus that can hold conservation easements throughout the state. As Utah Open Lands has gained experience with conservation easements, other Utah communities have begun requesting assistance. Today the organization spearheads numerous land conservation efforts throughout the state, including plateau region projects in the San Juan County community of Bluff and in the Book Cliffs region of Carbon and Emery Counties.

The Nature Conservancy's Utah Land Legacy Campaign represents a three-year, $7.2 million conservation initiative to preserve biological diversity, wildlife habitat, and open space on an unprecedented scale in Utah. This public/private endeavor will protect representative examples of the landscapes that Utah's pioneers once knew, which are now the most threatened habitats and ecosystems remaining in the state. Employing a balanced conservation approach, it seeks to protect the state's highest priority natural areas within five critical habitat types: Colorado Plateau canyon communities; Great Basin wetlands; rare species and ecosystems; mountain forests; and river corridors. Ultimately, these protected lands will become "living museum pieces," fragments of the pristine landscapes that dominated Utah when humans first arrived.[8]

REALIZING ENVIRONMENTAL AND ECONOMIC SUSTAINABILITY

Utah's Colorado Plateau region is clearly in a state of change. Its economy is undergoing a significant transition from one based largely on mining, grazing, and agriculture to one based on tourism, recreation, and other service-based industries. With these changes, the region's economy will increasingly depend on the quality of the plateau's environment and communities. The region's air, water, and open space as well as its accessible parks, forests, and public lands is already attracting millions of tourists and bringing new residents and businesses in search of a high quality of life.[9]

A healthy and sustainable economy is also important for the region. Until numerous jobs are available in industries not affected by the preservation of wildlands, endangered species, or pristine air and water, the plateau's rural residents will find it difficult to understand why preservation might be in their best interest. But a degraded natural environment and land base will ultimately undermine the region's economic activity, including its employment opportunities and quality lifestyle. At the same time, economic survival ability is fundamental to the long-term success of regional environmental conservation.

If the plateau is to prosper as a natural and a human system, regional residents and natural resource managers must better understand the linkages between the economy and the environment. Hindering this understanding is the widespread mistrust that exists between various governmental entities, the environmental community, and local rural residents—mistrust that has deepened throughout Utah's wilderness designation process. Yet the public comments regarding wilderness reveal that most state residents, regardless of where they live, care deeply for the land. Public opinion differs primarily in how, not if, Utah's public lands should be preserved and managed. Nevertheless, this mistrust holds the wilderness and other land preservation and management processes hostage on Utah's plateau, seemingly rendering productive dialogue or meaningful action futile.

What, then, is the solution? Can Utah's wild plateau lands be protected while establishing a viable economic future for the area? Are environmental preservation and economic growth and development compatible on the plateau? If the answer is yes, as Utah state government believes, then how can this be accomplished?

For environmental protection and economic growth to coexist on Utah's plateau, the communities, counties, resource managers, private and nonprofit groups, and governments must directly confront and surmount the divisive forces of mistrust and uncertainty. Working cooperatively, these groups must develop shared vision and understanding, and they must seek creative solutions to tired old conflicts. This will mean new institutional arrangements, improved working relationships, and better communication with an emphasis on listening and understanding. Furthermore, each group must participate actively in such cooperative planning efforts as the Canyon Country Partnership, the Colorado Plateau Forum, and others. Each effort represents a means for varying interests to have a voice and to begin establishing durable relationships built on mutual trust with formerly opposing parties. Small solutions may begin to surface, which will lead to larger solutions.

To ensure the region's economic future, diversified and sustainable local economies must be established. Besides tourism and recreation, viable roles should exist for agriculture, mining, manufacturing, and a wide range of service-based employment. Failure to diversify will weaken the region's ability to respond to inevitable changes. To build such an economy, the plateau's economic and community developers, working with local business and statewide business financing agencies, must utilize available tools and programs to create small increases in meaningful employment in various industries. Many financing programs and resources are available, including the Industrial Assistance Fund that has earmarked $1 million for rural economic development programs during the upcoming year. However, no one program, company, or industry represents the complete solution for rural economic problems. Rather, it will take a sustained and coordinated effort to accomplish necessary economic changes on Utah's plateau.

As we stand on the edge of a new millennium, it is increasingly imperative that we achieve a balance between the environment and the economy. Being creatures of the land, we must appreciate and protect its beauty and spiritual significance, as only humans can. And as the earth's creatures so dependent on the land's resources, we must also protect our ability to produce humanity's future wealth and livelihood.

NOTES

[1] This total does not include the 1,218 form letters and 10 separate petitions (containing a total of 17,433 signatures) received by the Utah Governor's Office of Planning and Budget (GOPB) as of June 1, 1995.

[2] Percentages are taken from analyses conducted by GOPB of public participation in Utah's wilderness designation process.

[3] Walter E. Hecox and Bradley L. Ack, *Charting the Colorado Plateau: An Economic and Demographic Exploration*, 1 (1996).

[4] The four MCDs located in Utah's Colorado Plateau region are the Uintah Basin, Central, Southeast, and Southwest. The Uintah Basin MCD contains Daggett, *Duchesne,* and *Uintah* counties; the Central MCD contains Juab, Millard, *Piute, Sanpete, Sevier*, and *Wayne* Counties; the Southeast MCD contains *Carbon, Emery, Grand,* and *San Juan* Counties; and, the Southwest MCD contains *Beaver, Garfield, Iron, Kane,* and *Washington* Counties. (Italicized counties are those located within Utah's Colorado Plateau region.)

[5] Randy Rogers, Utah Travel Council, "1994 Economic and Travel Industry Profiles for Utah Counties," p. 3 (1995).

[6] Walter E. Hecox and Bradley L. Ack, *Charting the Colorado Plateau: An Economic and Demographic Exploration*, pp. 10–11 (1996).

[7] Brooke Williams, "Escalante: Rural Transformation Through Small Manufacturing," (1994) p. 12. Work performed under contract for GOPB.

[8] The Nature Conservancy, "The Utah Land Legacy Campaign—A Centennial Conservation Initiative—A Proposal from the Nature Conservancy," (1996) p. 4.

[9] Walter E. Hecox and Bradley L. Ack, *Charting the Colorado Plateau: An Economic and Demographic Exploration*, (1996) p. 45.

PART V

A
TOUCH OF WONDER
CONSERVING WOLVES AND GRIZZLIES
IN THE NORTHERN ROCKIES

These diverse essays explore the controversy surrounding federal efforts, under the Endangered Species Act, to conserve and restore wolves and grizzly bears in the northern Rockies. Although not a scientist, Wallace Stegner fully understood and embraced Aldo Leopold's important insight that humankind is a member of a larger ecological community and owes a corresponding duty to this shared community, including the obligation to restore its missing parts. In the opening essay, the U.S. Fish & Wildlife Service's Rocky Mountain Wolf Coordinator, Ed Bangs, chronicles the political, legal, and other travails that the federal government and wolf proponents have faced in protecting naturally colonizing wolves in northwestern Montana and in reintroducing wolves to central Idaho and Yellowstone under special statutory provisions. Expanding upon that experience from his perspective as the longtime northern Rockies representative of Defenders of Wildlife, Hank Fischer examines the pitfalls encountered in the wolf recovery effort and outlines a bold new proposal to sidestep those problems using the Citizen Management Committee to oversee grizzly bear recovery in the Selway Bitterroot area of central Idaho. However, veteran Sierra Club Legal Defense Fund litigator, Doug Honnold, advocates a cautionary approach and counsels against compromising Endangered Species Act protections, noting that bears and wolves need big wilderness to ensure their survival and that critical biological concerns have not yet been adequately addressed. In total, the papers reveal the very real tensions and problems confronting controversial endangered species recovery efforts and the yet uncertain role that local populaces can—or should—play in that effort.

Chapter 12

RESTORING WOLVES TO THE WEST
Edward E. Bangs

THE EXTERMINATION CAMPAIGN

Historically, the gray wolf (*Canis lupus*) was common throughout nearly all of North America. But shortly after European colonization began, wolves and other large predators were persecuted as part of the settlers' belief that nature and wildness were to be conquered. Wolves were gradually exterminated from Mexico, portions of southern Canada, and the lower 48 states, except in Minnesota where a few hundred survived. By 1930 the U.S. Biological Survey's organized predator extermination programs had eliminated wolf populations from Montana, Idaho, and Wyoming. Yet as the last wolves were being hunted down, a few prominent wildlife biologists began to question whether this policy was good for the long-term health of the natural community. Reviewing *The Wolves of North America*,[1] Dr. Aldo Leopold, considered by many the father of modern scientific wildlife management, wrote: "There still remain, even in the United States, some areas of considerable size in which we feel that both the red and gray [wolves] may be allowed to continue their existence with little molestation. . . . Yes, so also thinks every right-minded ecologist, but has the United States Fish & Wildlife Service no responsibility for implementing this thought before it completes its job of extirpation?"[2] However, there was such widespread public support for destroying predators that the extermination of wolves was completed without remorse.

The fanatical zeal and rate with which this widespread extinction took place is still quite remarkable. Wolves that attacked livestock were not simply killed, they were clubbed, shot, burned, tortured, poisoned, and even roped by horsemen and torn apart. All wolves were relentlessly pursued even into the most remote areas, including national forests and national parks. Our harsh behavior toward wolves was only exceeded by our earlier treatment of Native Americans. With wolves destroyed, the disdain for wildness that the society of our grandparents held, would then be applied with vigor to the air, forests, rivers, grasses, and soil of the western landscape. With such a climactic and symbolic departure, it is no surprise that the grand entrance of wolves back into the West should be so traumatic.[3]

In the early 20th century, society's values toward wildlife began to change. Some species of wildlife (primarily those of consumptive value) began to be con-

sidered desirable. The promotion of scientifically based wildlife management programs led to recovery of deer, elk, and other wild ungulate populations throughout North America. Application of these scientific principles would, at last, also
be applied to predators. Wolf research, which began in the 1960s, shed light on
the importance of wolves and other large predators in the environment. As a
result of this scientific inquiry, the newly formed Alaska Department of Fish and
Game and several Canadian provincial wildlife management agencies began
efforts to end the persecution of wolves and to restore wolf populations in several
areas where they had been extirpated. This new information and attitude were
the start of the wolf's changing image.

RETURN OF THE WOLVES

By the early 1970s, wolf populations in British Columbia and Alberta were
expanding and the National Park Service openly suggested wolves be returned to
Yellowstone. Public reports of wolf activity were increasing throughout the
mountainous portions of Montana, Idaho, and Wyoming. In fact, in October of
1971, the first interagency wolf "team" met in Yellowstone National Park to discuss how to manage the increasing number of wolves, which these public observations seemed to suggest. In 1972, Dr. Bob Ream from the University of
Montana established the Wolf Ecology Project to confirm these reports and to
document wolf activity in the U.S. northern Rocky Mountains. In 1979 the first
wolf was located in southeastern British Columbia, just north of Glacier National
Park, Montana. That lone female was radio-collared and monitored until 1981.
No other wolves were found until 1982, when the "magic pack" mysteriously
appeared in the same area. Then, in 1986, a wolf den was documented in Glacier
National Park, the first in the western United States in over fifty years. Having
real wolves present began to change public opinion and the political landscape.
More and more people began to openly support wolf restoration.

THE ENDANGERED SPECIES ACT AND WOLF RECOVERY

The return of wolves to parts of the West, particularly Yellowstone National Park
(the world's first national park), has been one of the most polarized and emotional debates over man's relationship to the environment in this century. Wolves
were one of the first species listed under the 1966 Endangered Species Act, which
simply identified those animal populations in trouble. In 1974, wolves were again
listed under an amended version of the Endangered Species Act, a law which
actually had teeth and held federal agencies accountable for recovering listed
species.[4] In 1974 one of the first recovery teams formed under the new act was
designed to recover the wolf; it was led by the state of Montana. The team began

preparation of the Recovery Plan for the Northern Rocky Mountain Wolf , which was approved in 1980.[5] Although somewhat general, the plan recommended that a combination of natural dispersal and reintroduction be used to restore wolves to remote public lands in the mountainous portions of Montana, Idaho, and Wyoming. The plan focused wolf recovery efforts in areas like northwestern Montana, central Idaho, and the Yellowstone area. These areas contain millions of acres of remote public land, and hundreds of thousands of deer, elk, bighorn sheep, moose, and bison. Wolf packs living in such areas would minimize conflicts between wolves and people.

In 1987 a revised plan was approved by the U.S. Fish & Wildlife Service (FWS). It was much more specific about recovery tasks and established a recovery goal for wolf populations in the northern Rocky Mountains. The primary goal was to secure a minimum of ten breeding pairs of wolves in each of three recovery areas (northwestern Montana, central Idaho, and the Yellowstone area) for three successive years, or a total of about 300 wolves. Once established, wolf populations could be removed from federal protection and managed solely by Montana, Idaho, and Wyoming. The plan recommended that wolves be encouraged to naturally repopulate Montana and Idaho, but that they be reintroduced as an "experimental population" to Yellowstone. If wolves did not form at least two breeding pairs in Idaho by 1992, measures other than natural recovery were to be considered. The plan also recognized that wolves that attacked livestock must be moved or killed if local rural residents were expected to tolerate wolves, and that public information and education were key to a successful recovery program.

In 1988 the FWS established an interagency wolf management team to assist with the natural recovery of wolves in northwestern Montana. That ongoing program has four major components: (1) Attempts are made to place radio collars on one to two members of each pack, so that the status of the wolf population can be monitored; (2) wolves that attack livestock are controlled (relocated or killed) by the FWS or USDA Animal Damage Control, so that livestock losses remain low and local residents will tolerate the presence of wolves[6]; (3) research is conducted on wolf ecology and the relationship of wolves with deer, elk, moose, livestock, coyotes, mountain lions,[7] and people[8]; and (4) About 75 percent of the effort in the wolf recovery program involves an aggressive public information and education component. The team helped generate hundreds of newspaper, magazine, and book articles, television pieces, and has presented about 500 programs to local livestock, sportsmen, conservation, and civic groups. In addition, Defenders of Wildlife, a private group, established a compensation fund that reimburses livestock producers for livestock that is confirmed to have been attacked by wolves. The program appears to have been effective in building local tolerance of wolves. As of spring of 1996, about eight to ten wolf packs occupied northwestern Montana and public controversy over wolves and their management is waning.

CONGRESS AND WOLF RECOVERY

Because of the great public interest in wolves and the resulting controversy, Congress has been directly involved in the issue since 1988. In a compromise to pending legislation that would have required wolf reintroduction in Yellowstone National Park, Congress directed the National Park Service and the FWS to prepare an extensive series of reports on the potential impacts of wolves to that area. Completed in 1992, these reports addressed the possible effects of wolves on livestock, wild ungulates (deer, elk, and so on), hunter harvests, grizzly bears, small mammals, economics, land uses, and even sociology. The basic conclusion was that the wolves would not cause any serious biological impacts, would occasionally prey on livestock but those incidents could be managed, would result in positive economic impacts, and were ecologically desirable in the area.

In 1990, as part of another legislative compromise on a bill that directed preparation of an environmental impact statement on wolf reintroduction, Congress established the Wolf Management Committee. The committee was directed to develop a wolf reintroduction plan for Yellowstone National Park and central Idaho. The ten-member committee was represented by the FWS, National Park Service, USDA Forest Service, each of the state fish and game agencies in Montana, Idaho, and Wyoming, and four special interest groups (livestock, sportsmen, and two conservation-type groups). In a May 1991 report, a majority of the membership recommended that Congress specifically designate all wolves, except those in and around Glacier National Park, as a nonessential experimental population to be managed by the affected states. After an environmental impact statement (EIS) was completed, wolves would be reintroduced to Yellowstone National Park. Reintroduction in Idaho would occur only if at least two pairs did not naturally establish themselves in that area within five years. The report was strongly opposed by both conservationist representatives, who believed that the recommendation would allow so much wolf mortality that it would delay or even prohibit wolf recovery. The National Park Service abstained from the final vote. Congress also apparently had similar concerns and took no action on the committee's recommendation.

THE WOLF REINTRODUCTION EIS

In November 1991, Congress directed the FWS, in consultation with the National Park Service and USDA Forest Service, to prepare an environmental impact statement (EIS) on gray wolf reintroduction to Yellowstone National Park and central Idaho. Congress also directed that the EIS cover a wide range of alternatives. In October 1992, Congress further stated that the preferred alternative be consistent with existing law and that the EIS be completed by January 1994.

In early 1992, an FWS-led interagency team was established to prepare the

EIS. The team made a concerted effort to involve the local public throughout preparation of the document. The FWS funded the three affected states, the USDA Forest Service and Animal Damage Control, and the University of Montana to participate in the process. During the two years that the document was being developed, the FWS hosted over 130 public meetings, distributed about 750,000 documents, and received comments from over 170,000 people. The EIS mailing list contained addresses from all fifty states and over forty countries. The majority of all public contact by the FWS was directed at Montana, Idaho, and Wyoming residents, who lived in the vicinity of central Idaho or Yellowstone National Park.

The EIS contained several important predictions concerning the impact of a recovered wolf population (100 wolves) in each recovery area. It predicted that a recovered population annually would kill about 10 to 19 cattle, 57 to 68 sheep, and 1,200 to 1,600 wild ungulates; reduce hunter harvests of female wild ungulates zero to 30 percent but would not significantly impact hunting for males; not affect uses of public or private land, except for some use of M-44 cyanide devices that are used to kill coyotes; increase visitor use 2 to 10 percent; and increase the overall positive economic impact up to $23 million. From late 1994 until 2002, when wolf populations were expected to be recovered and delisted, the total cost for wolf recovery was estimated to be $6.7 million.

In summer 1994, the final EIS was approved by the secretary of the Interior and the secretary of Agriculture, respectively. It recommended that two identical nonessential experimental population rules (Section 10j of the Endangered Species Act) be developed, and that wolves be reintroduced to both central Idaho and Yellowstone National Park in late 1994. One rule covered most of Idaho and parts of western Montana[9]; the other rule covered all of Wyoming, and much of southern and central Montana. These rules attempted to address local concerns by allowing private landowners to harass wolves at any time (as long as they were not injured) and to kill wolves seen attacking livestock, and they guaranteed agency control of problem wolves. The rules also ensured that no land use restrictions would occur on private lands and only those necessary near den sites would be used on public land. The rules offered lead responsibility and funding for wolf management to the affected states and tribes, and allowed them to move wolves that were excessively preying on wild ungulates. Because of public mistrust on both sides of the issue, the rules contained two termination clauses. One clause stated that all reintroduced wolves would be removed if two naturally occurring wolf packs were discovered or if litigation removed the experimental status. The other clause stated that if the wolf population did not continually grow toward recovery levels, new management strategies must be employed that ensure increasing wolf numbers.

In November 1994, having completed the legally required rule-making and public involvement process required to establish experimental populations, the FWS prepared to capture gray wolves in Canada and release them in Yellowstone and Idaho. At this point, litigation was initiated against the FWS. The American Farm Bureau Federation, along with its affiliates in Montana, Idaho, and Wyoming, asked the court to prevent wolf reintroduction and to declare the plan illegal. At the same time, the Sierra Club Legal Defense Fund, representing the Audubon Society, Sierra Club, and several other environmental groups, asked the court to force the FWS to exclude any existing wolves in Idaho from the provisions of the experimental rule. In addition, the Urbigkits, a couple from Wyoming, asked the court to prevent reintroduction because they believed wolves always existed in Wyoming and that unique gene pool should not be contaminated by nonnative wolves. Although the litigation delayed the reintroduction program for about a month, the court ultimately denied requests to stop the program. The court, however, has not issued a final decision on the merits of these complaints, though that decision is expected shortly. Appeals and further litigation are considered inevitable.

In December 1994, arrangements were made to capture wolves in Alberta, Canada, and to transport them to the United States for release. The critical part of the program was to obtain healthy wild wolves from areas were they preyed on elk, mule deer, and moose, the types of prey they would find in their new homes. Working with local fur trappers and biologists from Canada and the United States, wolves were radio-collared and released. Those wolves were then tracked back to their pack, and other packs members were captured by helicopter darting. The wolves were placed in dog kennels with straw and fed road-killed ungulates. In January 1995 these wolves were then placed in individual shipping crates and flown to the United States. Fifteen young adult wolves, representing at least seven packs, were immediately released into the central Idaho wilderness. Fourteen wolves, representing three packs, were placed in three one-acre pens in Yellowstone National Park. These wolves were held until late March and then released. The FWS provided funding to monitor radio-collared wolves in Canada so the potential impact of the reintroduction on the source population could be determined.

In January 1996, this process was repeated in British Columbia. The Montana Stockgrowers Association and a local rancher filed suit to stop the release of wolves in Yellowstone, claiming that further analysis was required by law. After hearing arguments, the court again allowed the program to continue, and the suit was eventually dropped. When insufficient federal funding threatened completion of the 1996 reintroduction, the Wolf Education and Research Center,

Defenders of Wildlife, and Yellowstone Association raised nearly $100,000 from private sources to fund the project. Twenty wolves were released in central Idaho. In Yellowstone, seventeen wolves, representing four packs, were held in four pens before being released in early April 1996.

A STATUS REPORT

As of May 1997, the reintroductions have succeeded far better than predicted. In Yellowstone over 10,000 park visitors have seen or heard wolves, and visitation in local "gateway" communities nearest the wolves appears sharply higher. The three packs released in 1995 stayed together, spending a majority of their time in the park, and nine pups were born in two litters. In 1996, four pairs formed from wolves released in 1995. Two of four packs released in 1996 contributed to the fourteen pups in four litters that were born that year. In 1997 it appeared that eight breeding pairs had produced ten litters, with only one litter located outside the park. Wolves have killed twelve sheep, one dog, and no cattle in the Yellowstone area. Yellowstone National Park biologists continue to monitor wolves closely and are leading efforts to understand the relationships between wolves and ungulates in the park.

Fourteen wolves have died. Four were illegally shot. One person reported an accidental shooting immediately and was fined $500. Another person, after trying unsuccessfully to cover up the killing and losing several appeals to his conviction by a local jury, was sentenced to six months in jail, fined $10,000 and court costs, and lost his hunting privileges. Two other cases are still under investigation. Four wolves and two litters of newborn pups died because of territorial disputes between wolves. Three wolves have been killed by vehicles. One wolf was killed, pursuant to the experimental rules, after it attacked a sheep subsequent to being moved for previously killing two sheep. Two other wolves died from unknown causes during or shortly after being held in captivity.

The Nez Perce tribe has assumed responsibility for recovering wolves in central Idaho and has documented that the wolves have done very well. Wolves traveled far, as expected, but primarily settled on national forestlands. While no pups were born in 1995, three pairs produced pups in 1996 and seven to ten pairs were expected to produce pups in 1997. One wolf released in 1995 was illegally killed while feeding on a calf that had died from natural causes shortly after birth. One wolf accidentally drowned after being captured for killing three calves. One wolf was killed by a mountain lion and another one starved. No livestock were attacked by wolves in Idaho in 1995, but three calves and thirty sheep were killed in 1996. All livestock producers in the northern Rocky Mountains have been compensated for their confirmed losses by a private program administered by the Defenders of Wildlife.

Wolf recovery is imminent due to the two successful reintroductions into Yellowstone and Idaho, and the ongoing natural expansion of wolves in northwestern Montana. No further reintroductions are anticipated. In spring 1997, estimates indicate over ten breeding pairs in northwestern Montana, eight breeding pairs in the Yellowstone area, and seven to ten breeding pairs in central Idaho. At this rate of growth, the wolf population in the northern Rocky Mountains of Montana, Idaho, and Wyoming should be recovered and delisted before 2002, and at less cost than was originally estimated. While still an emotional issue, wolf recovery appears to be growing less controversial as local residents gain experience with wolves. As the U.S. Fish & Wildlife Service continues to manage wolves to reduce conflicts with local residents, public tolerance for wolves and trust in the program should steadily increase.

CONCLUSION

Along with Aldo Leopold, I believe that "every right-minded ecologist" now echoes the sentiments of Stanley P. Young, who documented the demise of the last wolves in the West. In his 1970 book, *Last of the Loners*, Young wrote:

> Hated, reviled, and feared, hunted, trapped and poisoned down through the centuries, always with a bounty on its head, to the extent of millions of dollars, as a symbol of the devil, and finally, as the progenitor of the domestic dog-man's best friend—no other carnivore rivals the wolf in the profound effect exerted on human affairs. May the wolf never cease to have a place in our North America fauna—a condition that, I am sure, can be made possible in view of the vast domain yet remaining in North and Middle America where it roams at will and where its presence is not in conflict with human welfare. In other regions of scant population it may be tolerated in reasonably controlled numbers. To that end, I have through the years given every support.

Now that wolves have been returned to the West, it is a different place. It is also, I believe, a better place for us and our children to call home:

"The very gentle glowing eyes of a dark wolf sparkle in the night."
(Tara Bangs 5th grade)

NOTES

[1] Young S .P. and E. A. Goldman, 1944. *The Wolves of North America*. American Wildlife Institute, Washington, D.C., p. 385.

[2] Leopold, Also, 1944. "Review of the Wolves of North America." *Journal of Forestry*, 42(12): 928–29.

[3] Kellert S. R., M. Black, C. R. Rush, and A. Bath, 1996. "Human Culture and Large Carnivore Management." *Conservation Biology,* 10(4): 977–90.

[4] U.S. Code, Vol. 16, secs. 1531–1543 (1996).

[5] U.S. Fish & Wildlife Service, 1980 and 1987. *Northern Rocky Mountain Wolf Recovery Plan*. Denver, Colo., pp. 67, 119.

[6] Bangs, E. E., S. H. Fritts, D. A. Harms, J. A. Fontaine, M. D. Jimenez, W. G. Brewster, and C. C. Niemeyer, 1996. "Control of Endangered Gray Wolves in Montana," pp. 127–34. In L. N. Carbyn S. H. Fritts, and D. R. Seip, eds., *Ecology and Conservation of Wolves in a Changing World*. Canadian Circumpolar Institute, University of Alberta, Edmonton.

[7] U.S. Fish & Wildlife Service, 1996. "1995 Annual report of the Rocky Mountain Interagency Wolf Recovery Program." Helena, Mont., p. 23.

[8] Tucker, P. and D. Plescher, 1989. "Attitudes of Hunters and Residents Toward Wolves in Northwestern Montana." *Wildlife Society Bulletin* 17: 509–54.

[9] Code of Federal Regulations, Vol. 20, sec. 17.84(I) (1994).

Chapter 13

MOVING PAST THE POLARIZATION
Wolves, Grizzly Bears, and Endangered Species Recovery
Hank Fischer

Yellowstone wolf restoration stands as a landmark conservation achievement, one that historians likely will use to demarcate the end of an era of predator persecution in the United States. This action will influence large predator conservation around the world, and people who participated in this epic struggle have every reason to be proud of their accomplishment.

But while Yellowstone wolf restoration may be a historic conservation achievement, it is a poor conservation model for at least three reasons: It took too long, it cost too much, and too many people are still angry about it. Conservationists may have won this battle, but we will lose the larger species protection war if we don't adopt more effective and less polarizing wildlife restoration strategies. Too many species need our help to spend so much time and money on one.

LESSONS FROM THE WOLF WARS

Aldo Leopold, whose work has profoundly influenced today's wildlife professionals, frequently reminded people that conservation's central goal should be to enhance not only how people relate to the land, but also how people relate to each other.[1]

It is instructive that the decade-long Yellowstone wolf debate has increased rather than decreased public divisiveness over wolf restoration. Pragmatic people might say that eggs must be broken to make an omelette. That is true, but the animals we seek to conserve can become casualties if segments of the public become sufficiently alienated from governmental decisions. Such polarization can spawn an attitude where illegal killing becomes socially acceptable—perhaps even righteous.

The greatest irony surrounding wolf restoration may be that the issue is so eminently resolvable. Wolf recovery needn't cause economic hardship, it requires few changes in land management, and it has a high likelihood of success. On a one to ten scale of difficulty, it's at best a two or three. Restore salmon or spotted owls? These are complex issues that require difficult economic and land use decisions. Wolves? A relatively easy species to restore.

Why then have we struggled so mightily? For one thing, our government is at war with itself. While it may be our national policy to restore threatened and endangered species, most western political leaders strive to block such efforts. Instead of encouraging warring constituencies to look for common ground, they encourage groups to throw dirt at one another. And I am not just talking about mossback Republicans who oppose all environmental initiatives[2]; I am also talking about Democrats who disappear underground whenever an issue gets heated.[3] Our current crop of politicians may be the nation's worst possible role models for consensus-building.

If I were to place blame for why we were unable to break past the polarization and find solutions to the Yellowstone wolf issue—and placing blame may soon replace baseball as our nation's favorite pastime—I would point a finger at our politicians who failed to provide leadership when it was badly needed.

Interestingly enough, the only politician from the northern Rockies who showed any leadership on the wolf issue is a person who at the time was widely regarded as the nation's leading enemy of the environment: Sen. Jim McClure from Idaho. It's a fact recognized only by those on the front lines that Yellowstone wolf restoration would never have happened without Senator McClure. Suffice it to say that successful conservation frequently involves incredible ironies and unlikely heroes. Solutions frequently arise from unlikely sources.

I do not mean to sound cynical, but waiting for leadership from our politicians is likely a prescription for frustration. And let's face it: Pointing fingers and blaming them isn't going to solve the problem either. There is only one way to fix our current broken system: People who care about the environment and restoration of endangered species must create new models for protection.

SEARCHING FOR NEW SOLUTIONS

Some battle-scarred veterans of the wolf wars decided to take a different course with a new initiative to restore grizzly bears to the large roadless expanses of western Montana and central Idaho. Instead of building an army to crush the opposition, we tried to analyze who would be the most vocal and effective opponents of grizzly restoration. While there were many players in the wolf issue, the livestock industry was always the opponent who mattered most. Similarly, we surmised that the timber industry and those associated with it—labor unions and local citizens—were destined to be the alpha opponents in the upcoming Bitterroot bear battles.

Our new tactic: Rather than launching a campaign and igniting a controversy, Defenders of Wildlife and the National Wildlife Federation decided to try engaging timber and labor interests in a collaborative effort to restore grizzly bears to the Bitterroot.[4] We sought to enlist our adversaries' support rather than engender their opposition. The Yellowstone wolf experience did help in one significant way: Perceptive industry leaders recognized that just saying no might not be a viable strategy.

A fact we did not fully appreciate at the outset of our efforts was that many of our so-called opponents did not have strong objections to the idea of restoring grizzlies. Many of them—like many of us—have serious outdoor interests, including hiking, hunting, fishing, horsepacking, and other wildlands recreation. It may be heresy for an environmentalist to say it, but let me say it anyway: Most of these people, even though they work for commodity interests, have a strong conservation ethic. They live in Montana or Idaho by choice. Most value the environment deeply. They are people who might be, should be, and sometimes are, card-carrying members of conservation groups.

At the same time, the timber interests we sought to enlist were highly threatened by the Endangered Species Act and the people who support it. They felt strongly that environmentalists were using the Endangered Species Act to restrict legitimate commercial activities, whether it was necessary for the conservation of a species or not. They were afraid of a grizzly recovery plan that left no room for people or jobs.[5]

It really did not take long for our disparate groups to reach philosophical common ground: Grizzlies should be restored to the Bitterroot area, but impacts on local economies and local people must be minimized. Nothing about this was too groundbreaking. Just words, really. Happy talk, some might criticize—and many did.[6]

But the next step was substantive and significant. Defenders and the National Wildlife Federation asked the two commodity groups—the Intermountain Forest Industry Association and the Resource Organization on Timber Supply—to cosign a letter to the Montana and Idaho congressional delegations seeking funding to initiate a Bitterroot grizzly environmental impact statement (EIS). They did so, and in 1995 the U.S. Fish & Wildlife Service received $250,000 to start the EIS process.

To put this in a broader perspective, the timing of this appropriation was particularly noteworthy. Congress approved this grizzly reintroduction plan at precisely the same time wolves were being reintroduced to central Idaho and the governor was talking about calling out the National Guard to stop it. It occurred about the same time a 6,000-person demonstration was taking place in Salmon, Idaho—a town of 3,000—in response to a judge's ruling to shut down all forest activities in order to protect salmon. The fact that this appropriation was able to win approval in such a hostile climate is testimony to our broad base of support.

Our nontraditional coalition began to work in earnest once the Fish & Wildlife Service initiated its environmental impact statement process. Our groups developed a question-and-answer booklet on Bitterroot grizzlies that agencies used as an information tool during early stages of the EIS process. Our objective was to ensure all citizens were operating from a common set of facts.

Next, our coalition also took the lead in hosting a series of local meetings where opinion leaders were invited to present their concerns. These meetings, held in several small communities in Idaho and Montana, alerted local citizens that a new, collaborative approach was being tried.

PUTTING CITIZENS IN CHARGE

But our coalition's most significant accomplishment was to submit a joint proposal to state and federal agencies that outlined our plan for how grizzly bears could be restored with minimal social and economic impacts. In July 1997, the Fish & Wildlife Service adopted our proposal as the preferred alternative in its draft EIS.[7]

Our coalition's proposal calls for reintroduction of grizzlies as an "experimental" population under section 10(j) of the Endangered Species Act (ESA). As with wolf reintroduction, this provision allows relaxation of parts of the ESA and increases management flexibility.

It is the second part of our proposal that breaks new ground in endangered species recovery. It calls for joint management of the grizzly recovery program by a locally based team of citizens and agency officials. We have termed our proposal the Citizen Management alternative.

Our coalition agreed that the most critical factor in gaining broader support for grizzly conservation is to give local citizens a larger and more meaningful participatory role in bear management. Conservation and scientific communities have faced increasing criticism in recent years for their perceived inattention to the needs of rural communities. Conservation biologist Dr. Peter Brussard suggests, "If people see that conservation goals are consistent with their own, they will become part of the solution rather than remain a major part of the problem."[8]

But before I get too carried away trumpeting this Citizen Management alternative as an innovation, it should be noted that Aldo Leopold beat us to the punch on this concept by nearly sixty years. In an essay about protecting rare animals, Leopold proposed that agencies should form a committee of diverse public interests to define the needs of endangered species. He viewed cooperation between agencies and private citizens as essential to their conservation and voiced optimism about the inherent tendency of humans to do what was right for wildlife. He summarized his citizen management concept by saying: "I am satisfied that thousands of enthusiastic conservationists would be proud of such a public trust, and many would execute it with fidelity and intelligence. I can see in this setup more conservation than could be bought with millions of new dollars, more coordination of bureaus than Congress can get by new organization charts, more genuine contacts between factions than will ever occur in the war of the inkpots. . . ."

According to the draft EIS, this Citizen Management Committee will consist of seven citizens from Idaho, five citizens from Montana, and single representatives from the Fish & Wildlife Service, the U.S. Forest Service, Idaho Fish and Game, Montana Fish, Wildlife and Parks, and tribal governments. The citizens will be appointed by the secretary of the Interior based on recommendations from the governors of Idaho and Montana.

While state and federal agencies will continue to conduct day-to-day bear management activities, the committee will set policy, develop biannual work plans, and oversee the controversial aspects of grizzly conservation. The committee will be required to abide by the same endangered species standard that federal agencies do: Their actions must lead to the recovery of the species, and they must use the best available science to make their decisions.

THE LEAP OF FAITH

This concept of citizen management admittedly takes a large step into uncharted waters. Endangered species management has traditionally relied on a "top-down" model of federally driven regulation and enforcement. Our "bottom-up" model is community based, and relies on federal control only as a safeguard in the event the actions of the citizen committee do not lead toward recovery.[9]

This vision requires a leap of faith. That leap of faith is whether ordinary citizens, informed by science, will make positive decisions for grizzly bears. It is our belief that investing citizens with more authority will also invest them with more responsibility. Our goal is to make endangered species recovery more oriented toward problem solving and less oriented toward regulation and litigation.

THE UPSHOT

Engaging in collaborative approaches is not necessarily about compromise. It is about getting what you want by responding to the legitimate needs of others. It is about defining a solution rather than simply stating a problem.

It took ten years and almost $6 million to get a Yellowstone wolf EIS initiated. It has taken two years and less than $.5 million to reach the same place for Bitterroot grizzlies.

If the initial steps in the Bitterroot grizzly process are indicative of future success, this collaborative approach to endangered species management could be an important conservation breakthrough. But perhaps even more important, the environment that Bitterroot grizzlies step into when they are reintroduced will be much friendlier than what Yellowstone's wolves have found.

NOTES

[1] Aldo Leopold, *A Sand County Almanac*, pp. 237–61 (1970).

[2] *Missoulian*, "Burns Aims to End Funding for Wolf Recovery Program," May 10, 1995.

[3] *Missoulian*, "Baucus Blasts Wolf Transplants and the People Pushing Them," February 11, 1996.

[4] *The Washington Post*, "Unlikely Alliance Finds Common Ground for Grizzlies," October 29, 1993, A3.

[5] *The Idaho Statesman*, "Idaho Fears Bears' Bite on Economy," October 7, 1995.

[6] *Wild Forest Review*, "A Dubious Plan For Grizzly Recovery in the Northern Rockies," January 1995.

[7] U.S. Fish & Wildlife Service, *Grizzly Bear Recovery in the Bitterroot Ecosystem: Draft Environmental Impact Statement.* Missoula, Mont. (July 1997), pp. 2–4.

[8] P. Brussard, *Society for Conservation Biology Newsletter*, February 1995.

[9] See M. Roy and H. Fischer, "Bitterroot Grizzly Recovery: A Community-Based Alternative," *Endangered Species Update*, December 1995, for a full treatment of this concept.

Chapter 14

WOLVES, BEARS, AND THE SPIRIT OF THE WILD
Asking the Right Questions
Doug Honnold

I face the nearly impossible task of trying to say something meaningful about wolves and bears in a short essay. It is difficult to bring those wild creatures, the very embodiment of wild places, into proper focus in our increasingly urban society. While my personal role in this drama has been as an Endangered Species Act litigator working to protect bears and wolves and their habitat, I will attempt to raise some larger issues about our relationship to wolves, to bears, to the landscape, and to the natural world.

In the West, we live in an era of explosive human population growth that has resulted in an assault on what is left of the natural world. Ecosystems are unraveling. Species like wolves and bears, which once roamed throughout the western landscape, are relegated to the few mountain retreats that have not yet experienced the wave of human expansion, development, and use. The fundamental question we face is: Do we have it in our hearts to carve out some space on the landscape where these wild animals can survive and their native habitats can be retained? Can we listen to our coinhabitants of this landscape, learn their needs, and make room for these creatures?

WOLF RECOVERY: SOME UNANSWERED QUESTIONS

Turning now to wolves. Although the government has expended considerable funds and energy to translocate wolves to Yellowstone and Idaho, wolves on their own have recolonized parts of the northern Rockies. As a result, we now have roughly 100 wolves in northwestern Montana. This natural recolonization story needs and deserves further amplification.

The first wolf that started the natural recolonization of northwestern Montana was initially observed near Glacier National Park in 1985. Because the origins of that wolf were unknown, the wolf pack that was documented the next year was referred to as the Magic Pack. What you may not know is that southern Canada is not a wild expanse of roadless wilderness filled to the brim with wolves and bears. In fact, in southern Canada, Alberta and British Columbia are subject to the same development pressures from agriculture, mining, oil and gas, and timbering that have fragmented and destroyed so much of our lands in the lower 48. You will probably be surprised to learn that the distance between established wolf packs in southern Canada and Glacier National Park is, in fact, a significantly longer distance than the distance between Glacier and Yellowstone. What is remarkable is that the Magic Pack, fully protected as an endangered species, has been able to multiply and naturally recover on its own. What was merely one wolf in 1985, two wolves in 1986, is now, in 1996, a wolf population of roughly 100 wolves in eight packs. I would note, parenthetically, that this natural recolonization of the northern Rockies has occurred with relatively little fanfare and comparatively little political opposition from any quarter.

In Idaho wolves were also continuing to recolonize wild places on their own. In the years preceding the government's translocation efforts, the number of confirmed sightings of wolves in Idaho increased exponentially. Instead of sightings in a few geographically isolated locations, wolves were documented throughout the wildlands of Idaho, in virtually every sector of the state. Radio-collared wolves from the northwestern Montana packs were observed migrating into Idaho. Population estimates by government scientists were as high as fifteen wolves residing in Idaho. And Fish & Wildlife Service scientists estimated that breeding and pack activity would be documented by government scientists within one to five years.

What was the U.S. Fish & Wildlife Service response to this natural recolonization of wolves in the wildlands of Idaho? The Service rushed to dart, radio-collar, and translocate additional Canadian wolves to Idaho. Under the government plan, all wolves in Idaho—both the natural wolves that made it there on their own and the ones that were given the free ride in government planes—would be treated as "experimental, nonessential" wolves. What this really meant was that the full legal protections of the Endangered Species Act that would otherwise apply to Idaho's wolves were dropped and the only protection these wolves received were the measures contained in the Idaho wolf special rule. Essentially, the Fish & Wildlife Service accomplished a de facto delisting of the wolves that were naturally recolonizing the wildlands of Idaho. Prior to the translocation efforts these wolves were fully protected endangered species; after the translocation efforts they were treated as "experimental" and no longer endangered. It is this feature of the Fish & Wildlife Service wolf relocation plan that we are challenging in court. We're not saying that you can't translocate additional wolves to Idaho. What we are saying is that you can't do it in a way that drops full legal protections—including the protection of habitat—for the intrepid wolves that are already recolonizing Idaho.

Ironically, from a political perspective, the federal government picked one of the worst times to undertake wolf translocation efforts: The right-wing, anti-federal government backlash, a revisitation of the Sagebrush Rebellion, was in full swing in the Rocky Mountain states. In essence, the Fish & Wildlife Service was engaged in a race against time, trying to translocate additional wolves to Idaho and delist the existing wolves so that rather than being bound by the legal dictates of the Endangered Species Act, the feds could make up the rules of the species protection game as they went along. But given the recent shift in political tides, the effort to buy political support for wolf recovery by trading away legal protections was destined to fail. The ranchers would not, in this political climate, support the government's wolf translocation program even if there were absolutely no legal protections for wolves and their habitat.

Let me return, however, to our two wolf stories, two very different approaches with radically different receptions, because I think the contrast illuminates some very deep societal values. First, we have the mediagenic Fish & Wildlife Service translocation effort, heralded in virtually every newspaper and television station in the country. The images, as we have seen today, are the images of wolves captured, wolves darted, wolves translocated, and wolves set "free" by man. Big government moving chess pieces on the land. I can't help but wonder whether this is nothing but another variation of the human desire to control nature that led—in an earlier incarnation—to the extirpation of the wolf from the western landscape.

I contrast that story with the story of wolves naturally, magically, on their own reclaiming their native lands. The wolves recolonizing northwestern Montana. The wolves recolonizing the wildlands of Idaho. And the radically different process that this suggests: listening to the land, listening to the species and their needs, remaining fluid in our approaches so as to incorporate new scientific information, letting nature heal itself where we can. Making room for species and their habitat needs. Truly sharing the landscape. Listening.

The irony here is that in our efforts to bring back wolves we alter, suppress, and destroy the very aspect of nature that the wolf symbolizes: the spirit of the wild. Instead we celebrate our imagined ability to control nature. We want to expiate our sin of extirpating wolves from the West through the use of high-tech management and control. We ignore the wolves' remarkable natural recovery. Their stories remain untold.

GRIZZLY BEAR RECOVERY: THE UNADDRESSED CONCERNS

My wife, Louisa Willcox, and I share a love of bears and an affection for bear totems. Often when I speak in court or other settings on behalf of bears I carry with me a bear fetish to remind me of the wildlands, the wild places, the special spirit that is inhabited by the great bear.

Bears are the very embodiment of wildness—a large predator that needs large expanses of habitat and remote refugia in order to survive. It is because bears are fundamentally incompatible with our human desire to control and manipulate nature that grizzlies have been relegated to a few mountainous redoubts in the lower 48 states. Bears simply don't get along with clearcuts, oil rigs, mining operations, cattle and sheep grazing, subdivisions, and all of the people with guns that go along with our human presence.

In reflecting on the plight of bears today in the lower 48, I'm reminded of the many *Far Side* cartoons depicting bears with radio collars, needles sticking out of their sides, and numbers assigned. I wonder how much of the wild we have already lost. Some biologists have noted that we are selectively thinning many grizzly bear populations by removing—eliminating—the aggressive, exploratory bears and retaining the more secretive, remote bears. Again, we must face the question of what remains of the wildlands when we are afraid to protect necessary habitat and instead opt for high-tech, intrusive management of what's left of our dwindling wildlands.

My concerns are perhaps best illustrated with two stories about bear biology. The first biological story concerns the habitat needs of the Yellowstone grizzly bear population, which is probably the most studied bear population in the world. For many years bear biologists studied intensively the foraging behavior of the Yellowstone grizzly bears. Over the many years of studying the bear, the biologists had never detected grizzly bears making any significant use of a plant species called sweet cicely. For more than ten years, the biologists had studied bear behavior and examined fecal material and the bears had not foraged on sweet cicely. Then, suddenly, in the eleventh year of these studies, virtually instantaneously, grizzlies throughout the Yellowstone ecosystem were using sweet cicely as a major food source. Now, obviously, the detection of this behavioral change raises all kinds of questions. Was there some nutritional element in sweet cicely that was important to bears in that year? Was the bears' need for, and use of, sweet cicely innate? Was it a learned behavior? Did bears individually learn from other bears how to utilize this important food source? How could such learning spread so quickly throughout the entire bear population?

This story also raises much larger questions and suggests some significant truths. Perhaps the most vital truth is humility. Few studies of the biological behavior and habitat needs of endangered species extend for more than a few years. Yet if this study had not continued to the eleventh year, we would never have discovered one of the significant food sources for the Yellowstone grizzly population. What other key species have we eliminated from the landscape without fully understanding their function and essential roles? This teaches us that we must preserve wild places, save all of the pieces of the landscape, because we don't have all of the answers, we don't fully understand the needs of other species. Again, we return to the notion of listening to the land, letting the species tell us about their habitat needs.

The second biological story concerns the role of the whitebark pine and its seed crops to the Yellowstone grizzly bear population. Whitebark pine seeds are one of the most important, if not the most important, food source for the Yellowstone grizzly population. Whitebark pines provide a crucial food source in remote areas of the ecosystem, far removed from human development and human presence. In years when whitebark pines produce good crops of cones, the bears are able to forage in the backcountry and avoid human presence. In years when whitebark seed production fails, bears must search far and wide for food, venturing into the low-elevation areas where people tend to congregate. We can even quantify the mortality risk associated with this behavioral pattern: Mortality of adult females, the most significant portion of the population, is 2.3 times higher than average during years of poor whitebark pine seed crops. What this tells us is that the Yellowstone grizzly bear population growth rate—whether the population is increasing or decreasing in size—is tightly connected to the size of the whitebark pine seed crops and the bears' ability to find food in the back-country.

Ignoring this behavioral dynamic, state and federal agency officials were ready to proclaim victory, arguing that the Yellowstone grizzly population was recovered because detected human-caused mortality was relatively low for a few years. But not surprisingly those years were good years for whitebark pine seed production. Then in 1994 and 1995, the pine seed crops failed, bears dispersed widely throughout the landscape in search of food, and bear mortality levels sky-rocketed to their highest levels in the past twenty years.

What is really frightening is that the bad years that bears experienced in 1994 and 1995 could become routine. Whitebark pine itself is threatened; it has been reduced or eliminated throughout most of its range in the Rocky Mountain states due to a blister rust inadvertently introduced from Europe. Some scientists specu-lated that Yellowstone's climate would not permit the existence and spread of the blister rust. However, in 1995 agency scientists documented many stands of whitebark pine in the Yellowstone ecosystem that have already been infected with blister rust.

In addition to blister rust, global warming also threatens to reduce substan-tially the size of whitebark pine seed crops. Whitebark pines are notoriously slow to regenerate and take decades before they will produce seed crops. Global warm-ing in Yellowstone could make much of the current whitebark pine habitat unsuitable for the pines because the sites would become too hot for the trees to survive. A few-degree increase in temperature would force the pines to migrate up the side of the mountains in order to find suitable climatic conditions. If global warming hits Yellowstone, we can expect a significant loss of whitebark pine habitat and, consequently, whitebark pine seed production.

Thus, we know enough now to know that the mortality of Yellowstone's bears turns heavily on the fate of whitebark pine crops. The future of the pines is in doubt. The only conclusion is that the future of Yellowstone's bears is tremendously threatened.

In the face of these behavioral dynamics and habitat threats, the state and federal agencies remain firm in their efforts to call the Yellowstone grizzly bear population biologically recovered and remove the bear from the list of threatened species. We sued the U.S. Fish & Wildlife Service, challenging the grizzly bear recovery plan because the Service failed to develop recovery goals for habitat, even though the loss of habitat was one of the major reasons that the bear was originally listed as a threatened species. A federal judge in Washington, D.C., agreed with our arguments and ruled that the grizzly bear recovery plan was illegal because it didn't include recovery targets for habitat. And yet, even faced with these developments, state and federal agencies continue apace in their efforts to delist the Yellowstone grizzly bear population. The politically driven efforts to delist continue, the habitat needs and threats to the bears' survival are ignored.

At a recent annual meeting of the Alliance for the Wild Rockies, there was a panel discussion of the merits and demerits of various proposals to reintroduce grizzly bears to the central Idaho wilderness complex. One of the proposals under discussion was a Citizen Management Committee proposal, which vests a community-based committee with responsibility for managing the reintroduced bears. At that meeting, a Native American from the Flathead Reservation rose from his seat in the audience to speak to the assembly. He posed a troubling question: "Did you ever stop to think: Are you doing this in the best interest of the bear, or are you doing this for you?" He went on to say: "Consider this from the bear's perspective. You're taken from your native lands, the lands that you know and love. You're taken from your family, your favorite berry sites, your favorite dens. You're shot with tranquilizers, outfitted with radio collars. Your blood is taken, your lip tattooed with a number. You're placed in a foreign land, removed from your people, your land, your culture.

"I want you to consider the similarities between this process and the history of moving the tribes to reservations. Taking away our lands and giving us new lands that you didn't want. And I ask you to consider: Can you guarantee that my new home will be mine forever? Or are you just giving it to me now so that you can take it away in the future? Can you guarantee that my new home will be safe from logging forever? Can you guarantee that my new home will be secure when the oil and gas companies want to drill in my lands? Can you guarantee that my new home will be safe forever from mining? Are you willing to protect my lands to the end of time?

"I ask you to consider," he concluded, "are you doing this for you, or are you doing this for the bear?"

And that is the question that I want to conclude with. What triumphs are we celebrating? Are we celebrating the triumphs of wolves and bears in all their wildness? Or are we celebrating our own efforts to control, to manage, to restrict, to confine the last vestiges of the wild?

PART VI

Its
RIVERS FLOW
TOGETHER
TIME, PEOPLE, AND THE GREAT BASIN

The following essays address the Great Basin region, an area still widely perceived as a vast emptiness largely forgotten by time. But that view cannot be squared with Wallace Stegner's experience, nor is it consistent with the vision that emerges from these essays. While sensitive to the rigors associated with the harsh Great Basin setting, Stegner also sagely observed the fundamental unity of this lightly populated area, noting that its rivers all flow toward each other. In a similar vein, writer Steve Trimble challenges conventional wisdom by rejecting the well-worn myths and surface barrenness of the Great Basin and by evoking instead a rich setting full of human and other complexities that cry out for more shared understanding. Writing from a range science perspective, Jim Young and Fay Allen review "the grand experiment"—raising domestic livestock on the cold desert of the Great Basin—and conclude that this still evolving endeavor has wrought significant ecological change without yet proving its long-term sustainability. In tandem, the essays suggest that the human relationship to the harsh Great Basin environment escapes easy characterization and is best understood as an evolving relationship built upon adaptability, cooperation, and sensitivity to the land's inherent limitations.

Chapter 15

LETTING GO OF THE RIM
Stephen Trimble

Wallace Stegner said, "The Great Basin is a unifying force; wherever you live in it, you flow toward every other part."[1]

People resist that fact. They cling to the rim—the only places hospitable enough for cities to grow—as they would cling with fear to the side of the pool before they learn to swim. The problem is just that: They do not know how to swim. They have yet to learn to see and to appreciate the Great Basin. It is too alien a landscape.

This is the forgotten desert of North America. The Great Basin Desert covers most of Nevada, the West Desert of Utah, the southeastern corners of Oregon and Idaho, and California east of the Sierras and Cascades. The ecological place called the Great Basin Desert overlaps the geological place called Basin and Range. Fault-block mountains and structural basins alternate relentlessly from east to west across this country. They have equal weight, but the basins challenge comprehension even more than the desert mountains—strange, still valleys without rivers that stretch away toward unknown and obscure horizons.

The entire region lacks the classically picturesque landscapes loved by art directors. Elsewhere in the North American deserts, saguaro and cholla cacti prick the skies of the Sonoran Desert, Joshua trees spread a latticework of tentacled arms over the Mojave, and the Rio Grande canyons gash and cleave the Chihuahuan Desert.

The Great Basin, instead, has sagebrush and shadscale and silence. Nowhere else in the West is there such a sweep of undeveloped country filled with such silence—a soothing bowl of wild basins and ranges sufficient, I have learned, for a lifetime of exploring.

In the early 1980s, I traveled throughout the Great Basin, researching and photographing for *The Sagebrush Ocean*.[2] When I returned to the basin in the 1990s, to photograph for a new project, *Earthtones*,[3] I discovered that my earlier book had become a historic document. The resurgence in gold mining that began in the mid-1980s had brought improved roads to mountain range after mountain range. New mining roads not on my maps crossed the old roads at unlikely angles. Backcountry faith—"This dirt track feels right and will go where I think it will"—no longer sufficed. Lonely two-tracks now were graded, graveled, and sometimes even gated.[4]

The boom already has peaked. The "world's largest mining machine" now clanks and blinks not out on some lonely range but in the lobby of the Silver Legacy Hotel in Reno. No sustainability here.

What will happen next? Can the Great Basin fill in—in the way so much of the West is filling in? In some places, yes. Subdivisions may yet reach continuously from Elko to Wells. In other places, surely not. Most of Nevada remains a place where it's prudent to gas up at every town, lest you run dry a few miles short of Gerlach or Jarbidge or Warm Springs. This is a land with limited water, limited resources, and limited amounts of what those attuned to the greens of Ireland, Bavaria, and Kentucky define as beauty. Such starkness is the salvation of the Great Basin as open space.

This is also, of course, its misfortune. Too many people see the Great Basin as a dumping ground, a place for nuclear waste repositories, bombing ranges, and missile test ranges (and, at Groom Lake, military uses so secret we aren't supposed to know the base even exists). After all, the politicians innocently assure us, there's nothing out there but empty, barren, useless, godforsaken desert.

The most easily perceived layers are harsher than the inner ones. Peel the outer skin, and surprises lurk beneath first impressions. The landscape reveals itself. The Great Basin reminds us to take nothing for granted.

Beginning in the summer of 1994, my six-year-old daughter, Dory, joined me on many of my trips westward from our home in Salt Lake City. Each time we let go of the civilized rim of the Great Basin and risked the plunge into its great spaces, we found ourselves engaged with the remoteness of the place. The approach was always a shock—the crossing of the Great Salt Lake Desert, its salt pan protecting the central Nevada mountains like a barrier reef. Mirages and glare hovered over the hard white crystalline surface, an unequivocal sign that we were entering new territory.

We reveled in the scent of sagebrush, pungent after a summer thunderstorm in Monitor Valley. We wandered in search of abandoned ranches and old mines; we camped alone at the end of the unmarked ruts that lead into Pete Hanson Canyon in the Roberts Mountains. We drove back roads for twenty-four hours without meeting another vehicle.

At the end of that twenty-four hours, we crossed Interstate 80 near Elko on our way from nowhere to nowhere, from the ghost towns of the Cortez Mountains north toward Tuscarora. We happened on the Carlin interchange when shifts changed at the Goldenstrike Mine. We waited for a gap in the stream of mud-spattered pickups headed back to Elko, then crossed the pavement quickly, turning off onto our next dirt road, and, within a half-hour, were lost again in a confusion of gated ranch tracks.

The congestion of the mine traffic seemed like a dream. It's so easy to become confused here. I love the fact that my daughter will take such experiences for granted, a matter-of-fact part of her childhood. Her younger brother, Jacob, soon grew eager to join her. At three, with a wistful look, he asked, "Dad, when I'm four, will I be old enough to go to Nevada?" Now six, he, too, has let go of the rim and explored with me into the Great Basin.

The paradoxes of this place traveled with us everywhere. Space and silence and a spare landscape left no doubt that we had entered the realm dismissed by the world. We also found ourselves in a place of rich complexity, with animal companions wherever we went.

Wild horses grazed through our campsite in the ghost town of Hamilton, high in a basin in the White Pine Range. When we came to rest in a small canyon above the Black Rock Desert, a desert horned lizard clambered away from our truck through contorted branches of sagebrush—the leaves redolent from bruising by our tires. A nesting pair of long-eared owls perched in an isolated aspen grove in the Hot Creek Valley. A buck mule deer in Denay Valley suddenly bounded away from his doe and fawn, arcing against golden grass.

The buck brought to life the huge, still valley. Tracing a line of bound and rhythm across the valley, springing upward and then jolting back to earth, planting his hooves in Great Basin alkali over and over, finally he ran out of sight while his family remained still, farther and farther behind. The sound of his hooves meeting earth came to us with a *clumppp*, softer and softer, until the buck was too far across the valley for us to hear.

We were left with silence, the silence that so many writers settle on as the defining descriptor of this place.

I'm not sure my children notice this silence. They focus on whatever falls close at hand. But I savor the silence that fills the basins, a precious quiet in a noisy world. I listen next for what fills the silence. The sounds of coyote, kestrel, cicada, and the calls of raucous bands of pinyon jays. Aspen leaves, spears of wild rye, brushes of juniper needles, and sprays of Indian rice grass—all speaking in the wind.

The poet Gary Snyder speaks of a "ghost wilderness"[5] that hovers around the edges of such landscapes. All the missing native bunchgrasses, all the legions of exterminated predators and herds of native grazers exist in our dreams, on the wind, as a background chorus. These ghosts, too, hum in the Great Basin silence.

Even emptiness and wildness are deceiving here. The Great Basin feels undeveloped, certainly, but everywhere we go, Paiute and Washoe and Shoshone hunters and seed gatherers, geologists, miners, cattlemen, and BLM range managers have been there before us. Introduced species of plants, livestock, grazing, range manipulation, and water development projects all have transformed this land—"shattered" the native ecosystems, in ecologist James Young's words.[6] This is a dynamic landscape, adapting constantly to changing climate, changing land use patterns, a landscape managed to produce revenue—a wilderness, with cows.

This "barren" desert isn't barren at all. An ecologist working here never uses the word. Neither would a sage grouse or a Great Basin spadefoot toad.

My children and I like to look for treasures. We sit on ledges and fill empty film canisters with quartz crystals eroding from Crystal Peak in the Wah Wah Range. We crack open rhyolite west of Ely and find garnets the color of old blood growing in miniature caverns in the stone. Ordovician brachiopods (the world's best) fall into our hands when we rap at the slate peeling away from Fossil Mountain in the Confusion Range. The Pony Express Road runs across Utah's West Desert through valleys that feel nearly as isolated as they did 150 years ago. Along this road, we find geodes between the shrubs.

We turn things over. The black desert varnish of the wind-faceted outer surface of rocks contrasts with the alkali-white base half-buried in the desert pavement. Scorpions, beetles, and rattlesnakes sheltering under rusted pieces of sheet metal around old miners' shacks race for shade when exposed.

These modest events play out on a huge expanse with little distracting detail, an enclosed arena—amphitheater of the continent. The Great Basin is a theater, and its largest playa, the Black Rock Desert, the ultimate stage.[7] When humans leave the wings, letting go of safe moorings, and walk onto this platform, every contact with the land has dramatic presence. On the Colorado Plateau, when travelers journey into the canyons, they enter the earth. In the Rocky Mountains or Sierra Nevada, people are dwarfed or enclosed. Here, in the Great Basin, each of us stands above basin floors and bald mountains, tall among the stands of saltbush or greasewood, piercing space and time, creating a scene, a drama.

One of my favorite quotes comes from Mary Austin, whose desert soul was largely shaped by the Great Basin, her *Land of Little Rain*. In 1920 she articulated what happens when a person lets go of the rim, steps into this natural stage. In that moment, what matters is neither the land alone nor a totally inward epiphany, but "a third thing . . . the sum of what passed between me and the Land which has not, perhaps never could, come into being with anyone else."[8] What matters is *relationship*, and the stark stage of the Great Basin highlights relationship.

The Great Basin leaves you alone to think about these relationships. Few other visitors intersect your path. Dory, at nine, summed it up this way. "In southern Utah, when we meet anyone in the canyons, they are our friends. In Nevada, the people we meet live there." True, we don't know every hiker in the canyons of the Colorado Plateau, but most of them are the same urban recreationists that we are, with a copy of *Desert Solitaire*[9] in their daypacks. They are familiar.

In the Great Basin, the local ranchers raise a finger from the steering wheel as they clatter by us on back roads. They hop in their pickups and drive over to investigate when I stop to photograph hot springs or haystacks on their land. They expect to be alone out here, and they keep track of new people.

On my most recent trip across the Great Basin with my daughter, we strung together a day of typically disorienting and delightfully dissonant events. We visited the Donner campsites on the west face of the Sierra Nevada, thinking about the emigrant families trapped for that long, lonely winter. We drove down to Palomino Valley, just north of Reno, watching the corralled herds of mustangs gathered from the BLM ranges for adoption, looking into their eyes until sunset, their wildness a hard fist barely contained by the tall fences. We ate a late dinner in the barrage of lights and tinkling gambling machines in the Nugget in Sparks, and then we drove out into the desert, headed for Pyramid Lake.

Although I had not been to the lake for ten years, I remembered a dirt track on the east side of this remnant of the great Pleistocene Lake Lahontan. The road, virtually untraveled, led eight or ten miles along the shore to the namesake tufa pyramid itself. With Dory sleeping in the seat next to me, and the stunning three-days-past-full moon above the eroded silhouette of the Truckee Range, I decided to drive us to the Pyramid to camp.

When I turned off pavement toward midnight, signs loomed in the headlights—signs I didn't remember, demanding that we have permits from the Pyramid Lake Paiute Tribe to be here. These signs disturbed the familiar Great Basin public-land mood of freedom. I felt like a trespasser. Since the shoreline lay within an Indian reservation, I *was*, but reservations in the West usually share an emptiness with surrounding BLM land. Tribes don't usually discourage backcountry camping. Though I rationalized that we could check in tomorrow in Nixon, after the fact, on this night, to my surprise, I felt tense. The tufa ridges rising up in my headlights spooked me.

I am sure much of my reaction had to do with where we had spent the previous week. We were returning from California, where the density of people and difficulty in finding a roadside campsite had made me a little desperate. At one of those California campsites, in national forest at the edge of gold country, we heard gunfire too near our camp for most of the night.

Was my new timidity simply the increase in responsibility that came with fatherhood? Generalized tension after the time in too-crowded California? A lack of adventurousness associated with (God forbid) aging? I wasn't sure.

I approached the Pyramid cautiously, hoping to avoid driving into someone else's campsite so late. I found that I could see farther by turning off my headlights and allowing the moon to illuminate the shoreline. Blue-black light showed the Pyramid rising along the lake, the ancient terraces banked around it, lightly vegetated with a few prickly balls of greasewood and a scatter of cheatgrass. I picked a level spot in the cauliform mounds of tufa surrounding the Pyramid, transferred Dory, still asleep, to the camper on the back of our truck, and took a stroll in the moonlight. The hummocks of tufa—crystallized from the lake's salty waters and exposed as it retreats—felt like the perfect place for rattlesnakes to coil, a pockmarked maze of eroded alcoves and niches. I didn't go far.

I had let go of the Great Basin rim, but I was out of practice. I needed to swim laps, drive the long reaches of the back roads, camp for a succession of nights. Great Basin solitude was overwhelming me. I felt timid and stiff and dismayed.

When I returned to the camper, another car came along the road toward us, driving slowly, shining a spotlight in circles. It must have been a tribal policeman on night patrol, though such attentiveness to the backcountry after midnight was certainly out of character with my past experiences here. The vehicle passed where we had turned off onto this spur, almost as if tracking us. The spotlight shone our way. I stayed in the camper, wording my response to the officer once he pulled up next to us. But there was no closer approach.

The patrol car swung down to the shore, shining the floodlight at the Pyramid, then drove over the hill to the north, returned, and drove away.

I tried to regain my comfort with the middle of nowhere. I set up the spotting scope and looked at the moon. Impact craters with star-shaped fractures led out over major portions of the sphere. Where the shadow of the earth lay across the moon, the crater rims stood out in extraordinary relief. Just below, I counted five moons next to Jupiter, one to the right, four to the left, one so close I had to squint to separate it from the planet, one far out and fragile, all strung in a gentle curve. I had never before seen so many of the planet's tiny companions with my not-very-powerful scope.

Excitement overwhelmed my discomfiture. I wanted to wake Dory and have her look through the scope, but I knew she wouldn't rouse enough to appreciate the magic.

The clarity of vision, the exposure, the sense of immeasurable distance back to the safe rim of civilization stirred me that night. Great Basin paradoxes were on the prowl: the opposing sensations of protection and threat created by the space of the place, the balance of tenseness and relaxation, watchfulness and exhilaration.

These are emotions that Great Basin people feel. *In The Year of Decision: 1846*, Bernard DeVoto imagined the shock that hit the overlanders of the 1840s when they encountered the Desert West: "this was an aggressive wilderness, its ferocity came out to meet you and the conditions of survival required a whole new technique."[10]

Only these new techniques can create Wallace Stegner's dreams for the West of a "society to match its scenery."[11] This is the crux of living here—an admission that the challenges of the land require creativity, cooperation, and communication. We need to admit these truths together—all the cultures of the Great Basin and the Desert West. Without understanding the paradox, without connection to the place and to each other, our lives are unmoored, our stories are rootless. We cling to misunderstandings, alternately romanticizing or fearful of the desert, dismissing the Great Basin as an empty wasteland.

We must remember that this land is not what it seems. Every trip out beyond the rim of civilization reminds us of this fact.

Dory and I camped one night in Joshua tree forest in Delamar Valley outside of Caliente, a place that felt as forgotten as any other huge basin stretching away from the paved "loneliest roads." Surely, this was a place for real solitude.

In the sky above us, bombers boomed through, low and loud. Fighter jets played war games in the night sky, practicing dogfights between the constellations. Dory was afraid to go to sleep—and we were camped in the middle of nowhere. Later I learned that this valley not only adjoins a military testing range but also is a premier place for UFO sightings.

Surprises always await us out here. Change happens constantly in this "changeless" desert. Great Basin silence fills with the din of life and land if we listen closely.

It's worth the risk. Let go of the rim.

NOTES

[1] From Stegner's "Walter Clark's Frontier" in *Where the Bluebird Sings to the Lemonade Springs* (Penguin Books, 1993), p. 174.

[2] *The Sagebrush Ocean: A Natural History of the Great Basin* by Stephen Trimble (University of Nevada Press, 1989).

[3] *Earthtones: A Nevada Album*, essays by Ann Ronald; photographs by Stephen Trimble (University of Nevada Press, 1989).

[4] See *High Country News*, October 4, 1993, pp. 8–15.

[5] *The Practice of the Wild* by Gary Snyder (North Point Press, 1990, p. 15.

[6] Jim Young, the preeminent ecologist of the sagebrush range, uses this phrase in many papers, see, for instance, *Cattle in the Cold Desert* by James A. Young and B. Abbott Sparks. (Utah State University Press, 1985).

[7] Barry Lopez described the Black Rock Desert as a stage in a television series on *The American Wilderness* in the 1980s.

[8] From a 1920 letter Mary Austin wrote to her guide and confidant, Professor Daniel Tremblay MacDougal, as she prepared to explore the Sonoran Desert. The letter is archived in Special Collections, University of Arizona Library, and quoted in Larr Evers' introduction to Austin's *The Land of Journey's Ending* (University of Arizona Press, 1983 reprint. Originally published, 1924).

[9] *Desert Solitaire* by Edward Abbey (Simon and Schuster, 1968) has become the guide to understanding the soul of the desert for two generations of backcountry devotees.

[10] *The Year of Decision: 1846* by Bernard DeVoto (Houghton Mifflin, 1942), p. 60.

[11] From *The Sound of Mountain Water* (E.P. Dutton, 1980), p. 38.

Chapter 16

THE GRAND EXPERIMENT
Raising Livestock in the Great Basin

James A. Young and Fay Allen

The Great Basin environment, as reported by early 19th-century travelers, was perceived as a place of repugnance and dread. The traveler's fear and rejection of these temperate arid regions—also termed cold desert landscapes[1]—is not hard to understand. The setting—dazzling salt flats surrounded by alluvial fans sparsely clothed by uniformly silver-gray shrubs—was foreign to them. It was an environment that did not obviously suit their agricultural backgrounds or goals.

The emigrant travelers reached the northern Great Basin in the fall season. Their transcontinental trip was timed by the occurrence of new grass on the Great Plains, which provided necessary forage for their draft animals. After crossing one of the world's great grasslands at the height of its growing season, they reached the Rocky Mountains with the uplands in the height of late summer splendor. But then, the weary travelers descended into the Great Basin in the early fall, after the basin valley vegetation had endured the long summer drought. Exhausted by continuous miles of travel across plains and mountains, the emigrant travelers and their draft animals were desperate to cross the Great Basin as fast as possible. They feared its inhospitable environment, as well as the prospect that early snowfall might close the Sierra-Cascade mountain barrier to the west.

Crossing the Great Basin gives the impression that the landscape is one mountain range after another. The mountain ranges are primarily north-south oriented, but often arranged in echelon, which allowed the 19th-century traveler to pass among and not over the mountains. The line of least resistance across the Great Basin avoided the mountains by plowing through the dust and salt crusts of the basin floors. Until the close of the Pleistocene, these basin trails had been under hundreds of feet of water from the Great Basin pluvial lakes.[2] As a result, the basin floor environments were sparsely vegetated, with the plants that existed striving for life in some of the continent's harshest growing conditions. In fact, the plants were subjected to a twin burden: accumulated salts from the evaporated lakes and atmospheric drought.

Not surprisingly, the Great Basin's sagebrush (*Artemisia*) and saltbush (*Atriplex*) shrub steppes were among the last North American environments where large numbers of domestic herbivores were introduced. The 19th-century emigrants who settled the Great Basin, although coming mostly recruited from northern European agrarian societies, had little experience in the open ranging of livestock in semiarid to arid environments and limited experience in temperate deserts.[3] Consequently, the Great Basin pioneers were the ultimate agricultural risk takers. They were engaged in a grand experiment to see if the range livestock industry was sustainable in the Great Basin. To further understand and assess this experiment, the following discussion examines the central and western Great Basin range livestock industry, which developed in the mid- to late 19th century.

TRANSPORTING CATTLE TO MARKET

Without a reliable transportation and marketing system, the Great Basin could never have supported a livestock industry. As it was, the Great Basin environment required a different system for transporting livestock to market than was used in other places. In the north-south expanse of the Great Plains, steers could be gathered in southern Texas and driven to Kansas for marketing. The animals would arrive in better condition than when they left Texas, provided they were allowed to graze on the grasslands they traversed. In contrast, the Great Basin is surrounded by deserts and mountains, which made driving animals to market impractical.[4] But once the Central Pacific Railroad was completed across Nevada in the late 1860s, it was possible to market cattle by rail in larger, distant markets. As a result, the livestock industry underwent a growth boom.

NOMADS IN THE DESERT

Because most of the Great Basin's cold desert landscape is unsuitable for yearlong large herbivore livestock production, the early livestock owners adopted a seasonal migratory pattern of livestock husbandry. Most cattle ranches maintained a permanent headquarters. The owner (or manager) and family did not move seasonally; rather, the cowboys and cattle were required to move. Cattle were left to fend for themselves, except for seasonal visits by branding or roundup crews working from mobile chuck wagons. The cattle would spend winter on the deserts, spring and fall in the foothills, and summer in the higher mountains. While the seasonal ranges would ideally be located within sight of each other, the reality was that the annual cycle often covered hundreds of miles.

With limited stock water and forage available, the Great Basin environment places extreme restraints on the number of large herbivores that can be supported. In contrast to humid environments, Great Basin grasses dry and cure standing in place, with adequate dietary nutrients for ruminants. The exception is digestible protein. The browse, mainly the twigs and persistent leaves of certain preferred shrubs, provides a high protein supplement to rations of sun-cured grass. Throughout most of the Great Basin, the growing season for herbaceous vegetation is a relatively short period, extending from April through June. The period can be limited by winter cold and summer drought. Although the growing season extends later in the higher elevations, snow cover can limit use of these areas. Bunchgrass ranges, found on the alluvial fans skirting mountain bases, can be grazed during the winter, but the grass only grows once a year on such sites. If the foothill forage is grazed in the spring, then it is not available until after the next period of growth. The lower basins remain largely snow-free during most winters, but available surface water is very limited. A northern Carson Desert study estimated that without artificial water development only 10 percent of the landscape is usable by large herbivores as winter range.[5]

Summer range is also often a limiting factor. Many livestock summer on mountain ranges and those that reach above 3000 meters have extensive areas of summer range. But the Great Basin uplands are limited in scope, and often further limited by the presence of poisonous tall larkspur (*Delphinium*). While blooming larkspur can be truly breathtaking, it is so toxic to cattle that grazing is not practical.

On winter ranges, the limiting factor is stock water. In wet winters, rain or snowmelt accumulates in small playas that occur in depressions on the basin floors. Cattle will use these shallow, dung-fouled pools until the last mouthful of water is sucked from a muddy track. With these temporary pools, utilizable winter range can be greatly extended. In cold, dry winters, however, the amount of utilizable range lessens. During the late 19th century, cattle sometimes starved on winter ranges when they were within sight of forage that was too far from water. With the growth of the range sheep industry during the late 19th century, water restrictions on winter ranges changed. Sheep could fulfill their daily requirements for moisture by licking snow that occurred on the basin floors. This simplistic animal behavior dramatically altered the Great Basin sheep industry.

REACTION OF VEGETATION TO GRAZING

Except for a few natural meadows, most Great Basin plant communities are shrub dominated. Above the salt deserts the landscapes are characterized by woody sagebrush species with silver gray foliage. Early Great Basin livestock producers absorbed a bitter lesson when they learned that cattle would not eat the dominant sagebrush. If forced to eat sagebrush by starvation, cattle would die. Although sagebrush leaves and twigs are potentially very nutritious, the foliage contains volatile chemicals that cattle instinctively avoid. If consumed, these chemicals inhibit microorganism actions that digest forage into absorbable nutrients in the rumen.[6]

Big sagebrush is a long-lived woody perennial, with the seed production characteristics of an annual. Whether 2 or 200 years old, sagebrush can produce abundant seed. Germination occurs in very early spring. Sagebrush flowers at the end of the summer drought and disperses its seeds in the late fall. Although seedling mortality may be high, their abundance ensures some establishment. Most native herbivores, including jackrabbits with voracious appetites, do not graze sagebrush seedlings.[7] The net result of livestock grazing, therefore, has been an increase in sagebrush density.

This cattle-sagebrush relationship has greatly influenced the Great Basin environment. Cattle prefer the native perennial grasses, and do not like the dominant shrubs. Most native perennial grasses are bunchgrasses (cespitose growth form), which means they reproduce from seeds and not vegetatively. Perennial grasses must annually renew their flowering stalks from the soil surface in order to reproduce. These perennial grasses grow and prepare to flower during the spring/early summer period. However, if the perennial grasses are heavily grazed every spring, year after year, they are not able to rebuild carbohydrates and reproduce, and in time will disappear.[8]

WINTERFAT

When their cattle refused to eat the dominant upland shrubs, the early Great Basin cattlemen were astounded to find that they relished a low-growing shrub found on winter ranges—winterfat (long known as *Eurotia*, with a name change to *Ceratoides* and more recently to *Krascheninnikovia lanata*). It occurs in large, nearly monospecific patches on the lake plains of the basins. If any one plant can be credited with making the 19th-century cattle industry possible in the Great Basin environment, it would be winterfat.

MAKING HAY

Great Basin ranchers initially tried to open-range cattle without any conserved forage for winter. Under the prevailing pristine conditions, there were few meadows that could be used for cutting hay. With irrigation, however, they were able to create artificial meadows and to enlarge natural ones. As a result, the Humboldt River valley and its major tributaries became livestock industry centers in northern Nevada. On rivers with beavers, the ranchers imitated their dam building; they impounded and spread spring runoff waters over the maximum area of floodplains. Gradually, this evolved into upstream diversion dams and ditches, which brought water to benches above the floodplain.

In the empty vastness of the south-central Great Basin, creeks with sufficient runoff to support meadows are rare. Consequently, the distance between ranches is extreme. The first settlers in a valley claimed the choice locations for ranch headquarters. Latecomers had to gamble that the annual runoff would be sufficient to produce enough hay so livestock could survive hard winters. At the same

time, these ranchers realized that they would never be able to expand hay production areas beyond the irregularly shaped, often stony fields that flip-flopped
from side to side along the creeks that meandered between pressing canyon walls.
Efforts to construct higher ditches down the canyon walls to irrigate a few more
acres were not always successful. Flooding was often caused by excessive grazing
that denuded the headwaters of steep watersheds used to irrigate meadows. Under
such conditions, excessive spring runoff could cause extensive damage, as could
high intensity summer thunderstorms centered on a particular watershed.

Hay meadows are still much too valuable to abandon. Therefore, when you
struggle up a rutted, rocky canyon road and find the stone walls of an abandoned
cabin beside a rabbitbrush (*Chrysothamnus*) infested field, it probably indicates an
early rancher's great expectations were not fulfilled because of insufficient runoff.

THE WINTER OF 1889 AND 1890

For Great Basin ranchers, the hard winter of 1889–90 proved that meadows were
absolutely essential for livestock raising. In the Great Basin, winters are greatly
variable. For northern Nevada, 1888–89 was the all-time driest season. The wettest
winter was the next season of 1889–90. Several earlier winters had caused severe
winter kills of cattle. With each subsequent hard winter, the effects grew more
severe. As the number of animals increased, excessive grazing decreased the quan-
tity and quality of forage.

On the northern Great Plains, the severe winter of 1887 decimated open-
range livestock east of the Rocky Mountains. It was such a colossal tragedy that it
was well publicized in the Great Basin. Certainly, John Sparks, the largest cattle
rancher in the intermountain area, who also maintained a ranching interest in
Wyoming, had personal experience with the dangers of overstocked ranges and
severe winters.

The winter of 1889–90 was severe in virtually all areas west of the Rocky
Mountains. Throughout the intermountain area, from the Columbia Plateau to
the Great Basin, the livestock industry, transportation systems, and town and city
dwellers suffered from prolonged cold and extreme snowfall. John Sparks, the
largest cattle rancher in the intermountain area, maintained a ranching interest
in Wyoming, where he had personally experienced the dangers inherent with
overstocked ranges and severe winters. Folk stories describe the winter. In the
spring of 1890, it was said, a person could walk for 100 miles along the Mary's
River in Elko County, Nevada, by stepping from one dead cow to another.
However, because Mary's River is much shorter than 100 miles, the story may
have referred to Salmon Falls Creek and its tributaries, which was the range used
by John Sparks.

Following this tragic winter, the Great Basin ranchers realized that a ton of hay was needed to feed each brood cow through the winter. Actually, the amount of hay varies from a half-ton on the edge of the southern deserts to one and one half tons in higher mountain basins. The average production of native Nevada hay meadows is not quite a ton per acre annually. This means that ranches running 2,000 to 4,000 cows, which was not uncommon in Elko County, required immense irrigated acreages and large seasonal crews for hay production.[9]

Such large-scale hay production requirements induced a land rush for irrigatable acres, and state lands were the target. After Nevada returned its original school sections to the federal government, a generous Congress gave the state 2 million acres of public land to sell. Nevada sold this land in forty-acre parcels, principally to ranchers, who could arrange these state lands in stairstep parcels roughly following irrigatable land along streams. Sold cheaply and on credit, most of the land went to large existing ranches. As a result, the little rancher either never existed in Nevada or he was quickly absorbed by larger ranches in most areas. Although some small ranches persisted, there are few compared with neighboring states. The great distances between natural meadows where ranch headquarters could be located, the finite amount of water available for irrigation, and the state land policies all favored a few large ranches.

HOT SPRINGS RANCH

The geology of the Great Basin's fault-block mountains accounts for numerous geothermal springs. A sufficiently large spring can provide an island of mesophytic vegetation in the desert. If the island is large enough or if it can be enlarged by an outflow water diversion, then a small ranch can be supported by the resulting wetlands.

The Walti Hot Springs in central Nevada is an example of such a ranch. It is, however, a "wrong side of the mountain" ranch. In the winter it takes half the day to get out of the shadow of the towering Simpson Park Mountains to the east; in the summer, the sun takes forever to set across the salt flat to the west. Walti Hot Springs is located in Grass Valley. It was first described by Capt. James H. Simpson, who visited the area in 1859 to locate a wagon road from Camp Floyd, Utah, to Genoa, Nevada. He reported grass growing up to the saddle stirrup in the southern end of the valley, which accounts for the valley's name. The grass was undoubtedly basin wild rye (*Leymus cinereus*), which still forms extensive stands in the valley.[10]

The Walti family settled around the hot springs. During winter the valley is surrounded by snow-covered peaks. In summer, the mountains are often not visible, due to aerial deposition of salt and silt eroded from the extensive playas to the west. The Waltis built with native rock because timber was scarce. They thatched juniper rafters with basin wild rye, and then covered them with six inches of dirt. Although there was plenty of hot water, it was heavily loaded with dissolved minerals, like magnesium sulfate, and had the consistency of runny egg whites.

The Walti ranch hay derrick was not very high, because little hay was produced. In June, long-billed curlews (*Numenius americanus*) frequent the saline/alkaline hay meadows below the springs, coming to nest on the relict wetlands. During the Ice Age, the valley supported pluvial Lake Gilbert and was surrounded by extensive riparian areas. The Holocene climate, however, has shrunk the Grass Valley wetlands to tiny mesophytic areas in an ocean of aridity. As a result, the Waltis and their livestock were just as dependent on these wetlands as the long-billed curlew.

STABILITY

The giant ranching empires of the western Great Basin, some of which were founded by John Sparks, have changed over time. The remaining large ranches are constrained by the environment. Some ranches have persisted in the same family for generations. In oral history interviews with the fourth-generation operators of the T Quarter Circle ranch near Winnemucca, Nevada, family members cite several factors to explain their long tenure on the range: (1) The property has always been passed on to a family member; (2) the family never borrowed money or took out a mortgage on the base property; and (3) the family has achieved sustainability by aggressively instituting changes in the management of their desert livestock operation. These changes have been based on a scientific understanding of the complex ecosystems where they raise cattle and a willingness to apply this science to management problems.[11]

ASSESSING THE GRAND EXPERIMENT

Now that livestock production has existed in the Great Basin for almost one and a half centuries, what are the results of the grand experiment? It is still too early to determine if true sustainability has been achieved. The players and practices in this range livestock industry drama keep changing. Livestock management systems, animal types and genetics, and attitudes toward natural resources have all undergone profound changes; climatic change is also a reality and must be accommodated. With water developments, native and domestic animals are now grazing millions of acres that previously would not support large herbivores. With the conversion of native perennial grasses to alien annual grasses, such as cheatgrass (*Bromus tectorum*), expansive and rapidly spreading wildfires are now more frequent. In short, grazing has produced more ecological changes in the Great Basin environment than have occurred in the previous millennium, and the ranchers are thus far proving adaptable to these changes.

NOTES

[1] Grayson, D. K. 1993. *The Deserts Past.* Smithsonian Institution Press, Washington, D.C.

[2] Houghton, S. G. 1976. *A Trace of Desert Water.* The Arthur H. Clark Co., Glendale, Calif.

[3] Young, J. A. and A. B. Sparks. 1985. *Cattle in the Cold Desert.* Utah State University Press, Logan, Ut.

[4] Young, J. A. and A. B. Sparks. 1985. *Cattle in the Cold Desert.* Utah State University Press, Logan, Ut.

[5] Young, J. A. 1994. "Changes in Plant Communities in the Great Basin Induced by Domestic Livestock Grazing," pp. 113–23. In K. T. Harper, L. St. Clair, K. H. Thorne, and W. M. Hess, eds. *Natural History of the Colorado Plateau and Great Basin.* University Press of Colorado, Niwot, Co.

[6] Nagy, J. G., H. W. Steinhoff, and G. M. Ward. 1964. "Effects of Essential Oils of Sagebrush on Deer Rumen Microbial Function." *Journal of Wildlife Management* 28:788–90.

[7] McAdoo, J. K. and J. A. Young. 1980. "Jackrabbits." *Rangelands* 2:135–38.

[8] Stewart, George. 1936. "History of Range Use." in *The Western Range.* Senate Document No. 199, 74th Congress, 2nd Session, Government Printing Office, Washington, D.C.

[9] McCormick, John, J. A. Young, and Wayne Burkhart. 1979. "Hay Making." *Rangelands* 1:203–6.

[10] Lesperance, A. L., J. A. Young, R. E. Eckert, Jr., and R. A. Evans. 1978. "Great Basin Wildrye." *Rangeman's Journal* 5:125–27.

[11] Tipton, F. H. 1994. "Cheatgrass, Livestock and Rangeland," pp. 414–16. In S. B. Monsen and S. T. Kitchen, eds. *Process Ecology and Management of Annual Rangelands.* General Technical Bulletin 313, U.S. Department of Agriculture, Forest Service, Ogden, Ut.

PART VII

The NATIVE HOME OF HOPE

STEPPING BACK TO THE FUTURE

The volume concludes with two poignant essays by authors William Kittredge and Terry Tempest Williams. Although ostensibly built around travel in southern France, Bill Kittredge's ruminations on prehistoric cave paintings transcend the immediate locale and address fundamental questions of importance to the American West of today. Inquiring into the continuity of human time, the creative influence of location on human understanding, and the powerful instincts attached to cultural conventions, Kittredge reminds us that past times are never as simple or pure as they may seem. Any effort to reclaim or resurrect a nostalgic past, he suggests, cannot ignore the hard lessons of history—a message that resonates with him as a sometimes nostalgic westerner. With these lessons firmly in mind, Kittredge may not object to using well-varnished history to imagine a western society of the future.

By contrast, Terry Tempest Williams's essay is firmly planted in the contemporary West, illustrating the powerful impact that federal endangered species legislation is having on the western landscape and those who inhabit it. Just as communities are split over ecological preservation versus development issues, families too are divided by deeply held beliefs and experiences. Did the government go too far when it halted construction in St. George, Utah, to protect desert tortoise habitat? That question is the subject of lively discussion at the traditional family Christmas gathering. If the gene pool is important to the human species, is it not also important to other species? Another provocative question that hangs over the narrative, sharpened by the government's announcement of a habitat conservation plan that will result in the "take" of over a thousand tortoises in order for real estate development to proceed. Is this compromise between species preservation and community growth satisfactory or just inevitable? Perhaps the fact that the tortoise is being accorded protected space amid rampant urban growth in the landlocked West signifies an emerging—and important—commitment to an evolutionary perspective.

If the West is indeed prepared to take such a long view, then a well-understood past may serve as prologue for an even more hopeful future.

Chapter 17

INSIDE THE EARTH

William Kittredge

The New Year's Day party in Missoula was more a celebration of endurance than a pure drift into pleasure. On the 5th of January 1992, we were airborne in the winter light, flying toward Paris, going to what I hoped would be a wake-up call. Like a boy of my time I most enjoyed imagining I was going to be standing at a bar where Hemingway stood, gazing from a great clean window into what James Joyce had called the lemon-colored light of Paris, bare forearms against the cool zinc, sipping gin. The part about gin came true sort of often.

Paris, after a few hours' meandering along the famous narrow streets on the Left Bank, evolved from exotic and strange into a playpen. We sat in the Brasserie Lipp and smoked while we ate very expensive oysters; I had another little cup of heavily sweetened espresso every twenty minutes; Gertrude Stein and Alice B. Toklas had lived just down the street from our hotel by the Luxemburg Gardens; I eyed the work of Vincent van Gogh in the Mussee d'Orsay as though it had been done by a neighbor in craziness; I went to bed drunk, and woke up wired.

From Paris we drove south to Venice and Florence, and then to Spain, checking out the cultural extravaganza as we went—the old bullfight ring in Ronda and the elegant court paintings of Velazquez and terrifying visions by Goya in the Prado, and the streets of Hemingway's Pamplona, casinos on the gaming coast of the French Atlantic.

Then, heading back to Paris and our flight back to Montana, we drove through ordered commercial forestlands to Les Ezyies on Vezere River in south-central France. Twenty thousand years ago bands of human beings lived in semi-permanent villages on sheltered ledges eroded deep into the limestone cliffs that look out over the undulations of the narrow and often stone-sided floodplain valley along the Vezere. We intended to see what we could of those legendary prehistoric sites.

In *The Autumn of the Middle Ages*, Johan Huizinga says, "Primitiveness of thought reveals itself in its weak ability to perceive the boundaries between things." Which is, ironically, how contemporary physics reveals itself. Huizinga also says, of reality as understood by animist cultures: "Thought attempts to find the connection between things, not by tracing the hidden turns of their casual ties, but rather by jumping over those casual connections. The connection is not a link between cause and effect but one of meaning and purpose."

In *The Savage Mind*, Claude Levi-Strauss says savage thought is as rigorous and systematic as scientific thought (if less factually informed). But scientists are schooled to accept their inability to know, and to say, "I don't get it." So-called savage thinkers push on, building structures of categorization and significance from implied, intuited, and magical connections between dreams and cosmologies and ideas of destiny and fate—and variously witnessed manifestations of energy, exploding volcanos and birds flying by. People in animist cultures, we think, from inside our mechanistic version of actuality, believe in magic.

Breaks in the earth are sometimes thought of as the source of all life. We've seen it, the metaphor—bean sprouts coming up, cracking the crust.

Many societies imagine themselves as having come forth from a break in the earth—a place of emergence. The Hopi think of their blue-water spring in the canyon of the Little Colorado, and the Zuni think of their emergence place as a small waterfall on the north side of the Grand Canyon. According to legend these are the places where their ancestors came out on the earth into sunlight—like seeds, growing and withering through seasons.

In our off-season hotel in Les Ezyies, Annick and I ate badly and slept worse. But in the morning, cool sunlight cut the mist as we wandered up to the little Museum of Prehistory tucked under a great overhanging limestone cliff in the center of town. The exhibits included items I'd seen in textbooks—most vividly an enormously ancient great-breasted little stonework figurine of a woman holding a ram's horn. I assumed, despite the thick glass separating me from it, that the figurine was a copy. But then workmen came to test the alarm system, setting off a rocketing electrical claxon. I realized that the Venus figure before me was the real thing. Otherwise it would not have been guarded so expensively.

There were others much like it, except for the ram's horn. Now that I had to take them seriously, in actuality and not in photographs, I found them deeply unsettling. They were utterly other, not depictions of any beauty I had been educated to imagine—tiny feet and wide hips, enormous buttocks, flowing bellies and great breasts, tapering shoulders, tiny heads. They reminded me of my mother as she grew old, heavy, and bedridden. I saw her naked only once when she was at that stage in her life; she was incapacitated; I looked away, and called the nurse, then left the room, trying to tell myself that my mother's vastness was only human. But, like a child, I was frightened. Her body cascaded with an amplitude I had not been taught to witness or admire. I couldn't think about it; my response at that moment in the room where my mother was to die a few years later was a terrible failure of empathy that haunts me even at this writing.

A number of such figurines have turned up over a belt of territory reaching from western France to the central Russian plain between the Ural and

Carpathian Mountains. They were made during the increasing cold as the vast glaciers moved south over northern Europe and Asia between 29,000 and 20,000 years ago. It seems likely that they were the product of a single tradition.

We wonder what people made them, and why. Notions of what people have taken to be sacred seem to connect. Images of flowing-breasted women struck from river stones, leaping pregnant animals inscribed on walls in caverns—it's easy to connect water and fecundity to images of springing free. But we have no idea and make vague statements about valuing feminine opulence. Maybe that wasn't the idea at all. Maybe the people who made those figurines weren't thinking about people like my mother or about femininity at all; maybe they were just making figures that fit the shape of an ordinary stream-washed stone after the wearing down.

Later that morning, Annick and I visited the cave known as Font de Guame, guided into absolute darkness by a woman with a flashlight, along narrow galleries winding into the earth, etched and painted and repainted with the figures of animals, a line of painted bison that I imagined as heading along the walls toward the entrance and maybe out into the sunlight and down to the green and grassy riverside.

I like to think that the people who drew those figures imagined that the cave was like the inside of a human head where animals might live in the imagination, illuminated when we think of them; such people perhaps thought the animals would vanish forever if no one imagined them once in a while. Maybe they believed that the animals they drew were like thoughts.

Maybe they thought they would own the animals if they painted them, like someone's idea of a god making up the world in its billion times billion complexity. A god might think of our world as necessary, beloved and not possibly to be foregone, but a pain in the neck since it had to be continually reinvented and redefined. People do think of imagining as creating. I tend to think imagining the future is a step toward inventing it.

The most interesting animals inside the cave at Font de Guame, for Annick and I, were not the line of bison heading out along the walls toward the daylight and good grazing along the banks of the river, in the daylight, but a pair of deer, a stag and doe, and what we took to be their devotion. Two curving black antlers and a line of backbone sweeping up from the antlers were painted on the wall and the rest was incised, minimalist and sexual when seen in the right light, the black stag licking at the head of a doe on her knees.

"Kissing," Annick said. Animals in a cave, painted 25,000 years ago, kissing. We laughed but in the manner of people who are trying to avoid a topic that isn't too altogether actually funny, deep in a cavern. We were, after all, together, in a cavern, and willing to care for each other.

There are many versions of the trip to the underworld, tours through the levels of darkness. Ulysses, Aneaus, Dante—they were seeking knowledge, talking to men and women whose lives were finished, witnessing the workings of fate in the lives of the dead. What, specifically, announced itself in that cavern? A sense that the world outside (outside the cave, the head, the brain) was sufficient and therefore holy, and we were part of it. Is this what we mean by annunciation, coming to see? The notion of kissing, life as a thing to be given, kissed away. Generous ways of going to the world were important in the vision of someone so long before us.

Three years later we were back in the Dordogne. On a warm, sunny day in late February 1995, spring all at once beginning, Annick and I drove a rented Peugeot up twisting roads over the limestone ridges with views of the Vezere River as it turned in undulations through plowgrounds—landforms scaled to dimensions obviously walkable and right for hunting, with the brilliant water always nearby.

Fields were drying, farmers were getting ready to plow, and I kept wanting to feel what it had been like to live there in one of those warming periods during the vast cooling of centuries called the ice ages (which go on—scientists say we're in another warming). Imagine great herds of horned animals grazing and migrating, on the move upriver.

But my imagining, I knew, was mostly sprung from my hope to see this place as some kind of lost Edenic never-never land, and by certain quite exact resemblances to Warner Valley, where I spent my boyhood—particularly the Lombardy poplar at the edges of fields. It is probably impossible to truly value the images on the walls of the caves at Lascaux and elsewhere along the Vezere if we cannot imagine the lives of the people who made them when ice covered most of Britain and Scandinavia and all of the Alps and the Pyrenees, and central Europe was open tundra where red deer and bison and wild cattle and horses wandered.

It is a stunning conjunction: those short difficult lives, and the startlingly evocative and sophisticated paintings on the walls in those caverns. We would weep if we knew what we were weeping for—courage, or what? Ourselves. In the *Iliad*, after Patroclus was killed, the women were said to be weeping in semblance for Patroclus but in truth for themselves.

Among the many ancient habitations we visited were the rock-shelf dwellings known as La Madeleine, and, a few kilometers upstream, Roque St. Christophe. The rock-shelves themselves—high and safe, easily defended, inaccessible, with views and a sense of shelter—reminded me of the prospect from the rim above Warner Valley.

What most beguiled me along the Vezere River was a feeling of being surrounded by millennia of human presence. In 1864 five years after the *Origin of the Species*, a round of mammoth ivory was dug up at La Madeleine. On it was incised an image of a woolly mammoth, the first depiction of an extinct species ever discovered.

Across the river from the shelter Roque St. Christophe was the village of Mousetier, the site of Neanderthal discoveries (Moutsterian is the name anthropologists use to designate an era in the lives of those people). A young man there to visit the lady taking tickets—the French charge admission to most sites—hiked across the stonework bridge to Mousetier (rock shelters were often near natural stream crossings), and carried lunches back in a brown paper sack. His hike was in continuity with thousands of years of humans on paths across the grassy fields. I was hungry, and turned to thinking about going to lunch in the little restaurant on the hill above the cave at Lascaux. It was just as I remembered—perfect soup.

Around those undercut limestone cliffs above the river there existed a continuity of human time from people constructing fires against the night to a fellow like me. There is no point in dreaming of a return to that old human existence—we've never left, there was nowhere to go; its rhythms are inscribed in us and will never go away.

That sense of connection has to be part of what people mean when they speak of consecrated places. What does that mean exactly—a holy space—is it a situation where humans, without panic, at the end of what is, eyeing death from close up, can feel securely that they're where they belong in the passage of things?

That's at least part of it, a feeling derived from a sense of participation. We were surrounded by rock walls people had used to back up their hearth fires for millennia. They lived on those ledges for thousands of years, embers burning down in the night fire, families and clans drying and getting warm while snow fell through the darkness and they dreamed of spring when the tundra would flower and the great animals would return. It is a possible dream of paradise. I wonder if it was theirs.

On our second trip, in 1995, after our soup and duck and a walk in the sun, Annick and I were treated to most of an hour inside the great sealed humidity-controlling doors to the cave at Lascaux (it's no longer open to the general public).

The first surprise, once into what would have been absolute darkness had it not been for the flashlight carried by our guide, was the size of the creatures painted on the white crystalline walls, great bulls painted in red ochre.

Deep caves like Lascaux are very different from the rock shelters. There's no evidence anyone ever lived inside at Lascaux even though it's likely that first vast gleaming calcite chamber was dimly lighted from outside before the roof over the entrance collapsed. The cavern opened to the west, toward the dying light of evening.

The culture responsible for the artwork at Lascaux, even in their time, was very ancient. The recently discovered paleolithic art in the Chauvet cavern in the valley of the Ardeche River, which flows from the central highlands to the Rhone in southern France, and the paintings and engravings found in the cave beneath the sea at Cosquer on the Mediterranean coast near Marseilles (the entrance is some 120 feet under water, drowned when glaciers of the last ice melted) are seemingly of the same tradition as the art at Lascaux, yet some 20,000 years older. No one knows what those artists thought they were doing as they painted those animals. Does it diminish the quality of their work to say maybe they were only entertaining themselves, creating decorations for the dance?

A dozen years ago, in a sparsely furnished house in a town called Port Alberni in the rainforest country on Vancouver Island, Annick and I talked to a gifted native artist named Ron Hamilton, who would not allow his work to be photographed much less sold. (Judging from the prices we saw on work that was much less impressive, he could have been wealthy in short order.) We asked him why, and he said, "It's only props, for the ceremonies."

His was a notion of primal value—that much of what we make is valuable only as props for the ceremonies we enact as we try bringing order into the chronology of our adventures. It was unselfish thinking of the kind that sustained anonymous craftsmen who worked on cathedrals over generations without hope of seeing the great project finished in their lifetime. Ron Hamilton was intent on keeping to his priorities. (I hope he got rich, not by selling art but by winning some lottery.)

As is usual with enduring art, the work inside those caverns has stayed alive over 20,000 years because, however it is ceremonially stylized, it is also individual and particular. As we know, each of us is idiosyncratically struck by woven textures of light. Clusters of work, likely executed by some individual or group, in caverns and shelters nearby to Les Eyzies, around the rest of the Dordogne, in the foothills of the Pyrenees, and in caverns like Altamira on the coast of northwestern Spain, are each uniquely evocative, reflecting an intimate, personal and specific slant-wise vision.

The kissing reindeer in the narrow passages at Font de Guame seem calm and quiet, as if they might be dreaming of the green light and the meadowlands outside, when imagined alongside the restless red bulls in the crystalline rotunda at Lascaux. In *The Creative Explosion*, John E. Pfeiffer remarks that there is more motion among animals depicted at Lascaux than in all other cave sites combined. The red bulls reminded me of Mexican steers my grandfather imported to Oregon from Sonora in 1945. As we were shipping them from the Klamath Marsh, hundreds of those steers escaped into the unfenced timberland of the Cascade Mountains. Some roamed for years.

What does the restlessness of those creatures imply about the artists who worked by the light of oil lamps to create the bulls at Lascaux? Why do those animals mostly face into the earth, downslope into the cavern and the interior darkness where our underlife lives with its secrets, peeping from dreams and our choice in fantasies?

Farther in at Lascaux, beyond the massive red bulls, are reindeer, antlers in intricate detail. The relationship of images leaves viewers with a sense of force in motion and slow delicacy counterpoised. The images at Lascaux are not at all "primitive." They are examples of utter quick virtuosity. The red bulls were never retouched. Probably they have always been understood as masterpieces, no doubt executed by a master or school of masters.

The rotunda at Lascaux made me think of standing just inside the cool darkness of the vast cathedral at Chartres and gazing up to the vivid storytelling windows on a bright day. My experience with the red bulls, as with the high brilliant windows at Chartres, did not mean specifically but radiated wholeness and a sense of reassurance, reminding me as absolute art always does of interconnected glories and sorrow, and that I could make my peace here as well as anywhere.

Deeper into the cave, created in what was absolute darkness, illuminated by oil lamps and torches when they were painted, the horses and the cows seemed to be always swaybellied and loomingly pregnant. In the figure of what has been called the Falling Cow, Annick saw leaping and joyousness. In a chamber called the Nave we saw the image of a creature called the Great Black Cow, inscribed with all the fulsome elegance of anything by Picasso. To my eye it is equal to the ink on paper depiction of the Chinese horse *Night-Shining White* by Han Kan, a masterwork from about the third century before Christ (which is my attempt at saying the Great Black Cow is as fine as any work ever done).

What must have been the central ceremonial section of Lascaux is called the Apse. Small figures and signs are engraved one over another again and again in the Apse, repeatedly redrawn, perhaps winter after winter or generation after generation, as if by a teacher before a succession of classes. It's reasonable to imagine that the Apse is a place where instructing, to whatever point, in whatever language, took place. I imagine spiritual leaders inscribing those figures on the walls over and over through hundreds and maybe thousands of years.

If that's what took place. It's easy to see why the Apse was named after the alter at the east end of churches (again, I think of Chartres, and the common spiritual situation shared by the people at Lascaux and Christians so many millennia later—confrontation with absolute mysteries).

Annick and I were tourists. We didn't get to visit the most truly hidden, interior place. The quintessential image in the cave at Lascaux is in a chamber behind the Apse, over a ledge and down some eighteen rockfall feet. Here we found the image of a bison trailing entrails in what must be the agony and rage of death as it goes toward a four-fingered man with the head of a bird, who is falling rigidly backward, perhaps killed, perhaps in a trance, penis erect, having lost his spear and dropped another shaft, which is topped by the full image of a bird.

Were the people who painted at Lascaux hunters who imagined they were connected to birds? We want to think these images were central in a system of belief. Perhaps the caves were ceremonial centers where initiates were taken to frighten and impress them (bring them to heightened awareness) while they were imprinted with a sense of the importance of their duties and obligations to their people, the most important of which may have been remembering the holy narratives that had to be repeated and repeated if ensuing generations were to know who they were and why (things learned during times of stress often seem to be irrevocably imprinted in our memories).

Before the invention of writing, people could not ensure that communal stories would survive except by imprinting them in the minds of the rising generation—all they knew, when to fish and where, how to bless the hunt, genealogies of communal heroism and perhaps reasons for the tribal connection to birds. There was nowhere else but in people's minds for knowledge to be recorded—which meant it had to be continually rerecorded. These were not simple people. So much was known. Remembering was the endless task.

Homeric texts, for instance, derived from an oral tradition, are thick with lists, repetitions, verbal formula, and aids to memory like stock epithets and a driving repetitive meter. Tellers re-created the stories from a stockpile of verbal icons.

David Abram, in *The Spell of the Sensuous*, suggests that the storytellers were like rap singers, riffing on lines and themes, combining and recombining a series of inherited memory-aiding clichés, reinventing the story as they spoke. Lists and repetitive forms, in poems of remembering and cultural celebration, can be acts of reverence, as in Whitman:

> I knew a man, a common farmer,
> the father of five sons,
> And in them the fathers of sons,
> and in them the fathers of sons.

Or, in cautionary poems, they can be acts of admonition, as in Sharon Olds, writing about her parents:

I want to go up to them and say Stop.
don't do it—she's the wrong woman.
he's the wrong man, you are going to do things
you cannot imagine you would ever do.
you are going to do bad things to children,
you are going to suffer in ways you never heard of.
you are going to want to die.
you are going to suffer in ways you never heard of,
you are going to want to die.[1]

Lists and repetitions can also lead us into imagining synathesia—seeing and smelling and hearing coming to us as one sense—the living world for a moment breathing its meanings into us, as in some passages of so-called nature writing, luring us into imagining ourselves contained within interconnections and flowing complexities that won't hold still for naming, as in this poem by Galway Kinnell:

> *Daybreak*
> On the tidal mud, just before sunset,
> dozens of starfishes
> were creeping. It was
> as though the mud were a sky
> and enormous, imperfect stars
> moved across it slowly
> as the actual stars across heaven.
> All at once they stopped,
> as if they had simply
> increased their receptivity
> to gravity they sank down
> into the mud; they faded down
> into it and lay still; and by the time
> pink of sunset broke across them
> they were invisible
> as the true stars at daybreak.[2]

One of the metaphors that helps me understand the world is the walkabout, as practiced by the Aboriginal people of Australia, or, more accurately, what I imagine as a walkabout, a journey through things, learning and relearning connection.

Until a few decades ago, the Aboriginal people were living traditional lives. Their distinctive art was everywhere. They developed what can be called x-ray painting, so as to see into an imagined interior of whatever creature is being depicted, so as to know the creature, the skeleton of the snake laid out in white within its undulations, alongside digestive organs.

To pass on accumulated knowledge of their place, and ways to conduct themselves, the Aborigines told themselves an almost literally endless sequence of tales about forebears who walked the land and sang it into being as they went, the act of naming understood as creating, things caught in the song, in the mind, known as intimately as in their paintings, as part of the extended self, caught in the breath, and thus likely to be beloved.

Aboriginal paths crisscross the land and are called songlines. Young men sing of the land and walk the songlines before initiation ceremonies centered on circumcision rituals. They paint the stories they have learned to sing on their bodies, and carve them into storyboards. Things learned during those vivid ceremonies are not forgotten. People memorize creation. The notion of ancient people walking the world, singing its glories into being as they went, naming each creature, plant or animal or insect, into actuality, is to me utterly beguiling because it rings of truth. We inhabit what we can name, we are what we can say. Is that the idea?

Hunting-gathering cultures that survive into the present age tend to be organized around rituals designed to encourage recollection. Women among bush people in the Kalahari Desert of southwestern Africa carry their children over great distances, always talking and telling the children the names of plants and when they bear fruit, the names of animals, when they can be hunted and where, naming and creating the world out of language.

Those women are naming elements and creatures in a garden they know intimately; they teach their children as they walk; with detailed knowledge of the routes where their people have always walked, their culture can endure. (Think of *Genesis*, where things come to exist forever once they have been named.) Recent research, reported in the April, 17, 1997, issue of *The New York Times*, indicates that children who are incessantly the focus of face-to-face talk with another person before the age of one are better equipped to deal with a world made of language when they become adults. Faced with complexity, our brains grow. Naming is a fundamental act that enables us to see.

According to anthropologist Keith Basso, in *Wisdom Sits in Places,* the Apache on the White River Reservation in eastern Arizona often name physical particularities of their territory—river crossings and rocky outcroppings—after incidents that happened there. Basso tells of Ronnie Lupe, chairman of the White Mountain Apache Tribe, suggesting that Basso make some maps. "Not whiteman's maps, we've got plenty of them, but Apache maps with Apache places and names. We could use them."

"Apache constructions of place, reach deeply into other cultural spheres,"

Basso says, "including conceptions of wisdom, notions of morality, politeness and tact in forms of spoken discourse, and certain ways of imagining and interpreting the Apache tribal past."

Basso found himself making maps with place names like Widows Pause for Breath and She Carries Her Brother on Her Back. Apache places are named after symbolically important events, so individuals in the tribe are continually moving in a webwork of places whose names embody the stories of their people. Living inside a mesh of significance constantly tells them who they are, where they reside in tribal history, and how to act if they wish their fellows well. It is a society attempting to be absolutely located, and thus secure.

Probably something like that was going on in the deep caverns at Lascaux. The psychic process of initiation in a cave is simple enough: Go into the darkness (go blind), learn the stories, light torches (see again), and be reborn into wisdom.

It is a sequence that metaphorically resembles the experience of bears emerging from a winter of hibernation. Those people no doubt saw the bears vanish into the earth, and come out again in early springtime. The resurrection of the bears may have led them to begin imagining the return from the caverns, of rebirth—the basis for our most hopeful religious story.

Ceremonies, which act out the storytelling, are like glue holding cultures together. Maybe the people during the end of those ice ages in Europe, at Lascaux and Font de Guame and Altamira, were solacing themselves with stories about the great animals they painted on the walls of caves, trying to assuage guilt over so much killing of fellow creatures. Or maybe they were attempting to magically re-create and give life to animals they killed for food, hoping to energize the deer and bulls and horses to return in slow migration with the next roll of seasons.

Inside at Lascaux, Annick and I were close up with the artwork of a hunting culture struggling to survive as humans do. The art at Lascaux might be an attempt to name those animals into eternal being. Hungry people, in a difficult climate, might want to institutionalize dreams of the lost paradise. Maybe they were preserving communal memories of a golden age when the hunting was easy. No doubt they were like us, like any child, simply yearning to confide, and to be reassured.

In *The Creative Explosion*, John E. Pfeiffer says "exalted individuals appeared . . . [from] shamans specializing in communications with the spirit world to hereditary chiefs and kings regarded as official representatives of the gods, and finally to superkings like the Pharaohs in Egypt who were gods in their own right."

Some people at Lascaux understood that control of information and defining the ways it can be understood is key to controlling a society. In what I intuit of the rituals that accompanied the art I see political manipulations, people of some description—good-hearted men and women, shamans and tricksters—attempting to deify the culture they loved, believed in, depended upon, understood as real, and could not bear to watch and share as it, like all cultures, over a vast sequence of generations, failed and disintegrated.

But insisting, as we know, can go terribly wrong. Hitler and Stalin, in grainy documentary films, on stone podiums in front of roaring thousands of true believers—think of them as shamans attempting to name and perform their beliefs into actuality.

In *Landscape and Memory* Simon Schama writes of Giby, where in 1945 "hundreds of men and women accused of supporting the Polish Home Army were taken to their death by the NKVD, Stalin's security police. The little hill had been given a fresh crown of yellow sand on which rested roughhewn slabs of polished granite. The stones were engraved with perhaps five hundred names. . . . But the real shock waited at the top of the mound . . . the ground fell sharply away to reveal a landscape of unanticipated beauty. A bright fringe of young trees marked the horizon floor, but at their back, like giants holding the hands of children, stood the black-green phalanx of the primeval forest."

Schama writes, "we are accustomed to think of the Holocaust as having no landscape . . . It is shocking to realize that Treblinka, too, belongs to brilliantly vivid countryside, the riverbed of the Bug and Vistula; rolling, gentle land, lined by avenues of poplar and aspen."

Sounds much like the valley of Vezere just down the hill from Lascaux, or Warner Valley were I learned to enjoy the green light. My reverence for images of the moving, searching animals we encountered inside at Lascaux is no doubt to some degree a result of sentimental nostalgia for what I, in my most condescending manner, take to be a simpler, more natural time, like my deeply reimagined childhood world. As with anyone who speaks out, I want to persuade readers to share my reverence for memories of waterbirds in a morning sky, and dark horses running the meadowlands.

We are incessantly naming and thus locating ourselves. But, followed too far, naming is our worst idea. However sweetly done, with all of an open heart, naming is always an imperialist act, a claiming. Building a wall, we tell ourselves about why we get to build, and about owning; we begin defining, containing, excluding.

On our way to Lascaux, Annick and I had snooped along the Ardeche Gorge in southern France, a great rivercourse canyon with gray-white cliffs where you could step off and fall hundreds of feet to the water. We were hoping to get inside the recently discovered Chavuet Caverns and sneak a look at the very ancient images of animals painted there. The chances of our getting inside turned out to be, properly, zero. Instead, we ended up witnessing the far dark side of cultural coherence, where the unthinkable lives.

We stayed in the tourist town of Pont de Vallon, a couple of kilometers upstream from a great natural bridge across the river. In the bar of our hotel, we sat with gin and tonic as the owner told of his parents leading their family into hiding during the German evacuation at the end of World War II, hauling their most precious possessions on a child's red wagon.

"We went to wilds," he said, in hesitant English. "Those were dangerous times. Now I find we were living at the ancient entrance to the painted caverns, which were collapsed for thousands of years. We didn't know it." His story resonated like a magical scrap of meaningfulness.

On his advice, the next morning, on highlands across the river a few kilometers, we visited the tiny rockwork village of Le Crotte, and saw how dangerous the Germans had been while evacuating in defeat. The Germans had shot and killed the entire population of Le Crotte—seventeen people.

Resting on a rock wall, I wrote some of their names on the back of a restaurant receipt (for some unremembered reason I didn't get them all), a scribbled listing that begins with "unknown."

Lucien Boyer *age 75*
Ernestine Boyer *age 68*
George Boyer *age 36*
Louis Brunel *age 47*
Josephine Brunel *age 44*
Adrian Mantacrier *age 45*
Madeliene Mantacrier *age 43*
George Mantacrier *age 17*
Noel Galizzi *age 44*
Theresa Galizzi *age 43*
Antoine Galizzi *age 17*
Micheal Galizzi *age 16*
Jacques Galizzi *age 15*

What do human beings think they are doing on earth? The wild violets in the fields were almost in bloom. The scatter of stone buildings stood empty until very recently. After fifty years they were being refurbished and lived in again. It seems to be in human nature to keep coming back, touching the wound, trying to heal ourselves and the world.

In *Twentieth Century Pleasures*, Robert Hass says "Nostalgia locates desire in the past where it suffers no active conflict and can be yearned toward pleasantly. History is the antidote to this."

NOTES

[1] Excerpt from Stegner's "I Go Back to May, 1987," by Sharon Olds in *The Gold Cell.* Reprinted with permission of Alfred A. Knopf, Inc.

[2] "Daybreak" in *Mortal Acts, Mortal Words: A Collection of Poems,* by Galway Kinnell. Reprinted with the permission of Houghton Mifflin.

Chapter 18

TO BE TAKEN

Terry Tempest Williams

"The revolutionary question is: What about the Other? . . . It is not enough to rail against the descending darkness of barbarity. . . . One can refuse to play the game. A holding action can be fought. Alternatives must be kept alive."

—Breyten Breytenbach

TORTOISE STEPS

Tortoise steps.
Slow steps.
Four steps like a tank with a tail dragging in the sand.
Tortoise steps—land-based, land-locked, dusty like the desert tortoise himself, fenced in, a prisoner on his own reservation
teaching us the slow art of revolutionary patience.

It is Christmas. We gather in our grandparents' home: aunts, uncles, cousins, babies—four generations wipe their feet at the holiday mat. One by one, we open the front door.

"Hello."

"We're here."

Glass panes iced are beginning to melt from the heat of bodies together. Our grandfather, Jack, now ninety, presides. His sons, John and Richard, walk in dressed in tweed sportcoats and Levi's, their polished boots could kill spiders in corners. My Aunt Ruth enters with her arms full of gifts. Jack's sister, Norinne, in her eighties, sits in the living room with her hands folded tightly, greeting each one of us with a formality we have come to expect.

Tradition.

On this night, we know a buffet is prepared: filet mignon, marinated carrots, asparagus and cauliflower, a cranberry salad, warbread (a recipe our great-grandmother, Mamie Comstock Tempest, improvised during the Depression when provisions were scarce and raisins plentiful), and the same silver serving piece is obscene with chocolates.

The Christmas tree stands in the center of the room, "the grandchildren's tree," and we remember our grandmother, Mimi, the matriarch of this family whose last Christmas was in 1988. We remember her. We remember all of our dead.

Candles burn. I walk into the dining room, pick up a plate and circle the table.

"What's new, Terrence?" my uncle asks ribbing me.

"Not a thing, Rich." I responded. We both look up from the buffet smiling.

I take some meat with my fingers. He spears vegetables. We return to the living room and find a seat. The rest of the family gathers. Jack sits in the wing-backed chair, his hands on both armrests. My father sits across the room from his brother.

"So how did the meeting go last week?"

"Terrible," Rich says.

"What did they decide?"

"Simple," my uncle says. "Tortoises are more important than people."

Heads turn, attention fixed on matters of the Tempest Company, the family construction business that began with our great-grandfather in the early part of the century, a company my brothers all work for, cousins, too.

"What are you talking about?" I ask.

"Where have you been?" my father asks incredulously. "We've been shut down eighteen months because of that—(he stops himself in deference to his aunt) that stupid Endangered Species Act."

I look at my brother Steve, who nods his head and looks at our cousin Bob who looks at his sister Lynne who shakes her head as she turns to Brooke.

"I attended the public meeting where they discussed the Habitat Management Plan," Rich says to us.

"And?" Lynne asks as she walks over to her father and offers him a piece of warbread.

"They ruled in favor of the tortoise."

"Which job is this, John?" Brooke asks, who at the time was working for the Governor's Office of Budget and Planning as the liaison between environmental groups and the state.

"It's the last leg of the information highway," Dad says. "Seven miles of fiberoptic cable running from the town of Hurricane to St. George linking rural Utah to the Wasatch Front."

"We're held up in permits," Rich explains. "A construction permit won't be issued until U.S. West complies with federal agencies."

"The government's gone too far," my great-aunt interjects.

"Too far?" My father says his voice rising like water ready to boil. "Too far? We've had to hire a full-time biologist at sixty bucks an hour who does nothing but look for these imaginary animals. Every day he circles the crew singing the same song, 'Nope, haven't seen one yet.'"

"The guy's from BYU and sits in the cab of his truck most of the day reading scriptures," Steve adds who is the superintendent.

"Thou shall not kill a turtle," someone mutters under their breath.

"Sixty bucks an hour," Dad reiterates. "That's twice as much as our foremen make! It would be cheaper to buy a poolside condominium for each mating pair of tortoises than to adhere to the costs of this ridiculous act."

"The government's gone too far," my aunt restates like a delayed echo.

"And on top of that we have to conduct a 'turtle training course.'"

"Tortoise, John," his granddaughter Callie interrupts. I wink at my niece.

"A turtle training course for our men, OUR MEN, so they can learn to identify one and then remember to check under the tires and skids for tortoises looking for shade before turning on the backhoes after lunch."

Rich stands up to get some more food.

"A hundred thousand dollars if we run over one," he says making himself a sandwich.

"Is that worth a hundred grand?" my father snaps.

"From the tortoise's point of view," Lynne says, pushing.

"What's St. George now, the fourth fastest growing community in the country?" Brooke asks.

"Not if the enviros have anything to do with it," Rich says.

"What do you kids want? To stop progress? You and your environmentalist friends have lost all credibility. One local told us a bunch of radicals actually planted a tortoise in the parking lot of the Wal-Mart distribution center just to shut it down."

"How do you know it didn't walk onto the asphalt by itself?" I ask.

"They had its stomach pumped and it was full of lettuce," Rich replies. We all roll our eyes.

Steve asks his cousin Matt, who is a first-year medical student, "Have you performed an autopsy on a desert tortoise yet?"

"Not yet," Matt responds. "Just human beings."

"Can I get anyone anything?" Ruth asks holding her granddaughter Hannah on her hip. She looks around. No response. "Just checking."

"And you wonder why people are upset," my father says turning to me. "It's easy for you to sit here and tell us what animals we should protect while you write poems about them as a hobby—it's not your pocketbook that's hurting."

"And is yours?" I ask fearing I have now gone as far as my father has.

I was not aware of the background music until now, Nat King Cole singing, "Have a Merry, Merry Christmas."

"I don't know," Jack says clearing his throat pulling himself out of his chair. "Why don't you boys tell them the real story?"

John and Richard look puzzled.

"What story?" Rich asks.

"Hardpan," Jack says.

"Never mind," my father says grinning. "Just keep that quiet."

Richard starts giggling like a little boy.

"Tell!" we beg our grandfather.

He placed his hands on the back of the lounge. "We had twenty-two crews during the war, put all the piping in the airbases at Tooele, Salt Lake, Hill, and Ogden. I never went to bed for five years: 1941, '42, '43, '44, '45, just dropped dead on this lounge from exhaustion every night. We even had work in Las Vegas putting in a big waterline to the north. I was away for weeks, missing Kathryn and the boys. Then one day, I was walking along the trench when I spotted what I thought was a helmet. I bent down. It moved. I realized it was a tortoise. I picked it up, its head and feet shot back into its shell. I put him in the back of my truck and brought him home for the boys. We named him, Hardpan."

He looks at his sons, smiles, and walks out of the room.

"Everybody else had a dog," my father says. "German shepherds, Doberman pinschers, black Labs. We drilled a hole in his shell and tied a long cord to it and walked him around the block."

We all look at each other.

"No kidding," Rich says. "Every day we walked him."

"Hardpan?" I ask.

"You know, the desert without rain—hardpan, no give to the sand." Dad's voice is tender.

"He was reliable, old Hardpan, you have to say that about him," Rich adds.

"Until he disappeared," Jack says returning to his chair.

Gopherus agassizii. Desert tortoise. Land turtle. An elder among us. Even among my family. For some of us he represents "landlocked" like the wildlands before us. Designate wilderness and development is locked out. Find a tortoise and another invisible fence is erected. The tortoise's presence compromises our own. For others, tortoise is a land-based sovereign on earth, entitled to his own desert justice. He is seen as an extension of family—human and nonhuman alike—living in arid country. His presence enhances our own. The tension tortoise inspires calls for wisdom.

These animals may live beyond 100 years. They walk for miles largely un-noticed carrying a stillness with them. Fifteen acres may be home range and they know it well. When they feel in their bodies that it is about to rain, they travel to where water pools. They wait. Clouds gather. Skies darken. It rains. They drink. It may be days, weeks, months before their beaks touch water again.

If native mythologies are true and turtles carry the world on their backs, the carapace of the desert tortoise is designed to bear the weight. It is a landscape with its own aesthetic. Three scutes or plates run down the vertebrae, hexagons, with two larger scutes on tope and bottom. Four plates line either side of center. The shell is bordered by twenty-four smaller ones that seem to hold the animal in place. The plastron, or bottom, of the shell fits together like a twelve-tiled floor. The desert tortoise lives inside his own creation like a philosopher who is most at home in his mind.

In winter the desert tortoise hibernates but not in the manner of bears. Hibernation for reptiles is "brumation," a time of dormancy where cold-blooded creatures retire, rock-still, with physiological changes occurring independent of their body temperatures. Much remains mysterious about this time of seasonal retreat but brumation among turtles suggests it is sparked by conditions of temperature, moisture, photoperiod, and food supply. They stir in their stone-ledged dens when the temperature rises, dens they inhabit year after year, one, two, maybe five individuals together. They leave. They forage. They mate. The females lay eggs in supple sands; two dozen eggs may be dropped in a nest. Buried. Incubated. Hatched. And then the quiet plodding of another generation of desert tortoise meets the sands.

It is genealogy of evolutionary adaptation until *Gopherus agassizii* suddenly begins bumping into real estate developers after having the desert to himself for millennia.

1996: A lone desert tortoise stands before a bulldozer in the Mojave.

My father and the Endangered Species Act. My father as an endangered species. The Marlboro Man without his cigarette is home on the range—I will list him as threatened by his own vulnerable nature. I will list him as threatened by my emotional nature. Who dares to write the recovery plan that regulates our own constructions? He will resist me. I will resist him. He is my father. I am his daughter. He holds my birth story. I will mourn his death. We face each other.

Hand over our hearts, in the American West united states do not exist even within our own families. "Don't Tread on Me." The snake coils. The tortoise retreats. When the dust devil clears, who remains?

My father, myself, threatened species.

I recall a statement made to me by another elder, a Mormon general authority who feared I had chosen not to have children. Call it "Ode to the Gene Pool," a manipulation of theology, personalized, tailorized to move me toward motherhood, another bulge in the population.

"A female bird," he wrote to me, "has no options as to whether she will lay eggs or not. She must. God insists. Because if she does not a precious combination will be lost forever. One of your deepest concerns rests with endangered species. If a species dies out, its gene pool will be lost forever and we are all the lesser because of the loss. The eggs you possess over which your husband presides [are] precious genes. You are an endangered family."

I resist. Who will follow? Must someone follow?

Clouds gather. It rains. The desert tortoise drinks where water has pooled.

Who holds the wisdom? My grandfather, the tortoise, calls for the story, then disappears.

Tortoise steps.

Tortoise tracks.

Tracks in time.

One can refuse to play the game.

Across from where I sit is a redrock ledge. We are only a stone's toss away from the city of St. George. I am hiking with my father. He has gone ahead.

Today is the spring equinox, equal light, equal dark—a day to truce.

I have followed tortoise tracks to this place, a den. It is cold, the air stings my face, I did not dress warmly enough. Once again, the desert deceives as wind snaps over the ridge and rides down valley.

The tortoise is inside. I wish to speak to him, to her, to them about my family, my tribe of people who lose money and make money without recognizing their own threatened status, my tribe of people who keep tortoises, turtles, as pets and wonder why they walk away.

"Have you heard the news today?" I pull the clipping from the local paper out of my pocket, unfold it and read aloud:

> If you're a desert tortoise living in Washington County, take this advice: Start crawling your way toward the hills north of St. George, Utah.
>
> Come March 15, any tortoise living outside a specially designated "desert tortoise reserve" could become subject to "taking"—a biological term for death of an animal or the destruction of its habitat.
>
> State and federal officials on Friday signed an interlocal agreement that will set aside 61,000 acres of prime tortoise habitat as a reserve that wildlife biologists believe will secure the reptile's recovery.
>
> On the flip side, the agreement also provides permission and means by which developers and others may take some 1,200 tortoises and develop more than 12,000 acres of tortoise habitat outside the reserve without violating the Endangered Species Act, under which the tortoise is listed as a

"threatened species."

Friday's signing ends six years of battles over the slow-moving animal, whose presence around St. George has created headaches for land developers and local governments.

"We feel confident that we're going to be able to work together and have a permit that provides for the recovery and protection of the tortoise," said Bob Williams, assistant supervisor for the Fish & Wildlife Service.

Sen. Bob Bennett, R-Utah, agreed. "This is clearly a very major step toward getting the endangered species issue resolved short of the train wreck of the spotted owl."

. . . Between 1980 and 1990, the Washington County's population increased 86% from 26,125 to 48,560. It is projected to have between 101,000 and 139,000 people by 2010.

Implementation of the Habitat Conservation Plan is scheduled to last 20 years and cost $11.5 million.

There is no movement inside the den.

"Tortoise, I have two questions for you from Neruda:
'¿Quien da los nombres y los números al inocente innumerable?'
(Who assigns names and numbers to the innumerable innocent?)

`¿Como le digo a la tortuga que yo le gano en lentitude?'
(How do I tell the turtle that I am slower than he?)"

The desert tortoise is still.

I suspect he hears my voice simply for what it is, human. The news and questions I deliver are returned to me and somehow dissipate in the silence.

It is enough
to breathe, here, together.

Our shadows lengthen
while the white-petaled heart of Datura
opens and closes.

We have forgotten the option of restraint.

It is no longer the survival of the fittest but the survival of compassion.

Inside the redrock ledge, the emotional endurance of the tortoise stares back at me. I blink. To take. To be taken. To die. The desert tortoise presses me on the sand, down on all fours. The shell I now find myself inhabiting is a keratinous room where my spine is attached to its ceiling. Head, hands, feet, and tail push through six doors and search for a way home.

Tortoise steps.
Land-based. Landlocked.
Land-based. Landlocked.
Learning the slow art of revolutionary patience, I listen to my family.

CONTRIBUTORS

Fay Allen is a research technician in the U.S. Department of Agriculture's Agricultural Research Service in Reno, Nevada.

Edward E. Bangs is the Northern Rockies Wolf Recovery coordinator for the U.S. Fish & Wildlife Service in Helena, Montana.

Brad T. Barber is the deputy director of the Governor's Office for Planning and Budget and state planning coordinator in Salt Lake City, Utah.

Rick Bass is the author of several books about the West, including *Winter, Nine Mile Wolves, The Lost Grizzlies*, and *The Book of Yaak*.

Aaron P. Clark served as a research assistant in the Utah Governor's Office for Planning and Budget while completing a degree in urban planning at the University of Utah.

Holly Doremus is an acting professor of law at the University of California-Davis, and a member of the Graduate Group in Ecology. She holds a J.D. degree and a Ph.D. in plant biology.

Hank Fischer is the northern Rockies region representative for Defenders of Wildlife and has authored several books, including *Wolf Wars* and *Montana Wildlife Viewing Guide.*

Dan Flores is the A. B. Hammond professor of western history at the University of Montana. His works include *Caprock Canyonlands: Journeys into the Heart of the Southern Plains* and *Horizontal Yellow: Nature and History in the Near Southwest.*

Martha Hahn is the Idaho state director for the U.S. Bureau of Land Management.

Doug Honnold is the northern Rockies region attorney for the Sierra Club Legal Defense Fund in Bozeman, Montana.

Teresa Jordan is a western writer whose works include *Cowgirls, Riding the White Horse Home, Graining the Mare*, and *The Stories That Shape Us.*

Robert B. Keiter is the James I. Farr professor of law and director of the Wallace Stegner Center for Land, Resources and the Environment, at the University of

Utah. His works include *The Greater Yellowstone Ecosystem* and *The Wyoming Constitution*.

Daniel Kemmis, formerly mayor of Missoula, is director of the Center for the Rocky Mountain West at the University of Montana; his books include *The Good City and The Good Life* and *Community and the Politics of Place*.

William Kittredge, a former Stegner fellow, is a professor emeritus of English and creative writing at the University of Montana; his books include *Hole in the Sky, Owning It All*, and *The Portable Western Reader*.

Thomas J. Lyon is professor emeritus of English at Utah State University and editor of the journal *Western American Literature, This Incomparable Land: A Book of American Nature Writing*, and *Great & Peculiar Beauty: A Utah Reader* (with Terry Tempest Williams).

Duncan T. Patten is professor emeritus of botany at Arizona State University and a research professor at Montana State University's Mountain Research Center.

Page Stegner is a writer and professor emeritus of English at the University of California-Santa Cruz, whose works include *Grand Canyon: The Great Abyss, Islands of the West*, and *Outposts of Eden*.

Stephen Trimble is a writer and photographer, whose books include *The Sagebrush Ocean: A Natural History of the Great Basin* and *Earthtones: A Nevada Album*.

Charles Wilkinson is the Moses Lasky professor at the University of Colorado School of Law and author of numerous books, including *Crossing the Next Meridian: Land, Water and the Future of the West* and *The Eagle Bird*.

Terry Tempest Williams is a writer and naturalist-in-residence at the Utah Museum of Natural History; her books include *Refuge, An Unspoken Hunger*, and *Desert Quartet*.

James A. Young is a range scientist for the U.S. Department of Agriculture's Agricultural Research Service in Reno, Nevada, and author of *Cattle in the Cold Desert* and *Endless Tracks in the Woods*.

DATE DUE

APR 1 5 2008

AUG ⁜ 2 2003

DEMCO, INC. 38-2931